Ordinary Democracy

Ordinary Democracy

Sovereignty and Citizenship Beyond the Neoliberal Impasse

ALI ASLAM

OXFORD
UNIVERSITY PRESS

OXFORD
UNIVERSITY PRESS

Oxford University Press is a department of the University of Oxford. It furthers the University's objective of excellence in research, scholarship, and education by publishing worldwide. Oxford is a registered trade mark of Oxford University Press in the UK and certain other countries.

Published in the United States of America by Oxford University Press
198 Madison Avenue, New York, NY 10016, United States of America.

Library of Congress Cataloging-in-Publication Data
Names: Aslam, Ali, author.
Title: Ordinary democracy : sovereignty and citizenship beyond the neoliberal impasse / Ali Aslam.
Description: New York, NY : Oxford University Press, 2017.
Identifiers: LCCN 2016018956 (print) | LCCN 2016031475 (ebook) |
ISBN 9780190601812 (hardback) | ISBN 9780190601829 (Updf)
Subjects: LCSH: Democracy—Philosophy. | Neoliberalism. | Political participation—Social aspects. | Protest movements. | BISAC: POLITICAL SCIENCE / Political Ideologies / Democracy. | POLITICAL SCIENCE / History & Theory.
Classification: LCC JC423 .A776 2016 (print) | LCC JC423 (ebook) | DDC 321.8—dc23
LC record available at https://lccn.loc.gov/2016018956

9 8 7 6 5 4 3 2 1

Printed by Sheridan Books, Inc., United States of America

To my family.

CONTENTS

ACKNOWLEDGMENTS

I have many people and institutions I wish to thank for their support. I had the good fortune of working with fantastic colleagues at the Princeton Writing Program who, along with my students, taught me how to pull together an argument. Chris Close, Anne DeWitt, Tim Recuber, and especially Keith Shaw have been valuable readers. Liz Markovits at Mount Holyoke College has been incredibly welcoming and supportive during the final stages of this project. Omaima Afzaal and Ricky Frawley provided valuable research assistance in the final revision stages. Thanks to the trustees of Princeton University and Mount Holyoke College for research support.

Parts of this manuscript were presented to audiences at Canadian Mennonite University, Colorado State University, Deep Springs College, University of Colorado-Boulder, University of Puget Sound, as well as panels at the American Political Science Association and Western Political Science Association conferences. The book is better for the challenging questions and thoughtful responses I received at each venue.

I must thank several colleagues who read and discussed parts of the manuscript with me, in some cases multiple times. I am grateful for all of their contributions, guidance, and encouragement. They include Cristina Beltrán, James Bourke, Kevin Bruyneel, Glen Coulthard, Sonali Chakravarti, Stefan Dolgert, Michaele Ferguson, Laura Grattan, Chris Huebner, John Lombardini, Patchen Markell, David McIvor, Joel Schlosser, and Isaac Villegas. Each conversation affirmed my love for political theory, not just for the political stakes of our work but for the relationships it has made possible for me. The errors and missteps in what follows are mine alone.

I had the privilege of being a graduate student at Duke University during a very special moment. Rom Coles, Peter Euben, Ruth Grant, Michael Gillespie, and Tom Spragens created an intellectually exciting and cooperative environment where ideas cross-pollinated and where learning had a sense of purpose. I learned so much from them and my fellow students James Bourke, P. J. Brendese, Stefan Dolgert, Laura Grattan, Alisa Kessel, David McIvor, Joel Schlosser, and Nick Troester. This book bears the imprint of so many of those conversations back in Durham and since then at conferences, dinners, and coffees whenever a chance to get together would beckon.

I am thankful to the late Wilson Carey McWilliams for introducing me to the work of Peter Euben and suggesting that I apply to Duke and for his friendship during the long stretch of time when I was figuring out what to do with my life. I was so lucky to have met Cristina Beltrán in the classroom during my first year at Rutgers. She continues to be an important mentor and friend. Even though I have never taken a class from him, I want to thank Patchen Markell for playing a similar role and for many great bicycle rides in Princeton.

My fellow "Demophiles," members of the long standing "Dinner and Democracy" reading group, David McIvor and Joel Schlosser deserve a special thank you. The most important elements of my thinking about democratic politics have been shaped through my participation. I look forward to many more dinners over the coming years.

Angela Chnapko and her staff at Oxford University Press have been incredible to work with. Angela lent early support for this project and provided important guidance along the way. I am grateful for two anonymous reviewers who saw the potential in the manuscript even if the argument was not all sewn together at the time. Their comments were transformative.

I wish to thank my parents, Razia and Sultan, and sister Jehan for all of their love and encouragement as well as the patience and support of the Ahmed family. I started writing this book just as Bart and then Aleena joined our family. They have been a wellspring of joy and a reminder of the kindness and generosity that surrounds us.

Finally, I wish to thank my dearest Rabia Ahmed without whom none of this would be possible. Thank you for celebrating each small step, helping me see beyond the present, and for giving me the life I could never have imagined on my own. Aaya Aslam arrived just as I was finishing this book. There has never been a better reason to finish. This book is dedicated to my family.

Ordinary Democracy

Introduction

Stop Reckless Spending
Stop Socializing America!
Warning: Constitution Under Attack!
We Need A Truth Czar
Size Matters, Reduce Government!
No to Obamacare!
We Will Be Forever Indebted to Obama Policies
Take Back America!
Honk for Capitalism!

They Got a Bailout. We Got Sold Out!
Arrest the Koch Brothers!
Impeach Obama. Protector of Wall Street Criminals!
End the Fed!
De-Privatize Democracy!
Standing up for the Change We Voted For!
The Obama we thought we had elected would be here with us, not ignoring us.
This is what democracy looks like!

The first set of messages were printed on signs carried by Tea Party protestors at an event in Flagstaff, Arizona, on August 31, 2009 that drew more than one thousand.[1] Protestors dressed in military uniforms and in Uncle Sam-style suits, carried flags bearing the image of a coiled rattle snake above the words "Give me liberty or give me death," as well as a modified, homemade version of the pirate Jolly Rogers, with a portrait of Obama's head in place of the skull sitting atop two crossed bones. The second set is a selection of signs observed in Zuccotti Park on the evening of October 6, 2011.[2] Read together, these signs register anger and frustration with democratic institutions and channels incapable of addressing the sense of powerlessness, distrust, and even betrayal that citizens feel.[3]

What caused citizens on both the left and the right to feel so estranged and devitalized? Part of it can be explained by acknowledging how much of day-to-day life is determined by forces beyond the control of ordinary citizens. The actions of powerful corporations, terrorist cells, and financial entities represent threats to national sovereignty that shape the decisions of governments and the terrain of everyday life but are unaccountable to citizens. Citizens also experience these forces in terms of compromised sovereignty, understood as their ability to act as self-determining individuals. Governments respond by strengthening the powers that remain in order to better react to these challenges. In practice, however, this has further distanced ordinary citizens from participating in decision-making, leaving them feeling as if they have little agency over both the factors that batter their sense of selfhood and how the government responds to those forces. The result is a citizenry without vitality, lacking energy and confidence in its own powers, which feeds into a widespread sense of impasse and impassivity. From the perspective of this devitalized citizenry, government is more responsive to the interests of corporations and the wealthiest 1 percent than to them, to the imperatives of economic growth than to democratic processes, to efficiency rather than to freedom. It is no small fact that citizens in groups opposed to mainstream political parties carried these signs. Instead, it is a measure of their lack of faith in the efficacy of established political channels that these groups have sprung up to mount challenges from the outside. For them, the political status quo represents an impasse or a deadlock where no progress is possible.

There are competing frameworks to explain the problem of devitalized agency among citizens today. Wendy Brown argues that neoliberalization of liberal democracies is to blame. According to Brown, neoliberalism is best understood not as a set of policies or institutions but in terms of the permeation and application of market rationality to all activities, including government. She argues that cost-benefit thinking has hollowed out democratic institutions and practices of citizenship by elevating efficiency, economic growth, and market freedom above justice, fairness, and equality, for example.[4] For Bonnie Honig, security and economic crises reflect the ascendency of emergency politics. Emergency politics refers to the extension of decision-making by powers unaccountable to democratic citizens far beyond the moment of emergency and crisis.[5] The normalization of emergency politics justifies both the reduction or privatization of formerly public functions characteristic of neoliberalism and the enlargement of executive powers over those functions that remain so that more decision-making is made unaccountable to ordinary citizens and the sense of impasse is deepened.

John Hibbing and Elizabeth Thiess-Morse offer a counter argument, suggesting that protests like these are out of step with how most citizens feel about being left out of political decision-making. They find many citizens may be uninterested in having a part in decision-making and, by implication, that they might welcome that decision-making has been left to others.[6] For these citizens, liberal democracy appears to have fulfilled its promise to relieve them of the responsibility for political life, freeing them to concentrate on the pursuit of the commodious life separate from the demands of popular sovereignty. As more of those desires are directed toward and understood through the marketplace, government's ability to safeguard the economy as a site where subjects realize their desires for agency has transformed how citizens view the purpose of government and their relationship to it.[7]

Just as preventing another terrorist attack once justified the executive to take whatever steps were claimed necessary to meet that goal, even if that meant violating civil liberties, licensing torture at Guantanamo, falsifying evidence of links between Al-Qaeda and Saddam Hussein's Iraq, and suspending due process, today the ability of government to prevent economic collapse and spur economic growth by whatever means necessary has become the measurement of legitimacy. According to this line of argument, securing the nation's defense and economic stability is incompatible with the slower pace of democratic politics, because crisis demands immediate and decisive action. While on matters of defense it has been the executive who has become the "decider," as arguments for the necessity of decisive action crossed from defense to economic security, expert administrative bodies have increasingly taken up that role. "Saving" the economy during and after crisis has fallen to central bankers helped by private management consultants who derive part of their authority from their use of social-scientific methods and neutral cost-benefit analyses.[8]

The protests suggest the incompleteness of each explanation, however. They register a desire for agency that remains unsatisfied by the market and survives despite the cumulative weight of emergency politics. Freedom, understood as the powers of self-legislation, has been the promise of modern democracy rather than the rule of the people that animated older, republican models of democracy that prioritized equality rather than freedom. It is the promise to secure individual freedom that establishes democracy as the only moral legitimate form of government today. As threats to individual sovereignty like terrorism and financial crisis indicate, individual subjects are linked to the collective body through the concept of sovereignty. As self-legislating individuals they mirror the sovereign state, which expresses the unified will of the people. Organized in a delimited territorial unit, the people are believed to have authorship over not just the laws and juridical policies of the state, but also the extra-juridical habits, norms, and dispositions, that legitimate, enforce, and normalize the exercise of state power.

Emergency political measures are prompted by threats to national sovereignty, such as terrorism and economic crisis. They represent efforts to secure and strengthen those sovereign powers that remain actionable, but in the process they reduce the people to passive spectatorship. During the 2008 financial crisis, states acted to stabilize the free fall of global capitalism by bypassing democratic processes and entering into direct negotiations with the heads of global banking firms and car manufacturers. John Locke associates sovereignty with the prerogative decision-making power of the executive, who is above the law and can suspend it to preserve the common good. At the same time, he also identifies sovereignty with the power of the people to rebel and dissolve the social compact if they believe the actions of the executive to be unjust.[9]

But neither of these sovereign powers can rule at the same time and the image of sovereign power that is unitary and undivided depends on one group sacrificing to another. Danielle Allen observes that like Thomas Hobbes, Locke identifies the Old Testament story of Jephthah (Judges 11) as the model of contract and consent, not Abraham's willingness to sacrifice his son. In the story, Jephthah was exiled from Israel because of his parents' illegitimate relationship but is asked to return to help the Israelites in battle. Promised rulership of the tribe in exchange for his leadership, Jephthah asks Yahweh for assistance, promising in exchange to sacrifice the first thing he sees when he returns home which, in his case, is his daughter. Allen notes that Jephthah's daughter saves her father by offering to sacrifice herself, but concludes that sacrifice is at the heart of contract theory and democratic citizenship even if these sacrifices are rarely avowed.[10] The sacrifices of indigenous communities both in the past and today are among the most egregious examples of this disavowal in settler-colonial states like Canada and the United States.

The sacrifices citizens make may be disavowed by calling them social rather than political, but they point to the gap between the promise of sovereignty and what citizens actually experience. Allen's point is that democracies have to develop rituals that help citizens generate the mutual trust necessary to honor these sacrifices since, as she says, the "hard truth of democracy is that some citizens are always giving things up for others."[11] Sacrifice happens at two levels then. Some citizens must sacrifice for others to preserve the common good; sometimes the will of the people must be sacrificed to prerogative power in the name of public wellbeing. Both events turn on defining those sacrifices as nonpolitical, either by calling them necessary or referring to them as private hardships.

Liberals solve the incoherence of sovereignty in Locke's writing by minimizing the role of the people to ratification of events and trying to deny sacrifice. This is done through liberalism's promise of political idleness. Citizens freed from having to participate in public life are idle citizens. Relieved from participating in political life, idle citizens can instead pursue self-rule and autonomy, or the ability to determine their own ends, as private individuals. The idea in liberal states that citizens are sovereign subjects made in the image of the state, as free and independent subjects, obscures the two dimensions of citizen sacrifice enumerated above. As a consequence, the idea of popular sovereignty that can act as the counterweight Locke imagined is transformed into an abstraction. As the skills and knowledge citizens require to act in common wither thanks to inactivity, understandings of sovereignty narrow to state actions. Sovereignty conveyed only through laws and juridical decisions made by administrative bodies erodes the trust necessary to manage sacrifice.

The desire for agency that survives amid conditions of emergency and impasse is evidence of the sacrifices made to preserve state sovereignty at the expense of the people. Specifically, the experience of political freedom that democratic citizens found in popular sovereignty has been sacrificed to safeguard what remains of state sovereignty. As the tension between prerogative and popular sovereignty has loosened under contemporary emergency conditions, sovereignty has been de-democratized. Sovereignty has been redistributed to state and corporate entities that are beyond the reach of ordinary citizens, so that sovereignty today appears closer to Jean Bodin's account of "absolute" sovereignty that is unitary and centralized in character.[12] Devitalized agency and citizenship has been the result of this transformation in sovereignty.[13] Lauren Berlant describes devitalized agency as agency that survives in a passive form, without the creative, world-making powers that draw citizens to public life because they believe it is receptive to their efforts.[14] For individuals, devitalized forms of sovereignty cleave connotations of self-authorization from the concept, leaving only the idea of sovereignty as autonomy or lack of dependence on another. Under conditions of devitalized agency the memory of more active forms of agency may survive but since political agency is increasingly frustrated, it is shifted toward other nonpolitical spheres like family, practices of self-care, and shopping.[15]

Even the cultivation of nonpolitical forms of agency underlines the affective links that binds citizens to the exercise of sovereign power at the state level, however. That is because citizens can either support the prerogative decision-making power of the executive or they can resist it through their actions. In other words, the practices of state sovereignty, or what I will also refer to as "macro-practices," are animated through the conduct of individual subjects that lie beyond the state and its laws, who give shape to juridical expressions of sovereignty through their actions. These subject-level "micro-practices" of sovereignty include relations, gestures, bodies, and habits that extend to the depth of society and which represent the extra-juridical component of sovereignty. They may complement or roughen macro-practices of sovereignty through action or inattention, but the point is that citizen micro-practices make possible macro-practices of sovereignty and are shaped by them in turn. In the case of the September 11, 2001, attacks, Elisabeth Anker argues that it is the experience of individual vulnerability that strengthened support for the War on Terror and state actions like the construction of a wall along the US–Mexico border meant to shore up national sovereignty.[16]

But the growth and influence of experts and administrative bodies in the wake of these emergencies have been made possible by diminishment of democratic assemblies and citizenship. Weakening them further, these macro-practices of sovereignty have made it increasingly difficult for citizens to imagine sovereignty outside the terms "necessitated" by emergency conditions. Felt legitimacy is Anker's term for identification with state power without processes of consent or deliberation.[17] Felt legitimacy compliments a deep sense of impasse and devitalized agency among the general public that rationalizes both passive, low-intensity citizenship and feelings of resignation that preempt the desire to seek change outside of a presidential candidate. Together these produce a form of common sense that causes citizens to view alternatives to powerful, undemocratic decision-making bodies skeptically, if not oppose them because they are impractical and inefficient.

William Connolly has argued that this common sense is the product of an assemblage that is complexly structured through relations of dependence, whose parts remain independent but generate a whole that is more than their sum.[18] That assemblage consists of not just corporate media but also religious dialogue, scientific and cultural institutions, government policies, and corporations that simultaneously produce affective hostility toward cultural difference, egalitarian policies, and government intervention to remediate systemic injustices. The resulting ideology seeps into and is reproduced by subjects through their micro-practices, as a body of knowledge, through habits of consumption, family relations, and religious practice, to craft the terms of everyday experience to which citizens add and then use to interpret their actions. This common sense is what makes the passive, devitalized citizenship that complements emergency politics possible and the associated de-democratization feel inevitable.

Ordinary Democracy turns to the crop of social movements that have emerged in the shadow of crisis to contest the necessity of emergency politics by democratizing sovereignty. Democratizing sovereignty involves restoring the tensional relationship between prerogative and popular power imagined by Locke but flattened under the pressure of crisis and emergency. Democratizing sovereignty entails both affective change and juridical reform: from passive to active citizenship, from solely being the object of power to having a measure of authorship over it.

Ordinary Democracy argues that contemporary social movements are working to democratize sovereignty by first addressing the widespread sense of impasse among citizens. The focus on animating popular sovereignty explains why these movements begin by documenting the sources of impasse. Studying their organizing practices reveals how they foreground the norms and dispositions that support emergency politics so that they can be unlearned and challenged. Chiefly, these micro-practices constitute the reasons why citizens believe they cannot act or that their actions are inconsequential. These movements concentrate on ordinary experience in terms of the dulling routines of the everyday that leave citizens worn out and unable to think beyond the needs of bare survival and that must be surmounted if citizens are to initiate any macro-level change. From this perspective, the use of documentary techniques which solicit and reproduce accounts of the everyday within these protests are meant to politicize the "necessity" of private sacrifices in order to produce solidarity and public dialogue around them. By publicizing sacrifices, what these movements do is help citizens measure the legitimacy of the sacrifices the polity have been asked—or pointedly, forced—to make in order to preserve the semblance of sovereignty, thus reestablishing sacrifice as a political question.

By publicizing the unaccounted costs of police violence and economic precarity resulting from "necessary" emergency measures, these movements help citizens scrutinize the political consequences of crisis management techniques that have elbowed them out of the way or which their passivity has made possible. Documents like the "We are the 99 percent" Tumblr page publicize the individual experiences of struggle and vulnerability and make it possible to build solidarity and action around this knowledge. Movements politicize the costs of idleness—the pursuit of agency in private domains and consumer consumption—but also fear of change that have left citizens more acquiescent and less able to contest non-democratic forms of decision-making. Occupations, public assemblies, dances, and prayers are practices intended to disrupt the habits of liberal-democratic citizens who are disposed to view politics, when they do at all, in juridical terms and who find ready fulfillment of their desires for agency in their identities as consumers. They represent micro, subject-level changes in affect, away from a form of low-intensity, devitalized citizenship toward the new forms of mutual trust and solidarity among citizens required to contest emergency actions taken to stabilize markets for capital investment and to secure borders.

Whether in shopping malls or in city squares, in front of police and citizens who consider them disorderly, I identify a range of movement practices meant to cultivate responsiveness and vitality among citizens habituated to low-intensity citizenship and therefore resistant to calls to action because they are skeptical anything might come of them.[19] Vitality originates in action-oriented associational practices that solicit and draw attention to existing opportunities for collective agency and democratic renewal. The attachments and knowledge that citizens acquire in these settings directly contrast with the resources available to them in more abstract and narrowly juridical renderings of citizenship, such as rights and voting, since these are inadequate to the task of challenging emergency politics.

Vitality mobilizes the energy, motivation, and mutual trust among citizens called on to take up collective action. I argue that such micro-practices of sovereignty are critical to challenging crisis and emergency because they rework the terms of what is thinkable and sayable, or what counts as ordinary political life.[20] These movement practices offer citizens the opportunity to join in association with others with initiative and for the purpose of creating the world in terms other than what is. Together, these practices are intended to rewire the attachments contemporary subjects have to the practices of sovereignty through embodied, associational practices that speak their desires for agency and attachment that differ from the "felt legitimacy" and unfreedom of emergency politics.[21] These challenges represent more than mere resistance to the directives of state power because micro-practices meant to generate vitality within movements are linked to efforts to make state power more responsive to citizens through laws, treaties, and constitutional reforms, which break up concentrations of decision-making power. Democratizing sovereignty involves transforming juridical institutions so that they are more responsive to the claims made by citizens and more participatory, as well as addressing the conditions of economic life which shape the ability of citizens to exercise their rights and routinely participate in public life. Without the vitality necessary to democratize sovereignty, sovereignty is experienced as acquiescence or domination.

Ordinary Democracy focuses on social movements inspired by the miraculous 2011 revolution in Tahrir Square to remove Hosni Mubarak from office, because these movements represent the possibility of ordinary citizens working together under conditions that have either funneled them away from political life or frustrated their entry into it. From this perspective, it views these movements not as unredeemed failures, but as examples of what Lida Maxwell has called "lost causes." According to Maxwell, lost causes draw attention to moments of democratic failure while simultaneously soliciting a public to affirm and act on the democratic possibilities that they represent.[22]

This turn to social movements claiming sovereignty diverges from contemporary democratic theorizing that has focused primarily on smaller-scale and episodic political phenomena.[23] The emphasis on sovereignty and democracy within state institutions in this book contrasts with a general move to separate the practice of democracy from its historical association with sovereignty and the state in democratic theory. Works fitting this trend include Antonio Negri and Michael Hardt's books, *Empire* and *Multitude*, which define democracy in terms of a self-organizing multitude of workers; Jacques Rancière's idea of democracy as the moment of disagreement and misunderstanding between citizens who use the same language to refer to different things; Sheldon Wolin's suggestion that democracy is limited to fugitive assemblies; William Connolly and Stephen White's efforts to describe democracy in terms of a reflective ethos of self-care; and Judith Butler's definition of democracy as embodied in practices of mutual generosity.[24]

The shift to define democracy in extra-juridical forms reflects a loss in confidence in the promise of liberty made possible through the state and its laws. Although the freedoms enumerated in the US constitution had, from the beginning, been predicated on the dispossession and domination of the nation's indigenous and slave populations, they remained vital because the dispossessed and dominated framed their aspirations of freedom in the same terms.[25] But as the gains of those movements have been slowly undermined or, more perniciously, predicated on the violent sacrifice of others,[26] the possibility of democratic agency and democratic agency without violence that they once represented feel increasingly distant.

For theorists who wish to separate democracy from sovereignty, democracy has been contaminated through its contact with sovereignty and the state, since these have been historically bound up with violence, empire, and exclusion. As Charles Mills and others have shown, the liberal democratic state is founded on a racial contract in which whites are the primary beneficiaries. Liberal contract theories, such as Locke's, imagined transforming "natural" or "pre-political" man into "political men" with rights.[27] In white settler states the establishment of this contractual society was premised on the denial, assimilation, and extermination of the already existing indigenous populations to effect this transformation, because sovereignty traditionally presupposes a unitary and uniform constitutional code that cannot tolerate diverse forms of citizenship.[28]

Xenophobic right-wing groups are evidence of the strong, mutually reinforcing circuit linking liberal democratic citizens, who understand themselves as free, autonomous, and self-legislating agents,[29] with state sovereignty generally and for white settler citizens, in particular, is closely associated with their positioning at the top of a racial hierarchy. These are strategies of racial control that are meant to secure the vestiges of individual sovereignty that remain under conditions of compromised national sovereignty, although the truth has always been that for democratic citizens the promise of sovereignty has always been chimeric. The fiction of undivided sovereignty is what animates emergency measures taken to preserve the common good even as it obscures the unequal sacrifices citizens must bear in the name of this sovereignty. The resurgence of right-wing populist groups in response to the perceived threats to national sovereignty is a reminder that the vitality of democratic citizenship has historically been secured through devitalizing possibilities for others.[30]

This legacy can help us understand support for the aggressive deportation of undocumented immigrants and militarization of the US–Mexico border; the murders of Trayvon Martin, Michael Brown, and Eric Garner; mass incarceration and disenfranchisement; the passage of racist anti-immigrant laws in Alabama and Arizona; and the fact that an entire segment of the population has become politicized in response to the election of Barack Obama.[31] The son of an immigrant, Obama is suspected by those on the right of wanting to loosen the country's immigration policies and extend amnesty to the undocumented in the interest of expanding the base of the Democratic Party with new voters whose culture, experiences, and languages set them apart from and, ultimately, against "native" whites. Or as one sign summed it up: "Obama's Plan: White Slavery."

The Arizona Minutemen, Oath Keepers, and, in Europe, groups like Red Dawn and Pegida, have grown in numbers and visibility because they present citizens a means of responding to compromised conditions of national sovereignty that are mirrored in their own experiences of devitalized agency, diminished status, and increasing vulnerability to circumstances beyond their control. On the right, anger at corporate power and special interests are overlaid with hostility toward "undeserving" citizens and noncitizens who take but do not contribute to the social safety net and strident calls to defend the borders from would-be immigrants who will overwhelm and overtake the nation's "native" population. Labeling the African American victims of Hurricane Katrina, "refugees" reflects this same effort. By calling them refugees, a term typically used to describe stateless persons or those who have left their homelands, the effect was to redescribe African Americans as outsiders to the nation, consolidating the identity of the nation and its promise of sovereignty in racialized terms.[32]

But to cede the state as theorists who wish to disentangle democracy from sovereignty have implied, is to leave the weakened but still formidable organs of the state open to takeover by either those who closely benefit from a political order organized to secure the conditions of capital growth, on the one side, or neo-fascists, on the other. The movements studied in *Ordinary Democracy* are unwilling to forfeit the state or the possibility of realizing democracy within it. They are seeking to expand political freedom and economic equality to a larger class of citizens; to reverse the narrowing of freedom to juridical terms that has exposed a larger gap between the promise and actual experience of freedom for many;[33] and curb the growth of US empire and corporate power. But primarily they seek to address the devitalized feelings of impasse and impassivity that often accompany the experience of emergency politics and which intensify those powers in turn. Examining the potential within these social movements is important because they may be able to transform everyday life on a scale larger than any single community, creating not islands of greater democracy but democratizing the conditions that contribute to the widespread experience of devitalized agency and unfreedom. These conditions include addressing the quasi-sovereign character of economic power, an area that other democratic theorists have neglected, in part because it is not clear how to democratize an entity without territorial boundaries.

PUBLIC PHILOSOPHY

Devitalized agency is the lens through which most citizens view events like the Egyptian Revolution or Occupy Wall Street, in part because they are so accustomed to identifying politics in monumental terms—as something that happens at the level of the state rather than at the level of citizens. But *Ordinary Democracy* looks at democracy in terms of the capacities of ordinary citizens to exercise power together under emergency conditions. In this respect, *Ordinary Democracy* follows a tradition that begins with Montesquieu's *Spirit of the Laws* and Alexis de Tocqueville's *Democracy in America*. Montesquieu's work is a study of not only constitutional design but also the sub-constitutional orders that animate the exercise of state powers. In other words, unlike earlier works of political theory that focused on the state and its leaders, Montesquieu combined an examination of the laws with an investigation into the subject-level micro-practices that gave form and shape to those laws.[34]

Likewise, Tocqueville chronicled the everyday habits, practices, and settings in which Americans lived as citizens. For Tocqueville, the genius of American democracy owed as much as to the design of institutions as it did the rich associational life of its citizens, the stabilizing role of a common Christian faith, and the passion for equality that permeated the habits and character of its citizens. He was prescient enough to observe how sub-constitutional orders apart from the federal government, which made the experience of exercising power in common part of the texture of everyday life, contributed to the freedoms and sense of equality that ordinary Americans enjoyed. For the same reasons, he worried openly about the pressure America's democratic culture faced from new forms of individualism emerging with the growth of capitalism.[35]

Appreciating the ordinary character of American democracy and identifying the presence of order against expectations of disorder, Tocqueville wrote, required a "new science of politics." He observed a restless vitality and organization in the rhythms of township and frontier life where others might have only seen unconnected activities or, with the memory of terror that followed the French Revolution in mind, feared the chaos and disorder within them. I am similarly suggesting that grasping how the normalization of emergency politics presents a challenge to, but also opportunity for, democratic practice requires a new approach to the study of politics that closes the distance between the study of politics and political life.

James Tully labels this approach to the study of politics "public philosophy." Public philosophy is written with and for citizens and citizen activists. Public philosophy refers to the self-conscious strategy, tactics, and theorizing that citizens within these movements create and distribute. I also classify my own engagement with these movements as public philosophy because the aim of this book is to illuminate the possibilities for citizen action and agency beyond unilateral assertions of state sovereignty. My claim is that much academic scholarship has inadequately responded to the way in which a devitalized sense of agency, the lack of first-hand experience of joining with others, and the easy draws of consumer culture have generated a sense of impasse and impassivity among contemporary citizens. Public philosophy therefore also represents a disciplinary argument about the study of political life.

Ordinary Democracy traces the possibilities for democratic life within these movements. By joining political theory to political practice under the conditions of devitalized agency, *Ordinary Democracy* adds a new dimension to public philosophy. For Tully, public philosophy names a form of theorizing that emerges in dialogue with the daily activities of citizens instead of being isolated from those concerns. Public philosophy does not privilege the position of the theorist who unmasks processes that are unfolding behind the backs of citizens or who identifies the preconditions for democratic flourishing. Rather public philosophy recognizes that citizens are already enmeshed in these questions and joins their attempts to clarify and sort through the challenges of living with dignity and justice. Taking philosophy to the streets, *Ordinary Democracy* is written with and for citizens engaged in making sense of their lives in the language they use to describe its possibilities even while it also underscores the usefulness of political theory for gaining a broader view on these disparate and seemingly unconnected forms of political activity.

Examining how citizens within these social movements make sense of the problems that define the conditions of their lives without falling into fear suggests that the sources of political knowledge today extend beyond the academy. The practice of public philosophy modeled in these pages consists of an engagement with and among citizens outside of the state and its institutions and the diverse representations of that experience—from documentary film to poetry to social media. My analysis of movement practices demonstrates *how* they illuminate the private sacrifices that are judged necessary to preserve the semblance of undivided sovereignty in order to reframe the possibilities that citizens have to act. I follow Tully in thinking about sovereignty as a set of governance relationships that include the state but extend well beyond its laws to include the new forms of political and, especially, economic power that organize daily life for many citizens and which drive emergency measures.[36] These governance relationships are increasingly the source of national and individual feelings of devitalized agency. They can be traced in the experiences of individual indebtedness, guilt, and shame, but also in the threat of lower credit scores for indebted countries in southern Europe; in unfulfilled yearnings for attachment and community; and the weight of impasse or the belief that nothing else is possible.

But studying these movement practices as examples of emerging counterpublics—associations whose members are defined by their opposition to prevailing norms—reveals that regenerating a desire for vitalized forms of active citizenship and vision for democratic life is integral to their protests.[37] This last point is an indication of how public philosophy is situated in and committed to practices of political contestation. Public philosophy is therefore distinct from understandings of philosophy that are committed to the discovery of universalisms or that believe that philosophy is incompatible with or separate from democracy. The normalization of emergency politics beyond the moment of crisis and the expansion of necessity to justify a much larger range of unilateral actions by sovereign powers means that there is no single truth that, once identified, could unlock the problem it represents. There is no universal ethic of responsibility or cosmopolitanism that, if accessed, would guide us out of the current situation. Instead of pursuing singular solutions, resistance has to be cultivated in the ordinary and unspectacular places where most people live their lives most of the time and which rarely hold the interest of most philosophers. By addressing problems that citizens face in these moments, helping them to realize small truths about those conditions, the dialogical character of public philosophy can be valuable.

That is because conflict within and about the content of public philosophy promotes the democratization of sovereignty since it reflects the relational character of sovereignty as well as the ambivalence and complications that define democratic collaboration with others. For this reason, a move to public philosophy offers better direction to the study of politics than the development of specialized discourses, conceptual innovations, or normative theories. The purpose of public philosophy is to guide citizens who see only impasse, to show that the only way around those impasses is to gather with people who feel the same and confront the structures of power that enforce those closures. For public philosophy, the loss of absolute truth is offset by the chance to offer hope and to multiply accounts of action that connect contemporary citizens to a democratic tradition that appears increasingly obscure to many of them. The most important contribution public philosophy can make is to offer new perspectives on the possibilities for citizens to act.

Among contemporary democratic theorists, William Connolly and Bonnie Honig carry forward Tocqueville's insight into how sub-constitutional habits and orders contribute to state practices of sovereignty.[38] For Connolly, juridical understandings of democracy are made possible and intelligible by sub-constitutional or extra-juridical practices of citizenship.[39] Connolly, for example, points to the absence of an ethos of pluralism among white Americans as the reason why President Jackson refused to enforce the Supreme Court decision recognizing the sovereignty of the Cherokee nation.[40] More recently, Connolly has suggested that strains of American evangelical Christianity, corporate power, and right-wing news outlets together represent an affinity of theological and secular spiritualties that has seeped into the "logic of perception"—the common sense I referred to earlier—supporting unilateral assertions of state sovereignty.[41] He names the refusal to sign climate change treaties, preemptive military actions, and efforts to make state laws adhere to religious codes resulting in attacks on minority rights, as examples of how this common sense has made the exercise of state sovereignty more one-dimensional and less respectful of pluralism. Connolly has called for microeconomic experiments guided by a spirit of ecological sustainability and egalitarianism to help citizens imagine alternatives to the current order of state priorities.[42]

Yet while an appreciation of the mutual dependence between juridical and extra-juridical practices of sovereignty has been consistent across Connolly's work, the emphasis within his scholarship has been on identifying the basis for citizens cultivating such an ethos. Connolly has sought the basis for this ethos across a wide variety of genre: through tracing an appreciation of mutual dependence and non-sovereignty among humans and nonhuman systems in film, neuroscience, and even in the complex mechanisms of climate science. His aim has been to identify the ethos—patterns of norms, judgments, and affects— that would make possible the more generous practice of sovereignty by pluralizing the number of legitimate theistic and nontheistic faiths that can be considered part of that ethos.[43] As Ella Myers has pointed out, though, the more generous ethos recommended by Connolly is one that is largely developed through individual reflection rather in dialogue or deep association with other citizens.[44]

Honig's concern for how citizens respond to top-down sovereign directives without being reduced by crisis and emergency to mere survival or endurance has taken a more diverse approach than Connolly's. While they span both juridical and extra-juridical responses, Honig's analyses of dilemmas of non-sovereignty tend to be grounded in historical contexts where democratic citizenship was practiced in situations very different from our own. Honig sees the decision by Louis Post, who was assistant secretary of labor during the First Red Scare, to use his knowledge of bureaucracy to create space for discretionary action as an example of moderating the exercise of juridical sovereignty. According to Honig, Post presented himself as rule-bound by citing adherence to administrative procedure, in order to insulate himself from threats by Attorney General A. Mitchell Palmer and J. Edgar Hoover, Director of the Federal Bureau of Investigation (FBI).[45]

Honig's recent study of the reception of Sophocles' *Antigone* is also motivated by the desire to highlight the political work that the play has and can perform to address efforts at resisting the sovereign authority of the state. Honig casts Antigone as invoking the language of sovereignty to authorize her own actions and undo similar claims by Creon. By suggesting that Antigone may have conspired with her sister Ismene against Creon, Honig introduces the possibility of contending sources of sovereignty within the action of the play. Honig turns to examples of these citizens acting differently: not succumbing to the demands of political necessity, but expanding their understandings of the term and, with it, their political choices to re-introduce this possibility to readers.[46]

But beyond identifying the link between micro- and macro-practices of sovereignty neither Connolly nor Honig closely investigates how social movements are seeking to democratize sovereignty and recast the imperative driving the unilateral assertion of sovereignty. The movements profiled in *Ordinary Democracy* build on Connolly and Honig's attention to ordinary practices and show how these practices also include aspirations toward democratizing sovereignty.[47] They model and project into the future emergent but not fully formed subjectivities and call others to cultivate and shelter those emergent practices. My account of the Idle No More movement in chapter 1 emphasizes the importance of generating new subjectivities to the project of democratizing sovereignty. Idle No More is an indigenous movement immediately motivated by Canadian Prime Minister Stephen Harper's claim that the passage of the 2013 Jobs and Growth Omnibus Bill, which nullified Section 35 of the

Constitution Act of 1982 guaranteeing indigenous communities the right to self-government, was necessary to ensure the nation's future political and economic security. By severely curtailing local control over land and water use by indigenous boards, the Harper legislation cleared the way for the construction of the Keystone XL and Enbridge Northern oil pipelines which would make development of Alberta's tar sands oil commercially viable.

For Idle No More, the first step to democratizing sovereignty involves addressing devitalized agency as one part of a larger norm of idleness associated with membership in the Canadian settler state. Idleness refers to the habits that justify the narrowing of the state's purposes to economic growth and which legitimate the "necessity" of Harper's legislation. These habits include patterns cultivating agency through consumer consumption rather than political association and identifying citizenship with fulfillment of low-intensity institutional obligations like voting. The decision taken by Idle No More protestors to dance the Round Dance in shopping malls and block highways disrupted patterns of idle consumerism and passive citizenship that disavow the historical sacrifice and present-day mistreatment of indigenous communities.

Once banned outright, the Round Dance is an embodied claim for indigenous self-determination and, equally, expresses the desire to unmake or decolonize the subject of the modern state beginning with its idleness and passivity. The affective vitality of the Round Dance is a micro-practice of sovereignty that does not mirror the unitary body of the traditional sovereign. Importantly, dancers claim self-determination as members of a group moving in time together. Bodily resonance binds them in a dance that can be alternately defiant, celebratory, mournful, and joyous, but ultimately works to undermine the image of the sovereign self patterned after the unitary sovereign of the modern state. The Round Dances performed in shopping malls were organized as flash mobs, spontaneous assemblies that blended political activity with the pleasures of spontaneity and surprise that strongly contrast with the site of low-intensity citizenship for members of the liberal democratic state: the voting booth, which is experienced privately and individually. The performance of Round Dances at shopping malls, in particular, were meant to compete with the pleasure and agency citizens seek in consumerism, since these represent forms of citizen idleness that legitimate the necessity of Harper's actions.

The refusal to accept Harper's action extended beyond generating public opposition to them to include the reinstatement of Section 35, in order to regain control over critical boards governing local land and water use, even if these governing institutions are widely recognized as creatures of the settler state, and the restoration of treaties signed between indigenous communities and the Crown. Knowing that the settler state has been successful in bending indigenous resistance to serve its own ends, some members of Idle No More have also pushed for the restoration of treaties, since these were signed between indigenous nations and Canada as equal, sovereign partners. These macro-level efforts to democratize sovereignty are dependent on micro-practices like the Round Dance and blockades that work to unmake the passivity of the settler citizen.

In the second chapter, I argue that Occupy sites in over two hundred US cities as well as online documents associated with the movement, like the "We are the 99 percent" Tumblr, presented citizens with participatory forms of engagement and association that contrast with the depoliticized character of felt legitimacy. The participatory dimensions of the movement's documentary practices helped dramatize the difficulty of paying attention to how emergency politics have transformed their hopes for the future. They did so by generating spectacles of subjects worn out and down by the sacrifices that emergency and crisis had coded as "necessary" and their resulting experiences of devitalized agency. Occupy Wall Street helped mobilize a public to scrutinize the consequences of actions that were judged necessary, such as the federal government's 2008 claim that it had to bail out banks because they were "too big to fail," and which helped normalize the concentration of decision-making powers in nondemocratic bodies.

Unmasking the fiction of the self-reliant, sovereign individual by revealing the unacknowledged sacrifices that citizens have been compelled by "necessity" to make was, I argue, the value of Occupy Wall Street's public philosophy. Specifically, Occupy's use of documentary techniques produced an archive of shared suffering and vulnerability that publicized and reframed private hardships as consequences of political choices justified in terms of the common good and not inevitable. The protests were meant to reveal the losses of agency that citizens had to bear to preserve the image of undivided sovereignty and the loss of trust that resulted from those sacrifices in political terms. Immediately, those sacrifices included joblessness, mortgage default, and homelessness, and other private hardships stemming from the 2008 economic downturn that have collectively undermined the terms of citizenship, for which work is a substantive precondition.[48] Occupy also undermined the ideal of the sovereign individual that legitimates the exercise of emergency powers by opening up space for citizens to discuss and begin to work through without resolving sacrifices made by women and communities of color that had not been acknowledged.

Acknowledgment of mutual vulnerability among citizens may represent the first step toward forging new forms of association and attachment, but what are the limits of conceiving of democracy in terms of mutual vulnerability? The third chapter investigates the role of mutual vulnerability in helping initiate democratic change by examining the basis and limits of conceiving democracy in terms of micro-practices of ethical care and generosity through Judith Butler's writing on "precarity" and her analysis of the 2011 protests in Tahrir Square to remove Hosni Mubarak from office. Butler has argued that the occupation of Tahrir Square suffused the protestors with an ethos of shared vulnerability and generosity, because sleeping, eating, and living in the square engaged citizens in micro-practices of mutual care.[49] For Butler, the experience of this precarity or the recognition of non-sovereignty is the defining instance of what Aletta Norval terms "moments of democratic identification," which allows citizens to see aspects of the present in new terms.[50] In Cairo, according to Butler, the task of satisfying the obligations of the body bound protestors to an ethic of nonviolence that was indifferent to sectarian divisions among Muslims, Christians, and secular humanists that had long split Egyptians. Butler suggests that the experience of intercorporeal visibility and vulnerability particular to contemporary street protests are the distinguishing features of democracy and democratic citizenship. For her, democracy can only be understood in terms that contrast with the juridical practice of sovereignty and state institutions.

Yet the ethic of nonviolence Butler highlights was not the product of indifference to sectarian divisions but rather a conscious effort to address them through spectacular displays of interfaith cooperation in Tahrir Square. Borrowing Norval's insight into the dynamics of aspect change, I suggest that organizers in Tahrir Square actively worked to inspire and cultivate democratic imaginaries among citizens. I argue that organizers were keenly aware of the need to address the fear—fear of the police and fear of sectarian violence—that the regime had used to extend its rule. They addressed this fear by organizing exemplary spectacles of interfaith cooperation during the eighteen-day revolution involving human chains of Christians protecting Muslim worshippers on Fridays and Muslims standing guard during Sunday Mass. Together, these spectacles conveyed and generated evidence of cooperation and trust among all Egyptians.

Second, Butler misjudges the aspirations and understandings of democracy that guided the protestors when she focuses on ethical practices alone. The protestors in Tahrir Square sought constitutional reforms to protect the gains of the revolution. Moreover, they continued to occupy Tahrir to demand these reforms after the removal of Mubarak and to register their opposition to the constitutional changes initiated later by the nation's first democratically elected president, Mohammed Morsi. Just as with Idle No More, the Egyptian protests suggest that citizens understand democracy to be meaningful only if it spans extra-juridical and juridical forms of sovereign power.

Still, micropolitical practices of individual initiative and mutual aid were undoubtedly important to the ability of Egyptian protestors to hold Tahrir Square and remove Mubarak from office. The fourth chapter examines the value of individual initiative and mutual aid efforts in building the capacity of citizens to act under conditions of devitalized agency. Individual initiative and mutual cooperation were central to the do-it-yourself (DIY) ethos of Occupy Sandy, the mutual relief organization that sprang up in the aftermath of Hurricane Sandy in 2012 and which was broadly praised for its good works. Scholar Lauren Berlant has suggested DIY citizenship represents the most promising model for citizenship under contemporary conditions of crisis and emergency. Indeed self-initiative and mutual cooperation are routinely identified as key elements of American democratic culture, stretching back to Tocqueville.

This chapter questions the macro-practices of sovereignty that the actions of citizen mutual aid makes legible, however. While scholars like Berlant have praised DIY citizenship for its capacity to direct desires for creativity and attachment toward public life at a moment when formal political institutions are less receptive to them, I argue that, taken alone, the DIY ethos is situated too closely to the dominant logics of the networked, neoliberal economy. Even though the origins of DIY lie in anarchic movements and strongly influenced the anti-capitalism of punk music and Occupy Sandy's emphasis on mutual aid contrasts with the experience of competition in the labor force, I suggest that Occupy Sandy's organizational resemblance to the project-driven economy reinforces rather than softens the drive subjects in the neoliberal economy have to develop themselves as human capital. My claim is that DIY citizenship represents a bundle of micro-level practices that works with instead of against the grain of emergency politics. Specifically, they support the necessity of economic growth and efficiency over democratic processes and privatization and downsizing of state responsibilities.

Although critics within the movement have also dismissed Occupy Sandy's volunteerism because it compromises a continued focus on criticizing the income inequalities that produced the "99 percent," I argue the attempt to use the storm and climate science as the basis for critiquing capitalism as Naomi Klein, Bill McKibbin, Andrew Ross, and other activists recently have will only be partly successful. That is because these arguments do not adequately tend to the reasons why contemporary subjects willingly support and attach themselves to the contemporary economy, despite the injuries they suffer as a result of those choices. Drawing on research conducted by sociologists Luc Boltanski and Eve Chiapello into what they call the new spirit of capitalism, I suggest that addressing the excess demands of neoliberal capitalism must originate within a reconsideration of the desires that draw subjects to the free market. Building on Max Weber's idea of the spirit of capitalism, or the non-coercive dimensions of capitalism that animate and legitimate capitalism ideologically, Boltanski and Chiapello identify three reasons why workers consent and support the configuration of the contemporary economy. These are desire for freedom, flexibility, and public good. I argue that the desire of storm victims to rebuild communities suggests that they value stability and public good as much as they value their freedom. Freed to be mobile human capital, they refuse and insist on rebuilding their communities. I suggest that organizing around other desires that sustain attachments contemporary subjects have to the market may resist claims of economic necessity justifying unilateral state action.

This argument is indebted to Michel Feher and Wendy Brown's analysis of human capital development and its implications are taken up in the final chapter,[51] which considers the challenge of organizing citizens beyond the boundaries of formal political institutions by asking what it would mean to democratize the economy.[52] The complexity, scale, and interconnections of the global economy seem to put it out of the reach of any particular sovereign body, whether juridical or extra-juridical, leading Wendy Brown to describe capital as possessing a kind of sovereignty of its own. Moreover, critics like Brown and Jodi Dean argue that democracy does not offer the resources necessary to mount a resistance to the force of neoliberal capital.[53] They suggest neoliberalism represents an intensification of liberal democracy where citizen-consumers come to see freedom and the free market as interchangeable and where traditional virtues of democratic citizenship—the opportunity for creative world making, spontaneity, and diversity—are the same features for which capitalism is celebrated.

I challenge their calls for post-democratic forms of sovereign power by suggesting that the assumption that radical change must be external to immanent conditions and experience does not always hold. I take up the question of the transformative potential of ordinary democracy in this final chapter by examining the politics of debt resistance. I highlight the role of micro-practices within the Strike Debt movement that are meant to change how citizens understand debt within a moral economy that sees debt as the source of shame and shameful pleasures connected with over-consumption. I argue the movement's debt forgiveness parties represent an effort to shift the association with debt from shame to taking pleasure in forgiveness. Along with this micro-practice, I proffer that experience with the debt minimization and resistance techniques outlined in the *Debt Resistors' Operations Manual* help make the movement's call for the kind of Debtors' Jubilee described in the Bible and Qur'an intelligible and less utopian, enabling it to serve as the aspirational horizon for those efforts. In this case, my suggestion is that micro-practices create room for imagining new forms of extra-juridical sovereignty that vitalize emergent practices of debt resistance.

As a work of public philosophy, *Ordinary Democracy* responds to an urgent need to comprehend and develop new practices of democratic citizenship. It identifies both obstacles to political agency and practices that strengthen and generate the desire for participation in common action, focusing on how movements try to inspire and renew the courage required for citizens to act. The movements profiled in *Ordinary Democracy* represent more than just ordinary citizens doing ordinary things, but performing those actions with vision and purpose. Their diversity confirms that there is no single response to the challenges of neoliberal impasse but suggests common features involved in democratizing sovereignty and revitalizing agency.

1

Idleness Is the Problem

"So I think this absolutely needs to go ahead, but you can rest assured that making our emissions targets, including in the oil sands sector, is an important objective of the government of Canada." The "this" Prime Minister Stephen Harper was referring to in his question and answer session with Bob Rubin at the Council on Foreign Relations on May 16, 2013, was the Keystone XL pipeline.[1] Harper, in his previous remarks to the council, had outlined his plan for "preparing Canada for leadership." His plan would advance "security, prosperity, and democracy" and its cornerstone would be the development of Canada's oil sands reserve.[2] As he told the audience assembled that afternoon, construction of the pipelines would achieve energy security, reducing dependence in North America on "foreign oil"; it was good for the environment since, according to Harper, emissions from oil sands represented "almost nothing globally," and, finally, it would grow jobs on both sides of the border, a fact that citizens of neither country could afford to ignore. This is why, Harper concluded, the project had such broad public support.

That Harper ultimately justified the pipeline in terms of necessity indicates the driving role that economic growth and security have assumed in legitimating state action today. Sheldon Wolin and Wendy Brown have argued that neoliberalism, as a system of governance, does not seek to eliminate government, but to redefine its purpose. Governance refers to policies, laws, regulations, but also habits, norms, and dispositions, that legitimate, enforce, and normalize the exercise of state power.[3] Neoliberal privatization and cuts to the social safety net achieve the stated goal of reducing bureaucracy and regulation while simultaneously strengthening control over the remaining security and economic functions of the state. With the reduction of its responsibilities, the state is increasingly measured by its ability to deliver on its surviving functions. Indeed, threats from outside the state, including terrorism and economic competition, put greater pressure on leaders like Harper to concentrate what state powers remain in order to hold onto the semblance of sovereignty, entailing the powers of self-determination and autonomy that traditionally define the nation-state.

Although these threats to national sovereignty are increasingly coming from nonstate and even nonhuman actors, the latter in the form of viruses and the quasi-sovereign character of capital for instance, the concern for security is locked into the definition of sovereignty. Locke maps sovereignty onto physical territory and Max Weber identifies a monopoly on violence within a territory as the mark of the sovereign.[4] Wolin observes the roots of increased state power in the Cold War, when the threat of nuclear war with the Soviet Union justified military spending, enlarged executive powers, and privatization of government services. According to Wolin, upholding norms of freedom and the free market licensed "forms of power and magnitudes of power hitherto unknown."[5]

If Harper's proposal had such broad public support though, why was it couched in the language of necessity? After all, to call the proposed pipelines necessary was to suggest that they were beyond debate. Perhaps Harper was hoping to interpellate a sense of felt legitimacy, sidestepping the need for deliberation or consent.[6] But if that was what it was, there was already evidence back home that it was not working. Harper's last statement to the audience in New York omitted the fact that thousands of indigenous persons and their supporters had been protesting the measures he had unilaterally taken the previous fall to secure his government's ability build the pipeline.[7]

The formation of modern Canada was predicated on the violent assimilation and destruction of indigenous peoples and cultures, which were sacrificed to generate a singularly settler state. And as Harper turned to strengthen Canada's economic position in the current global hierarchy by developing the commercial viability of the tar sands region, he once again did so at the expense of the indigenous peoples of Canada. The legislation introduced by Prime Minister Harper violated both existing treaties and the provisions of self-government outlined in Section 35 of the Constitution Act of 1982.[8] Section 35 stipulates that the Prime Minister will "invite" aboriginal representatives to discuss any future proposals that would affect the constitutional status of aboriginal sovereignty.[9]

Yet Harper introduced the legislation during the autumn of 2012 without consulting with representatives from indigenous communities.[10] The bills introduced include: S-6: First Nations Elections Act, which limits the ability of bands to protest elections; C-248: Indian Act Amendment and Replacement Act, which undercuts the ability of First Nations to pass their own laws and relieves Ottawa of the duty to consult tribal bands on decisions that affect them; S-212: First Nations Self Government Recognition Bill and FPNOA, which privatizes tribal lands and nullifies local governance; C-27: First Nations Financial Transparency Act, which undermines the financial independence of bands under the guise of reducing corruption; S-2: Family Homes on Reserves and Matrimonial Interests or Rights Act, which allows tribal lands to be transferred to non-First Nations person in violation of current treaty agreements and Court rulings; and Bill C-45: The Jobs and Growth Act (Omnibus Bill), which would restrict the number of protected waterways from nearly three million to less than one hundred, in violation of current treaties. It also removed stipulations that require the federal government to consult with Canada's aboriginal peoples before proposing projects that would be sited on indigenous tribal land and/or affect those communities. Bill C-45 would alter the Navigable Waters Protection Act of 1882, which makes it a crime to "block, alter or destroy any water deep enough to float a canoe without federal approval," by reserving this protection for only named bodies of water.[11]

The Harper legislation represents a reversal of Section 35 and continuation of the earlier settler practice of seeing Canadian territory *as terra nullius*, virgin and unclaimed. *Terra nullius* is predicated on the denial of aboriginal sovereignty. Indigenous activists understand *terra nullius* as the philosophical justification for settler colonialism: the unjust and ongoing imposition of alien rule. Despite the Royal Proclamation of 1763, which acknowledges aboriginal title, and a series of treaties signed between the Crown and tribal bands, in which the signatories recognize one another as nations of equal standing, Canada's indigenous people have been treated as minor partners. For the most part, aboriginal peoples entered Canada unwillingly and as unequals, and their land was taken from them unfairly, by violent and lethal force. Members of the First Nations tribal bands, for example, were removed from their traditional lands, either forced onto reservations or forcibly assimilated into Canadian society. Many children designated "aboriginal" by the state were violently removed from their family homes and sent to state-run homes where they were forbidden to speak tribal languages or observe indigenous customs.

The response to Harper's actions is part of a long history of indigenous resistance and self-determination efforts. Idle No More was started online in 2012 by a group of indigenous and non-indigenous women to draw attention to the consequences the Harper legislation would have on indigenous rights to self-rule and control over land and water use. By identifying the incipient movement in terms of behavior it would no longer accept, Idle No More activists suggested that the first step to countering Harper's prerogative power would require practices to unmake the norm of passivity or idle citizenship that characterizes membership in the settler colonial state. Ryan McMahon, a member of the Anishinaabe Nation, names unlearning the settler mentality among both indigenous and non-indigenous activists a top priority for the movement: "Idle No More is not only unsettling the larger Canadian population but it's about unsettling ourselves as Indigenous Peoples—the hard work of decolonization is happening right in front of us in real time, on Twitter, Facebook, and in shopping malls . . . we have a lot to *unlearn*."[12]

Unlearning idle citizenship represents the first step to democratizing sovereignty by decentralizing decision-making power in assemblies and institutions that serve to counteract prerogative state power. The Round Dance dramatizes indigenous sacrifice and survival in relation to the formation of modern Canada. Performing the Round Dance in shopping malls during the Christmas holiday season and blocking busy highways and intersections is the reminder to both indigenous and non-indigenous persons of how citizens participate in the exercise of sovereignty through their actions or inactions. The coordinated movements and embodied performance generates feelings of vitality, attachment, and cultural pride among dancers that contrasts sharply with feelings of shame, indifference, and passivity that circulate broadly in the general population. The Round Dance represents a form of active citizenship that is meant to awaken creative, world-making powers among citizens acting together in order to combat the deep sense of impasse that short-circuits desires for agency.

But the Round Dance is more than merely disruptive of state sovereignty. Unlike radical democrats like Wolin who confine democracy to irruptive and episodic moments, democratized forms of sovereignty represent the aspirations of Idle No More activists. Though they disagree on whether or not to restore Section 35 and broken treaties signed between Canada and indigenous nations, they wish to pluralize the sites of decision-making and distribute those powers across multiple legal jurisdictions.

UNMAKING IDLE CITIZENS

Idleness in the context of Idle No More refers to more than just the comportment of the settler citizen; it also challenges a stereotype about indigenous peoples that works to undercut their political activity in two ways. Both are micro-level practices that sustain the Canadian nation-state's macro-level structures of sovereignty and governance. The first is manifest in the stereotype of the lazy or idle indigenous person who benefits from government social programs. Canadians incorrectly believe that indigenous peoples benefit from free education and social welfare programs, but this is not the case. Nonetheless this misperception generates feelings of resentment among white settler citizens and those of other (non-indigenous) races over what are thought to be unearned entitlements and privileges, especially when these are claimed by indigenous persons living not on land that is recognized as indigenous territory but in Canada's cities.

From their perspective, Harper's move to cancel these entitlements and to reduce "corruption" and "bad government" among indigenous leaders do not register as racialized arguments but are understood in terms of fairness and dollars and cents.

Stereotypes of lazy or idle indigenous peoples are also a source of shame and feelings of inferiority for many indigenous persons that must also be unlearned, writes Chickadee Richard. According to Richard, the internalization of this stereotype has made indigenous communities more docile and governable. For Richards, contesting this stereotype also requires independent media, given how corporate media amplifies messages that are in line with the government and its allied interests, especially the petrochemical industry. Richard writes: "I believe we have been taught to think in a certain pattern and this makes us easier to control. Sometimes our people think that thinking for oneself is wrong, especially if it's against chief and council, government, men, or so forth. Over time you see how the media works against certain ideas and in the favour of the government and multinationals, trying to create pretty pictures. . . ."[13] Richards is describing how aboriginal subjects have been shaped as subjects of power not just through state institutions but through an array of independent yet interlocking institutions that function as an assemblage to produce what citizens understand as common sense. McMahon elaborates this common sense in terms of feeling ashamed at being Anishinaabe. Recalling his experience in the Indian Residential School system, which was designed to assimilate indigenous youths by separating them from their communities, he writes, "There was a lot of weird 'don't talk about it-ness.'" McMahon describes the resulting feelings of inferiority and insecurity as a "major scar" that contributed to his struggles with alcohol abuse as a young adult in Toronto.[14]

Until this passivity or idleness and the associated feelings of shame are unlearned, McMahon and Richard suggest that indigenous communities permit settler citizens to live innocent of the knowledge of the violence directed toward indigenous peoples in the past and how it continues into the present. The political idleness of the settler citizen is arguably gained by the overshadowing of public life by private pursuits. Through a combination of impasse and hyper-individualism, agency is funneled into consumerism. These private pursuits distract citizens from deeper forms of political engagement and from reckoning with the hidden processes that sustain them—in particular, the extraction of natural resources, burning of fossil fuels, and the environmental damage resulting from overproduction and consumption.

Indigenous scholars and activists have identified the subjectivity of the settler citizen as an obstacle to self-determination, observing that indigenous subjects are just as likely to be magnetized by the hegemonic culture of the settler state as non-indigenous persons. This is one reason that so many indigenous scholars are wary of the institutions of self-government specified in Section 35. Glen Coulthard observes that as creations of the Canadian state that do not require recognition from aboriginal communities, institutions of indigenous self-government set up by the constitution do not recognize indigenous sovereignty or subjects on their own terms.[15] Instead, self-government enlists and calls on members of indigenous communities to cultivate an attitude or affect that is suited to the terms set by the colonial power.[16] The expectation of compliance with state directives and acceptance of the ultimate sovereignty of the state's juridical powers is evident, Coulthard writes, in the 1997 Delgamuukw decision. In that decision, the Canadian High Court declared that the federal government could infringe on aboriginal title for reasons it deems "compelling and substantial."

This wariness explains the emphasis on cultural regeneration within indigenous political movements and within Idle No More. The Idle No More protests featured practices intended to both disrupt the normal routines and idleness of the settler state and model an alternative form of citizenship. By blocking rail lines and busy metropolitan intersections and highways during rush hour, as well as rural routes through indigenous lands traveled by oil and logging trucks, Idle No More activists wanted to interrupt the smooth function of the economy to suggest the illegitimacy of Harper's actions. By introducing "inefficiencies" into the regular function of the economy and patterns of capital circulation, the protestors provoked a backlash from settler citizens who resented them for putting the steady accumulation of capital in jeopardy. Yet by destabilizing the economy and preventing its regular function, Idle No More activists drew attention to the Harper government's failure to safeguard the conditions required for economic security and growth it had identified as its raison d'être.

The road blockades and protests in shopping malls, in addition to more conventional "political" sites such as outside parliament house and the prime minister's offices in Ottawa, disrupted state sovereignty at both the macro- and micro-level. At the macro-level, obstructing traffic disrupts the regular order of the city and state. It tests the powers of the state and the commitments subjects have to those powers. The criticism lobbed at Idle No More protestors for troublemaking and causing disorder on talk radio and in the opinion pages during this period testifies to the strength of the attachment that most Canadians have to the state and to state imperatives. But these actions also reveal a level of dissonant citizenship that directly addresses resistant fellow citizens as well as the government. Idle No More's micro-level practices of citizenship involve affective appeals to all Canadians to join in popular action to challenge the necessity of the government's actions.

Idle No More's micro-level practices of sovereignty create the conditions for re-imagining macro-level practices of sovereignty in more democratic terms. Just as the sovereignty of the liberal subject is the microcosm of the sovereignty of the liberal state, Idle No More's micro-practices of sovereignty aspire to generate a reinforcing loop among citizens who recognize the possibilities for action beyond submission to the necessity of state directives. These movement practices produce forms of popular sovereignty that contend with the dominant forms of idle citizenship as well as forward juridical claims to sovereignty in the form of self-governing institutions and treaties that rival the powers of the Canadian state.

They do so by attempting to rewire citizens' attachments to idleness as expressed through low-intensity citizenship, on the one hand, and the pursuit of agency and creativity through consumer activity, on the other. The Round Dance disrupts, as it competes with, the patterns and norms of thinking and doing associated with idleness. This is a form of association that contrasts with depoliticized forms of identification. It depends on active participation and is embodied and sensual rather than abstract and passive. The resulting vitality is necessary to politicize the sacrifices of earlier indigenous communities in order to demand redress. Understood within the context of indigenous struggles for sovereignty and self-determination within and outside of the settler state, Idle No More invokes the language of sovereignty to authorize its actions and undermine Harper's claim.

GENERATING VITALITY: DANCING THE ROUND DANCE

Neal McLeod's poem "Nothing Will Ever be the Same: Idle No More" conveys the aspirations of the protestors as well as identifies the spaces and habits of racism, consumerism, and history that contextualize the Round Dances. A portion of McLeod's poem is quoted below:

> kayas ago
> I remember all of the time
> I would go to malls
> in Saskatchewan
> kisiskaciwan-sipiy-askiy
> racism, in your face 'em
> redneck hollers
> leaving nothing
> under their collars
>
> now the drums
> of our young people
> make new sounds
> and tear away, beat by beat
> the closed spaces
> to create new places
> for the ones that come after us

kinanaskomitinawaw ka-nikamawak
I thank all of the singers, ahaw!

ironic colonialism
caused neechies to
create new testimonials
makes people dig deeper
when they come back
with rich, heavy sound

there is nothing that
can hold back that sound
no Bill can constrain it
no Indian Act can stop us
from our neechie acts

the sound fills our marrow
and makes our bones shake
and nervous settlers quake
with dreams of our ancestors
become real in this moment
for the osk-ayak[17]

McLeod describes his dancing of the Round Dance in shopping malls where he had previously experienced racial animosity as a transformative act. For McLeod, this act was transformative of commercial, consumer-oriented spaces as well as the dispositions of idleness associated with them, both in terms of the political idleness that is the by-product of lifestyles organized around the satisfaction of capitalist desire for consumer goods and the inferiority and shame of not belonging that many indigenous persons experienced in these "closed spaces." Representing a break with forms of protest marches and demonstrations clearly recognizable to members of the settler state, this dancing is an expression of indigenous identity that transforms spaces into "new places," signifying the transition from abstract membership (spaces) to embodied belonging and association (places) the dancers experience. The poem both reflects and generates growing cultural pride and confidence among indigenous dancers. This confidence appears in the incorporation of indigenous words and languages into the poem itself, given indigenous youth were once punished in Canadian settler schools if they spoke in anything but English or French and made to feel ashamed of their "backward" culture. The aim of these schools was to break students' ties to their languages and culture in order to assimilate them as members of the liberal state. The settler state's success at separating and individuating subjects is reflected in McLeod's use of the first person singular at the outset of the poem. By the end, however, his language shifts to first person plural.

For McLeod, this transformation is linked to sounds of the drums that resonate through bodies dancing together. This new collective body is the source of sounds that re-enter and reinvigorate the body ("sound fills our marrow"). The drumming joins the dancers together while at the same time the spectacle unnerves settler citizens who come upon the dancers. These dancers are acting in defiance of juridical instruments like the Harper legislation and the earlier Indian Act to generate new forms of community and sovereign power. The performance is disruptive but durable since the new places it creates are "for the ones that come after us" and it is only possible thanks to the collective act of dancing and singing together ("I thank all of the singers, ahaw!). Dancing and singing invite participants to form new attachments with one another and with future and preceding generations ("for the ones that come after us/with dreams of our ancestors") that allows desires for political agency and attachment to slide from the abstract and unexercised agency possessed by citizens of the settler state to dense, embodied forms.

McLeod's language conveys the experience of vitality, or the belief that the world is responsive to one's actions and efforts, found in the Round Dance. Specifically, he refers to a confidence found in association with others that makes collective dreaming and action possible. According to McLeod, these dreams and actions "Become real in this moment." Realizing this power to act together at once scares and exhilarates dancers who feel their "bones shake" with knowledge of their own collective being and potential. The weight of that strength is implied in the description of the sound generated by the dancers and singers, which is "rich, heavy." That heaviness allows McLeod to recognize the Round Dance as a counterweight to the state. Neither the Harper legislation, nor the legal measures that deny indigenous sovereignty (the Indian Act), will stop the dancers from articulating those demands.

The vitality of the Round Dance, specifically its ability to awaken the creative dimensions of citizenship in ways that low-intensity forms do not, can be traced to its embodied, participatory, and spontaneous character. Many of the Round Dances in shopping malls were organized as flash mobs, which have their origins in DIY grassroots political events that were intended to collapse the distance between performers and the audience that they summon into being. Such mob events were often held in public spaces in order to surprise and elicit reactions from passersby but, as Mary Elizabeth Anderson observes, this audience has grown to include those who would view the events later online thanks to the widespread availability of digital video recording machines. Anderson argues that even with the commercialization of mob events, they retain their ability to move watchers emotionally. She argues that flash mobs should be understood in terms of authoring the kind of public rituals Victor Turner identified as part of the instruments for making and remaking society and which Emile Durkheim saw as experiences of "collective effervescence."[18]

For Anderson, flash mobs are distinguished by the appearance of spontaneity as participants use "sudden, unusual movements in public spaces in order to effect a series of 'surprises.'"[19] These include surprise invitations to participate, the discovery of the other participants, the surprise of those who happen to witness the event in person, and the surprise of those who learn of the event later. Reflecting on her own experience viewing the Oprah Feelin' flash mob, which was organized in Chicago to surprise Oprah Winfrey by the producers of her talk show and involved many thousands of dancers, Anderson locates the experience of joy in watching the dancers dance in recent research into kinetic receptivity conducted by neuroscientists. Kinetic receptivity describes the active, embodied rather than passive, responses that spectators of such dances experience. According to Wolf Singer, these experiences are organized according to prior experiences and there is a kind of physical pleasure, or possibly frustration, that is experienced when the brain tries or fails to map this new experience onto memories of older ones. Dance scholar Ivar Hagendoorn suggests that the experiences of joy or frustration originate in the viewer's expectation of the movement and the dancers' actual movements, similar to the experience of either catching or not catching a ball.[20] Writing in the context of demonstrations for immigrants rights that took place in several US cities in 2006, Cristina Beltrán has described those protestors as embodying "festive anger," a term that expresses a "complex (and interconnected) set of civic emotions, including indignation, determination, irony, outrage, and joy" originating out of the experiences of "exploitation, hostility, and state-sanctioned violence" toward immigrants.[21] Understanding the Idle No More protests as festive anger makes it possible to grasp both the transgressive and inaugural potential of the affect generated there.

This research suggests that viewers of the Round Dance experienced it as something new and disruptive and were alternatively moved by it to experience a feeling of resonance and connection, frustrated by it or, possibly both. Certainly an element of surprise is visible in videos of the Round Dances available online. Shoppers can be seen stopping, drawn in by the sound and the crowd of bodies surrounding the dancers, to take in the performances. Some stay before wandering off, but the dances disrupt the circuits of Christmas-holiday shoppers who are in the midst of the most intense retail period on the calendar. Similar protests on city streets, on highways, and even on rail lines, blocked the regular circulation of goods and bodies, disrupting the smooth operation of the economy. Because these disruptions had symbolically and materially significant impacts on the flow of goods and services in the economy, settler citizens took notice of them and the government's inability to put a stop to them. In other words, the performance of these micro-practices undermined the legitimacy of Harper's assertion of state sovereignty since it was visibly unable to guarantee economic productivity, the very thing it has come to be measured by.

This break in the chain connecting state sovereignty to micro-practices of idleness makes way for the possibility of democratizing sovereignty by introducing forms of popular power that vie with the state's exercise of prerogative power. As Simon Critchley has argued, indigenous performances like the Round Dance "have the effect of calling into question the entire legality of the state and calling for redress to a massive historical wrong."[22] At the heart of these alternatives are dances themselves, which were once banned outright in North America. While these performances neither represent nor are intended to represent "authentic" expressions of indigenous culture because they have evolved and continue to evolve as a result of the colonial experience [23] activists frame them in terms of practices of decolonialization anchored in a long history of indigenous resistance. Originally identified with the Cree, since the middle of the twentieth century the Round Dance has been adopted and localized by other North American indigenous groups, especially those whose traditional teachings had been wiped out by the settler state. The Round Dance spread among First Nations during this period as many looked to regenerate local tribal cultures by learning from other indigenous spiritual traditions and cultures.[24] The Round Dance is both a healing dance and a social dance, part ceremony and part a call to resistance and cultural renewal. Pamela Green and Norman Moyah identify the modern Round Dance as the most "intimate and communal expression of Aboriginal spirituality" but it is a regular feature of political gatherings such as the annual meeting of the Women Against Violence Against Women to mark the murder and disappearance of more than 1,000 indigenous women in Canada.[25]

For participants, the Round Dances are important opportunities to experience unity outside the terms of felt legitimacy particular to membership in the settler colonial state and to work against the shame and stigma that contribute to their passivity. To begin with, the dancers are collective assemblies made possible by the co-presence and contributions of those who dance, drum, and sing. Traditionally the Round Dance is performed to honor ancestors or to generate and affirm a sense of community among those gathered. It celebrates membership in a community rather than the individual, and given the political history of the Round Dance, it foregrounds acknowledgment of the losses suffered by indigenous communities in the past and through the present. Moving together side by side in time with the drumming, clasping hands, the dancers experience being part of a group that is larger than the individual and which is claiming autonomy and the right to self-determination as a group.[26] John Protevi and William McNeil have argued that collective bodily movements like communal dances and military exercises produce an affective joy in being and acting together in the company of others.[27] Collective movements and rhythms resonate in the body to generate what Protevi calls a "spiraling intermodal feedback" among participants that transforms them into a new body politic that is unwilling to accept invocations of necessity in the name of sovereignty—what McLeod conveys above in the language of "new sounds/new places." Such micro-practices can shape larger macro-practices of sovereignty, just as Michel Foucault identified military drills and institutional spaces like hospitals and prisons with the production of subjects of the modern nation-state.[28]

Instead of being linked to the sovereign individual of the liberal state though, the counter claim to self-determination is articulated through the collective body. Niigaanwewidam James Sinclair underlines this remaking in his poem, "Dancing in a Mall":

> Back
> in the Beginning
> repeating these stories
> like a drop
> pooling
> in fountains of time
> linoleum waves
> in circles of ancestors
>
> Naanaboozho is here, she is here.
> here. here. here.
> born with a stone
> dropping dripping
> into ndns gathered

from children.
of sacrificed mothers
and windy fathers.

sent
on journeys
to closed store windows
here
our lives are born
exploding through breath
into pipes filled with black.

two steps
now
don't pause
to
dream see
the
earth move
howa

there is no end
there is no end
there is no end
That is the story when we tell it.
The flood
Is always a beginning
a return.

writing with our feet.
we speak.
in the air conditioning.
the drum
like petals
on hide
our link

so in winter we
danced
looking for
mom
and dad
we spoke we walked we danced
we dreamed
and we said no more

we remade
we remade
we remade
the paper walls.
we remade
we remade
we remade
the world

here, in our repeating
floods
our fables
our births
our families
in the hole of fluorescent light
we continue

Ha ya hey ya
we live
Ha ya hey ya
we live
Ha ya hey ya
we live
Ha ya hey ya
we live[29]

For Sinclair, the protestors speak as a collective body and "write" with their footsteps. He refers to "we" rather than the rights-bearing "I" privileged by the settler state. Like many indigenous activists, Sinclair identifies the endurance of indigenous communities and languages despite all of the violence directed toward them by the settler state—an experience he likens to breathing through "pipes filled with black"—as a source of strength ("we continue"). The colonial state has nearly wiped out indigenous communities, whose children, mothers, and fathers have been sacrificed to it. But if floodwaters can overwhelm, they are also a source of renewal, restoring the land and peoples who live on the land without trying to master it. Sinclair indicates this generative relationship with the language of "repeating floods" from which "our fables/our births/our families" emerge. For him, the flood and the settler nation and culture it represents is not an end but "always a beginning."

Dancing the Round Dance in a shopping mall is a gesture of beginning. Beginning is a collective exercise that disrupts the habits of the settler citizen immersed in the habits of idleness and consumerism at the mall. Unlike the settler citizen mall shopper, who publicly identifies with her interests rather than opinions that are shared and refined through dialogue with others, participants in the Round Dance are engaged in an associational practice of singing, speaking, and walking together. The experience of collective beginning produces a sense of vitality ("we live") that contrasts with the impasse felt by citizens of the settler state. This vitality allows Sinclair to believe that the barriers that previously held members of his community in place are less sturdy than they were believed to be. Thanks to the protests and the experience of speaking, walking, and dancing together, they are revealed to be "paper" capable of being refashioned. Sinclair's poem implies the creation of subjects who are attuned to their vitality and powers of agency in contradiction to the expectations of impasse and passivity held by members of the settler state—emphasized in the repetition of "we remade" in the eighth stanza. The experience of dancers and viewing the dancers works to reframe the expectations both indigenous and non-indigenous populations have about the feelings of shame and inferiority that have made indigenous communities passive and governable. The dancers and drummers augment agency through its exercise, forging attachments to others that help them confront the feelings of loss, abandonment, and helplessness experienced by youth and adults like McMahon.

The bodily experience of agency and pleasure in the company of others directly contrasts with the minimalist experience of membership in the settler colonial state. If voting is the political practice that marks membership in the settler colonial state, the contrast between that environment and the Round Dance is striking. Voting is an individual activity where decisions are made in secret and not disclosed to others. Voting is discrete and bounded; it involves choosing from already formed options and requires the citizen to invest a minimal amount of time, which also suggests that not much should be expected from it in return. The Round Dance is a creative and embodied collective activity. It presents citizens with an experience of unity and vitality that runs against the grain of the felt legitimacy and idleness characteristic of the exercise of popular but non-democratic acts of sovereignty taken by the Harper government.

The Round Dance is a dramatic performance in which citizens must publicly identify with their desires for mutual attachment and publicity. The desire to identify publicly as a political actor is itself counter to the norms of citizenship associated with the liberal democratic state, as much as the refusal to submit to state directives is. Subjects are constituted and constituted differently through these actions. The Round Dance and blockades are evidence of citizens who are unwilling to accept government policies taken in their name and the notion of state-centered, juridical understanding of sovereignty that operates according to the assumed consent of the people. Performing these micro-practices under the language of indigenous sovereignty calls a public into being around that claim, so that subjects are pulled by the idea that they are sovereign while at the same time generating that sovereignty together. It is not only the question of governance and sovereignty over indigenous lands that is at stake in the protests but also the kind of relationship that citizens should have to the modern state. The protests represent attempts to flip the question about legitimacy around so that it is the actions of the state that are held questionable, rather than actions initiated by citizens.

CONCLUSION: DEMOCRATIZING SOVEREIGNTY

Subject and cultural transformation are the purpose of Idle No More's Round Dances and blockades. They represent a refusal of the norms of idle citizenship that is generative of vitality and active citizenship. Active citizenship and popular legislative power are the first steps to democratizing sovereignty and challenging emergency politics, because active citizens break the cycle of acquiescence and domination that characterizes the passive relationship idle citizens have with state power. Unlike idle citizens, who identify citizenship with the fulfillment of low-intensity obligations like voting and paying taxes and institutional designs that do little to draw desires for agency that have been directed toward the market, Idle No More's practices seek to nurture vitality among citizens. Vitality is at the core of McLeod's and Sinclair's separate accounts of performing the Round Dance.

Dancing the Round Dance in shopping malls, in city streets and squares, blocking rush hour traffic during the 2012 Christmas holiday season disrupted the normal circulations of idle citizens. These disruptions drew attention to the Canadian government's inability to perform the roles that have come to define its purpose and legitimacy in the shadow of emergency politics: to secure the conditions necessary for job growth, capital investment, and economic competitiveness. Idle No More's activism expressed a refusal to believe Harper's claim that growth of the tar sands industry would benefit all Canadians in spite of the environmental costs to indigenous communities, land, and water sources.

Idle No More's demand for sovereignty vis-à-vis the Harper government, both in terms of the renewal of treaty agreements and the restoration of self-governing provisions outlined in Section 35 of the federal constitution, draws attention to the relational and sacrificial character of sovereignty. The concept of *terra nullius* is central to the founding of Canada; Canadian sovereignty is founded on the sacrifice of indigenous groups and their sovereign rights except where these have been recognized in treaty agreements signed between the Crown and indigenous nations as equals. Even though the terms of these agreements have not been honored by Canada, they stand as evidence of the historical and continuing sacrifices made by indigenous peoples for Canadian sovereignty. Idle No More's commitment to the necessity of democratizing sovereignty, however, sets it apart from the way in which contemporary theorists are trying to separate democracy from sovereignty and its historical entanglement with the nation-state. Furthermore, the emphasis on the role that revitalization of indigenous culture must play in such efforts casts democracy as much more than just a practice of refusal of state prerogatives. Beyond a politics of refusal, Idle No More gestures toward the importance of sub-constitutional and extra-juridical orders that make such actions possible.

Idle No More's organizing practices suggest that democratizing sovereignty involves unmaking the affective circuits that bind sovereign individuals to the state and legitimate its emergency actions. The Round Dance is an associational practice that generates a sense of resonant vitality among participants. The vitality that dancers experience addresses the feelings of impasse that are the conditions of possibility for emergency politics. The continuation of demonstrations and blockades in Elsipogtog, New Brunswick, against hydrofracking operations, anti-pipeline actions in British Columbia, and protests against tar sands production in Alberta are evidence that the indigenous resurgence and subject transformation initiated by Idle No More are taking root and the 2012–2013 protests against Harper were not episodic eruptions of indigenous resistance but the start of a sustained movement to democratize sovereignty. The spread of direct action and confrontation represents a break with the cycle of negotiation and co-optation that has marked the last few decades of indigenous relations with the settler state.

If indigenous resurgence and remaking subjects are at the heart of efforts to generate the popular legislative power necessary to democratize sovereignty, the juridical forms of these efforts are less clear. That is because the groups that identify with Idle No More do not agree on what exactly should constitute those juridical claims: the restoration of treaty agreements or the reinstatement of self-governance provisions specified by Section 35? Those differences have their origins in the different arrangements that indigenous groups have with the Canadian federal government, even as the general public barely have any idea of the distinctions among these groups. The three groups falling under the category of Canada's indigenous peoples specified in the constitution each have a different status: First Nations, Métis, and Inuit. The group First Nations consists both of tribal nations or bands that have signed treaties with the federal government and are seeking for the government to uphold those treaties and those nations or bands that do not have treaties. The Canadian government interacts with First Nations through the Indian Act of 1876 and its amendments, which recognize official bands and reserve lands. The Indian Act also specifies the governance structures of band councils, but these councils are controversial because critics regard them as ultimately accountable to state, not local, power since they are creatures of the state. These critics see moving away from the Indian Act and band councils as the only way forward, while other groups have been trying to pursue reforms and the restoration of treaties through the council structure. Neither the Indian Act nor treaties govern Canada's relations with Métis and Inuit who make up the other two groups of indigenous peoples recognized by the state. Their concerns do not center on the reserves, the council system, or the restoration of treaties. Instead, their agenda focuses on access, addressing the poverty, discrimination, and second-class citizenship many aboriginal peoples experience in Canadian society, as well as high rates of violence in their communities.

That Idle No More's juridical claims are unsettled reflects this diverse history and experience. The movement has sought to restore and democratize the institutions of self-government specified in Section 35 of the Constitution which the Harper legislation gutted. It has also called upon the government to redress the violations of existing treaties. These efforts have coexisted with critiques of settler colonialism, the most radical of which maintain the complete incompatibility of the indigenous lifeworld with the settler state and capitalism. This is the position of scholar-activist Taiaike Alfred.[30] Citing the cycle of co-optation that accompanies cooperation with the Canadian government, Alfred argues that strategies of noncooperation are the only means of undermining the legitimacy of the

Canadian government and the principle of *terra nullius*, which deny prior aboriginal claims.[31] For him, indigenous peoples have only two choices if they reject self-determination: exclusion and marginalization from settler society or assimilation.[32] From Alfred's perspective, the provisions of self-government extended by the Canadian government represent paths to both assimilation and marginalization for indigenous "citizens" of Canada. Because the right to self-governance is extended at the discretion of the federal government, it is paternalistic and fails to acknowledge that aboriginal rights are *sui generis*.[33] The history of seeking recognition from the Canadian government has left many indigenous groups wary of becoming entrapped in juridical structures that have been used to assimilate and depoliticize indigenous claims of self-determination.[34] For this reason, activists like Alfred see the renewal of treaty agreements as the only viable form of juridical sovereignty since they are premised on mutual recognition between Canada and indigenous nations as sovereign powers.

But perhaps because the entanglements between indigenous and settler territories and communities are real and well-entrenched, Idle No More activists have also responded to Harper's actions by trying to reclaim self-government despite their ambivalence about how self-government may compromise autonomous self-determination. In demanding the restoration of Section 35, Idle No More has also sought to democratize these institutions by gaining greater control over local land and water use boards. With respect to the pipelines, local governance will have national and even international implications for the viability of the Canadian tar sands oil industry and growth of the Canadian economy. Local governance would represent a victory for the climate change advocates allied with Idle No More, who object to tar sands oil because of the high levels of carbon dioxide released during the production process and who worry that access to cheap oil sources will only delay the introduction of overdue efforts to curb fuel consumption in the United States.

Each of these juridical approaches to sovereignty is anchored in practices of unmaking the idle subject of the modern nation-state. The process of unmaking and remaking the subject is key to the movement's understanding of contesting and democratizing sovereignty, with the two sides of the sovereignty/subject equation being related to one another. The movement's critique of settler colonialism raises the issue of racial privilege and indigenous sacrifice explicitly. While Idle No More has partnered with environmental groups opposed to further development of the tar sands oil and other natural resources, the movement has not articulated other practices that would help reshape the desires for consumer consumption at the micro-level that contribute to the state's macro-level assertions of sovereign power. But the critique forwarded by Alfred suggest that the exploitation of indigenous peoples is connected to the exploitation of their land and that the latter cannot be curbed without also addressing a system of exploitation in which settler citizens have and continue to benefit from the unjust exercise of power against indigenous communities. Working on desires that are increasingly part of the state's raison d'être suggests the degree to which contesting necessity must involve addressing the everyday political and economic practices that sustain that order.

While I have offered an initial sketch of democratizing sovereignty in this opening chapter based on the lines of thought that emerge through an analysis of Idle No More's public philosophy, the remaining chapters will develop these lines more fully. The coming chapters examine other movements out of an acknowledgment that these movements have emerged in tandem, influencing, borrowing, and sharing among one another. They have experimented and co-developed a range of practices to nurture vitality and democratize sovereignty and I turn to them to explore a set of themes and questions that are part of the Idle No More's story but were inflected differently and therefore are more audible elsewhere.

Like Idle No More, these other movements must penetrate a deep layer of passivity and sense of impasse that keeps citizens from believing that they can act or that anything could come from their actions. These movements operate in a context where the desire for agency has been undermined by depoliticizing forms of togetherness. Barack Obama's 2008 presidential campaign and his promise of "Yes, We Can!" tapped a desire for "change" among many Americans, especially younger voters and minorities who had previously felt marginalized by candidates and the larger political process. But his campaign failed to convert this groundswell of popular support into a democratic organization. As Jeffrey Stout has argued, the transformation of the Obama campaign organization into a re-election committee combined with the intensification of executive power under President Obama generated deep cynicism among those his campaign had once inspired to believe change was possible.[35] Movements seeking to democratize sovereignty face the formidable task of addressing themselves to a citizenry that is alternately skeptical, pessimistic, and devitalized.

The coming chapters explore how other movements have addressed desires for agency that survive under this arrangement of state power and the micro-practices through which they have been kindled and cultivated. They also explore how these citizens have been able to help one another see opportunities for action under conditions that ordinarily appear intractable, exploring a range of questions including: How to pay attention to, imagine, and generate the possibilities for vitality among conditions that wear ordinary subjects out, devitalize agency, and legitimate emergency politics? How to shift affective attachments to forms of sovereign power that rely on acquiescence and domination to the forms of vitality necessary to democratize sovereignty? What movement practices affect these shifts and how do they operate on individual and collective bodies? How does the imbrication of liberal democracy and capitalism affect the understanding of these practices? Along the way, we will visit in greater depth some of the elements that were crucial to Idle No More's organizing strategy, including the role of DIY practices, independently generated amateur media, critique of hegemonic forms of sovereign power, and sources of solidarity and hope.

2

Out of the Ordinary

It took an extraordinary event of police violence for the Occupy Movement to garner attention from the mainstream media. Although protesters had been occupying Zuccotti Park in lower Manhattan since September 17, it was not until a week later, on September 24, 2011, when NYPD officer Anthony Bologna was filmed pepper spraying four white female protestors and walking away from his screaming victims, that the movement received any television news coverage. Mainstream news coverage, moreover, came only after the clip had "gone viral" and had been viewed thousands of times online. At the center of the initial coverage of Occupy Wall Street was the spectacle of the screaming victims, not what they and others gathered in Union Square to protest.

The attention on police violence directed toward the women (just as later attention would be focused on how campus police overreacted in pepper spraying peaceful student protestors at the University of California, Davis) reflects a political culture in which openly aggressive policing provokes outrage but the less visible offenses motivating the protestors barely register as politically salient. Leaving aside the fact that the outrage was not over the regularity of police violence directed toward young African American and Latino men for a moment, how did Occupy Wall Street unfold and assemble a counterpublic in an environment where the public viewed the protests as, yes, an expression of free speech, but ultimately unproductive? The perception that Occupy was unproductive was due in part to the great number of causes that protestors proclaimed, but it was also due in part to the movement's refusal to conform to the narrative-driven, issue-oriented lens through which citizens today commonly understand politics as well as the flattened confidence that ordinary citizens have in their own abilities to affect change.[1]

Occupiers were not playing by the rules of idle citizenship. Sleeping and eating in public squares and on the street, with their endless assemblies and comical hand gestures, they also looked as if they were engaged in something that coded them as unproductive citizens.[2] Too close to the homeless eager for a free meal, Occupiers were apparently leisured in a political culture which values work and having a job, and in which workers work longer and longer hours to get by. Economically but not politically idle, they were expected to feel embarrassed by their personal failures. Debt and joblessness were sources of shame and therefore not the basis of meeting and organizing with strangers. Others saw them as "complaining" about either not having jobs or not having well-paying jobs and wrongly looking to the government for assistance, which invited a backlash from other citizens facing the same circumstances and those who had played by the rules. Instead of complaining and protesting, why were these people not out looking for jobs? Why were they seeking government redress when they clearly were not working hard enough to better their situations? These questions reflect a widespread belief in individual resilience and responsibility among Americans today that has roots in a tradition of self-reliance that is directly connected to the exercise of sovereignty and emergency politics. Self-responsible individuals are miniature sovereigns. Like the state, sovereign individuals are thought to be free, independent, self-legislating beings.

My argument in this chapter is that Occupy's main achievement was reworking the terms of common sense and political possibility among citizens. In particular, Occupy's documentary practices enabled citizens to bring into the public realm accounts of private hardship that had contributed to their sense of impasse and devitalized agency and make them the basis for collective identification and action. This represents a form of public philosophy that contests the circuit linking individual sovereignty to the reassertion of state sovereignty during and following crisis and emergency by dramatizing the widespread failures of the state to deliver on the promise of sovereignty, understood in terms of individual self-determination. Indebted to the techniques of documentary film, which spotlight slices of ordinary life, sites like the "We Are the 99 Percent" on Tumblr, which documented the personal hardships and routines of ordinary citizens, dramatized how the normalization of emergency and crisis has transformed the terms of everyday life and citizenship. Cumulatively, the density, diversity, and mundane character of this archive points to the comprehensiveness of those changes and the difficulty citizens have paying attention to those changes.

By producing an archive of individual suffering, Occupy generated spaces for citizens to apprehend how the ideal of sovereignty promised to them had been sacrificed to preserve the sovereignty of large financial institutions, economic stability, and growth, even if they had not been identified as sacrifices. Yet by publicizing these personal sacrifices, Occupy's documentary archive enabled citizens to form mutual attachments around admissions of vulnerability rarely tenable as the basis for solidarity. These new associations diverged from the discourse of self-reliance that feeds into support for emergency powers by allowing citizens to question the necessity of their personal sacrifices and the invocations of necessity that justified but disavowed those sacrifices. By identifying those sacrifices, Occupy illuminated the sacrificial and relational character of sovereignty. Through soliciting and publicizing accounts of personal sacrifice, Occupy generated new spaces and forms of attachment that enabled citizens to address feelings of impasse that sidelined them and kept them idle. Still, if Occupy injected vitality into citizens who had felt ground down by their personal hardships and circumstances, that vitality was experienced unevenly: while the movement's rhetoric highlighted how, for example, the dreams of homeowners and college students had been sacrificed to the interests of financial capital, it had difficulty admitting how the sovereignty whites had enjoyed had benefitted, both historically and through the present, from the sacrifices people of color had been forced to make to preserve that sense of sovereignty.

THE COMMON SENSE OF FELT LEGITIMACY AND THE NECESSITY OF EMERGENCY POLITICS

In order to grasp the significance of how Occupy's documentary practices were able to prompt a reconsideration of sovereignty by generating public identities among those whose sacrifices had been disavowed, it is necessary to place them against a backdrop distinguished by spectacles of sovereign state power that generate popular but uncritical support for those actions. Elizabeth Anker argues that the War on Terror and efforts to shore up America's economic security expressed a desire to overcome feelings of vulnerability through the extension of sovereign identity, a desire that is best understood through the genre of melodrama. Anker traces the development of melodrama in US politics to the beginning of the Cold War. Analyzing speeches by Presidents Truman, Nixon, and George W. Bush, as well as coverage of the attacks on the Pentagon and World Trade Center, alongside melodrama as a literary genre, she argues that melodrama explains American responses to conditions of devitalized sovereignty. Just as in melodramatic film and literature, she observes that US presidents and media cast the nation as a victim-hero, where injury animates the desire for sovereignty.

According to Anker, melodrama is a genre that is closely linked with state power. Melodrama anticipates the triumph of the hero who overcomes challenges along his path. Anker argues that when arguments for the political necessity of state action are conveyed in melodramatic terms, they short-circuit the processes that legitimate power in democracies. By framing the response to terrorism in moral terms or bank bailouts as necessary for the stability of the economy, melodramatic genres produce affective identification with unilateral and unaccountable state actions. Anker calls this sense of authorizing state power through affective identification with state sovereignty "felt legitimacy."[3]

Anker argues that the US emphasis on self-reliance intensifies the link between sovereign individuals and sovereign states present in liberal political discourse. Combined with a notion of personal freedom that is articulated as freedom from interference by the state or other citizens in the work of liberals like Locke and John Stuart Mill, self-reliance means that failure to realize the sovereignty promised to citizens is understood in terms of personal failure whose causes are, by extension, social rather than political in origin.[4] Anker writes that US melodrama depicts lone individuals struggling against injustice and frames these as individual struggles rather than collective problems requiring common action.[5] That is because US melodrama frequently simplifies the forces of injustice by portraying villainous individuals as their cause, a move that wipes away explanations that are in tension with American beliefs in self-made individuals.[6]

Melodrama elicits tremendous audience sympathy for its victim-heroes. When transferred onto national discourses, this sympathy attempts to unify citizens both in the immediacy of their affective identification with national injury and to the expansion of state power as a response to that injury. Thus, President George W. Bush explained the attacks on the Pentagon and World Trade Center in terms of the motivations of Osama bin-Laden and as an assault on the freedom that Americans enjoy.[7] In calling for the creation of the Office of Homeland Security, Bush claimed that it was "essential" to defeating terrorism and made the defeat of terrorism a moral imperative for the nation. Stating that the nation had suffered a "great loss" but that in the resulting "grief and anger" it had found its mission, Bush identified that mission in civilizational terms for "all who believe in progress and pluralism, tolerance and freedom" against those who "plot evil and destruction."[8] Anker observes that Bush's melodramatic framing of America's War on Terror in terms of defending freedom and liberal values obscures how these terms were deployed to justify imperialism in the past and disavows any explanation which would consider the legacy of those policies in shaping the motivations of the 9/11 attackers.

The portrayal of the War on Terror in melodramatic terms produced a citizenry that was unified in opposition to "foreign elements" and which had licensed the expansion of state power to aggressively police Arab and Muslim-Americans as well as the country's southern border with Mexico. This example clearly demonstrates the racialized but never avowed aspect of the desire to restore sovereignty. In 9/11 discourse, but also discourses that justify the necessity of sovereign state actions to safeguard the nation's economic security, the victim-heroes are whites.

Nonwhites are caught in the gap between the universal character of this national discourse and the racial particularity it enfolds. The individuated terms of melodrama casts racial discrimination as something that is both perpetuated and suffered by individuals, minimizing its systemic and social character. The effect is to undermine arguments that locate the origins of racial inequality and discrimination in ongoing, systemic patterns of behavior that accrue benefits primarily to whites and disadvantage blacks and other minorities. The consequences are seen in the belief that laws punishing overt racial discrimination represent the elimination of all obstacles that had previously barred progress for black Americans as well as arguments that frame social inequalities in terms of individual responsibility that call for greater bootstrapping on the part of the less fortunate. Melodrama thus depoliticizes citizens and political inquiry into the causes of political crisis beyond individual actions at the same moment that it draws them toward identification with state action.

For William Connolly, popular support for strongly racialized assertions of individual and state sovereignty in response to political and economic crises can be traced back to the forces that shape the agenda of the US political right. Corporations, evangelical Christianity, the electronic news media, and the leaders of the Republican Party, he argues, have worked to shape how Americans approach and comprehend political questions and possibilities. In other words, he argues the attitudes ordinary citizens have toward politics is reflected in their understanding of common sense, which is significantly shaped by the sounds, words, and images put forward by institutions that make up the US right wing. While not identical, the leaders and members of these groups overlap significantly and are considerably involved with one another, borrowing and furthering ideas born in one domain in other contexts.

In a similar analysis, Philip Mirowski concentrates on university faculty, think tanks, and talking heads, who pick up, reinforce, and legitimate one another over the airwaves, in print, and online. Mirowski argues the result of this "debate" is what he calls "agnotology," which represents the effort to propagate doubt and confusion among the public by presenting contending but extreme or marginal positions among the "free market of ideas" in their coverage of issues. According to Mirowski agnotology is instrumental in contributing to public impasse and impassivity. Using the climate change "debate" as his example Mirowski explains how the actions of members of the collective work together to alternatively deny or debate scientific fact and to generate a debate over short-, medium-, and long-term responses that delay and, effectively block, meaningful change until the "debates" are settled.[9]

To the degree to which these institutions support the strong assertions of sovereignty characteristic of emergency politics, they define the terrain of what citizens broadly recognize as common sense. Common sense captures the legitimacy and conventionality of their support for emergency measures, by which I mean the naturalness of such thinking and how it makes alternatives uncommon and increasingly unimaginable.[10] With the electronic media acting as its mouthpiece, the citizen's understanding of the political landscape as well as her imagination has been significantly altered. Connolly's analysis explains how the desire individuals and nations have for economic security and sovereignty mutually reinforce one another to narrow the range of possibilities that citizens and states have available to them. Thus, he sheds light on the logic and force of "necessity" that compels efforts to secure sovereignty out of feelings of vulnerability. Feelings of vulnerability direct many citizens fearful of losing their status to direct their hostilities toward a range of groups making claims for equal status. Thus, gays and lesbians; women; African Americans; secularists, atheists, and Muslims; are seen as threats in a zero-sum understanding of status and sovereignty.[11]

Still, Connolly sees the possibility of developing a more generous attitude toward difference and plurality through a diverse set of practices that involve a "high visual intensity." Connolly writes, "It is important to achieve high visual intensity, so that the images we form both activate creative thinking and filter into affective dispositions to action."[12] Connolly regards films, especially those that are viewed by citizens assembled together in public forums for the purpose of watching films, as "crack[ing] the mold" defining these genres and "scrambl[ing] old habits of attachment."[13] By foregrounding the viewer's role in making sense of and organizing what was rendered on the screen, Connolly believes that film presents the opportunity for citizens to reconsider the terrain of the ordinary world from a new perspective.[14] Although he briefly mentions social movements as performing this role, Connolly tends to describe the process of imagining alternative practices of sovereign state power in terms of micro-practices of visualization that are self-reflective.[15] Connolly tends to describe the generation of this ethos as an individual, not a collective practice—although he is careful to stress that acting on these commitments requires individuals to act in the company of others.

Together Anker, Connolly, and Mirowski's analyses account for a broadly depoliticized political culture in which the concentration of decision-making power means there are few opportunities or resources for initiating collective action to address conditions of impasse that have left more Americans feeling vulnerable, unable to comprehend those experiences outside the language of personal failure, and helpless to change their situations. Felt legitimacy acts powerfully to bind Americans in an experience of popular but undemocratic unity that legitimates the exercise of emergency powers in the name of protecting the common good, just as a complex media assemblage works to justify and naturalize the exercise of those emergency powers. Melodrama's emphasis on the achievements of heroic individuals battling villains who embody the challenges to freedom further acts to weaken receptivity toward analyses that identify the roots of crises in complex political histories and events that require collective political action.

In other words, Anker and Connolly's analyses define a terrain of ordinary life in which there are few expectations of anything different from the status quo and where even frustration with this status quo struggles to establish a larger resonance. Ordinary in this context refers to not only the mundane texture of the day-to-day but also the degree to which everyday experience is understood as the baseline for normal without the recognition that it is normalized. Michel Foucault referred to this aspect of ordinary experience as what makes it feel natural or inevitable so that it is difficult to theorize differently.[16] Yet the degree to which the practices of state sovereignty and sovereign individualism are expressed through affects, attachments, and behaviors that subjects reproduce everyday also suggests how they can be generated differently via the cultivation of an alternative set of affective attachments. Occupy Wall Street unfolded against this backdrop and, as an aspiring popular movement, its initial task was to re-present ordinary life as receptive to political action. In the next section I suggest that the movement's documentary practices were essential to this goal by allowing Occupiers to reframe their experiences of vulnerability not as personal failures but as caused by political decisions taken in their name by officials who were not publicly accountable. I argue these documentary practices were the basis for collective action within the movement to the degree that they undermine the image of the sovereign individual.

WHOSE SOVEREIGNTY? WHOSE SACRIFICE? OCCUPY'S PUBLIC PHILOSOPHY

In the last chapter, I suggested that sovereignty always involves sacrifice, even if these sacrifices are seldom avowed. That is because citizens rarely realize the sovereignty they have been promised. Historically, women and minorities have been denied and forced to forfeit their claims to sovereignty so that white males could experience sovereignty. Sacrifice continues to be part of the texture of democratic life, however. Just as women and minorities were once disenfranchised and their concerns were not recognized as political, today sacrifice is often bounded in private experience. For instance, in 2009 US homeowners were sacrificed so that banks would not fail. Calling banks "too big to fail" allowed policymakers to close off political debate over whether or not to bail out the banks—the question instead became, how big should the bailout be? Yet the decision to let banks live on after their near collapse sacrificed homeowners with underwater mortgages. Homeowners received no bailout and their mortgages remained private obligations even if they could not afford to pay back their bank loans and were forced to walk away from their homes.[17]

The example of ballooning mortgage payments in the months leading up to and after the 2008 crash suggests why when one group is sacrificed for another in democracies, those who are sacrificed do not use the language of sacrifice to describe their situations. At one level, this is because their sacrifice was not acknowledged in the terms of the government bailout. At another, they experienced making or trying to make their mortgage payments as obligations that could not be passed onto others and which wore them out. Both the intensity and immediacy of daily life makes it difficult to apprehend that life in terms that differ from how it is singularly felt and experienced by subjects. There is no single moment that could explain how or why homeowners found themselves holding underwater mortgages. Instead, their situations seem to come into focus with the steady, uneventful accumulation of time. The sheer banality of ordinary life is what makes most of it uneventful, even if its pressures can wear subjects down. It is also what makes it hard for citizens to imagine everyday life in terms other than what they have come to know.

My claim in this section is that Occupy's use of documentary techniques allowed some of these sacrifices to be named, even if they were not always satisfactorily addressed or resolved, and that publicizing these sacrifices allowed citizens to undermine the image of autonomous sovereignty linking individuals to the nation described by Anker and Connolly. Occupiers around the country as well as those who visited and contributed to the movement's online archive participated in a form of public philosophy that I suggest allowed them to examine what kinds of sacrifices have and have not been acknowledged. I turn to documentary here because it is a genre that is concerned with examining ordinary life and, often, stories that are hidden in plain sight. The genre of documentary film is difficult to define, but scholars concede a few basic features.[18] Documentaries, they agree, deal with reality and are organized around the stories of real people participating in historically verifiable events. The latter informs the storytelling character of many documentaries. "They tell us what leads up to actual events or real changes, be they the experience of an individual or an entire society," writes Bill Nichols.[19] The subjects of such stories play themselves and not fictional characters imagined by someone else.

Beyond these basic elements, Elizabeth Cowie argues documentary film is characterized by a series of paradoxes. Its relationship to reality is not straightforward, even if it is grounded in the substance of reality. As she notes, documentary film is concerned with representing reality, but in doing so creates a new reality. It draws on a desire to know and the belief that the world as it appears can be interpreted and deciphered, but at the same time evades our attempts at mastery and sovereignty. By highlighting our dependence upon sensory knowledge while also reminding us that the senses can deceive and be deceived, documentary underlines the contingent status of knowledge and its inherent incoherence. The documentary film is simultaneously a vehicle for serious inquiry into political and social life that informs and educates the public and a spectacle offered up for entertainment. The active, creative, and provocative act of documentary filmmaking, she notes, is always, moreover, threatened by passive reception.[20]

Documentary filmmaking is thus animated by a concept of representation separate from the idea of one class of individuals representing another associated with democratic institutions of the modern nation-state. It is better captured by the set of meanings implied by the Latin word *repraesentare*, which means to make manifest or present again. Most often used to refer to inanimate objects, it could mean literally presenting that object again, presenting another object in place of a missing object, or to suggest that an object actively embodies an idea. The verb could also mean to hasten an event or bring it to the present.[21] As a representative art, the promise of documentary film is to depict objects that have a strong descriptive likeness to what they claim to represent. At the same time, documentarians have historically sought to hold up a mirror to objects, such as marginalized groups or cultures, which have been marked in society by their relative absence rather than presence. In these circumstances, the subject or objects of such films can be said to symbolize a larger question or concept.[22] Yet in these films the degree to which an object can be judged to symbolize a larger idea depends on the audience's willingness to accept the symbolic association offered.

Certainly, as the techniques of documentary filmmaking have expanded to new contexts, including faux-documentary "reality" television programs, such determinations have become more complicated. For John Corner, the expansion of documentary-as-diversion at the expense of its traditional use in publicizing dominant modes of citizenship (the government propaganda newsreel of the early 20th century), as tool for journalistic inquiry, and instrument of radical interrogation and alternative perspective has meant that the term documentary is better understood in adjectival form rather than as a noun which refers to a concise set of techniques or subject areas.[23] He writes, "To ask, 'is this a documentary project?' is more useful than to ask 'is this film a documentary?' with its inflection towards definitional criteria and the sense of something being more object than practice."[24]

With Corner's observations about "post-documentary" forms of representation in mind, I suggest that in its multiple practices the Occupy Movement might be considered a documentary project. By allowing citizens to name how their own experiences of sovereignty had been compromised through sacrifices they had made or had been forced to make, Occupy's documentary practices worked to democratize sovereignty. Through these practices, I argue that Occupy helped to repopulate the terms of common sense by letting citizens acknowledge and form attachments around their shared experiences of vulnerability. Visitors to Occupy sites around the country, for example, were encouraged to document their own perceptions of the conditions of possibility for themselves and the nation by writing public responses to the following prompts: "What is wrong with our country?" "What is right with our country?"[25] Many of these responses, along with a catalogue of the discussions, sometimes with transcripts or meeting notes, that sprang up in general assembly and committee meetings were made available online.[26] Those unable to visit or join in these documentary activities firsthand were able to follow live streaming webcasts from many of the Occupy sites, along with websites updated in real time in multiple languages announcing the planned schedule of activities and recording the detail and outcome of various discussions among participants.[27] The proliferation of these documentary materials from multiple sources and perspectives, across many different genres, from participants occupying sites around the country, curious visitors, and those eager to share their own stories in words and images worked to undermine the force of the dominant common sense. Together, citizens and noncitizens working within these sites and responding to them produced a stream of counternarratives about the private sacrifices they had been asked to make to preserve the semblance of sovereignty for banks and credit-holders.

The "We Are the 99 Percent" Tumblr page is an example of how Occupy sought to break the circuit linking the sovereign nation and sovereign individual by politicizing experiences of vulnerability that were understood to be personal hardships to be overcome through individual effort, including joblessness, indebtedness resulting from family illness, and costly tuition bills. Readers and potential contributors to the site were instructed to submit a photo of themselves holding signs with a single sentence summarizing their "circumstances" along with the words "I am the 99 percent." Most of the messages are longer than a single sentence. Visually and in terms of content, they resemble the kind of hand-written signs carried by homeless men and women that report personal hardship.[28] The following post from December 22, 2011, depicting a woman holding a sign that partially obscures her face is representative of the testimonies on the site:

> I am a 40 year old full-time college student with 4.0. I work full time. I live with MS. I can't get insurance. I get no medical needs met because I don't have insurance. I pay my taxes. I am the 99 percent.[29]

The woman's testimony condenses themes that are repeated in many other posts. Accounts of students and families struggling with medical care costs, lack of access to affordable insurance, working full-time jobs without benefits or living wages, empty savings and retirement accounts, and underwater mortgages, represent what Timothy Recuber calls "micronarratives of suffering" that point to how the current political and economic climates are rendering family and work life.[30]

Read together, the "We Are the 99 Percent" Tumblr presents an archive that competes with the melodramatic narratives that reinforce state sovereignty and the associated ideology of self-reliance that shield state actions from scrutiny. This archive redirects melodramatic identification from the state back to citizens. By publicizing personal hardships that had not been avowable outside the private sphere of close familial relationships, they attempt to remove the shame that enforces silence. By allowing contributors and readers to publicize the hardships that constrain their agency by indicating how their agency has been restricted by challenges that texture the experience of everyday life, the accounts draw persons into the public eye, invite them to form attachments with others, and allow them to begin to address their experiences of unfreedom.

Visitors to the website and other Occupy sites learn that they are not alone in their experiences of economic vulnerability, knowledge that helps them break the stranglehold that melodramatic narratives of sovereignty, which code these experiences as personal failure, have on their self-understanding. Cowie cautions that what viewers initially experience taking in these scenes is uncertainty, however. She explains that this moment of uncertainty in the eyes of the viewer constitutes the "event" or action of the documentary project, especially in its spectacular form. "An event is an action: something happens, becomes classified as an event, and is extracted from the ongoing, contingent reality of a multitude of actions and happenings. Events entail the temporal as action that, located in time and space, become identified as timely and caused."[31] Comparing the documentary event to scientific experimentation, she writes that in both instances an event "enables new knowledge or changes understanding."[32] Once it is possible to see that one's personal misfortune is widely shared, it becomes possible to see it differently. Understood as public philosophy, documentary practices insert reflective distance into the immediacy of everyday life that is necessary to imagine that life in different terms.

Likewise, the Occupy encampments enabled homeless citizens to acknowledge the sacrifices they had been asked to make to preserve public order. Routinely harassed by police for sleeping and living on the streets and intimidating others with their presence alone, members of the homeless community, whose ordinary lives can be said to be both visible and hidden in plain sight, joined the encampments at a number of Occupy sites. For some, their participation sprang from political convictions. For others, their interest was more pragmatic. The encampments allowed them to live in the streets in communities free from nightly harassment from the police and pressures to accept beds in shelters. Many of the Occupy sites also offered free food and relief from the monotony of surviving on the streets. What they discovered though was that their presence and knowledge of surviving on the streets was crucial to maintaining the spectacle of the encampments, even if some protestors felt that their presence along with the energy required for a community to live together in an open space was a distraction from Occupy's "true" agenda. Members of Occupy Philadelphia, for example, proposed a "dual-site restructuring of the encampment" to separate the political goals from the needs of living out in the open.[33]

In other cases, the homeless became important partners in shaping the content of the movement's politics and its articulation of the sacrifices citizens had been forced to make.[34] In Eugene, Oregon, homelessness came to occupy a central position in the movement's discourse as greater numbers of the homeless joined the city's encampment.[35] With members of the homeless community contributing to the counternarratives generated by participants, efforts to document the lives of the homeless and the structural forces, attitudes, laws, and discourses, that enforced their marginalized status emerged alongside critiques of economic and political inequality at the heart of the accounts of the ordinary life put forward by citizens at other sites. In Eugene, at least, discussions of the national mortgage crisis were entwined with the fact of homelessness. The worry was not just that families defaulting on mortgages might face homelessness but that homelessness itself constituted a crisis long tolerated and invisible.

Occupy Eugene was able to highlight the forces that had deemed the homeless issue and community invisible in the past. As coverage of Occupy Eugene progressed, members of the homeless community like Jackie Millet, age 60, whose photo accompanied a December 8, 2011, *Associated Press* article about the encampment, increasingly became its face and spokespersons. Millet is quoted, "For the homeless we need a place to be. We don't want to be criminalized."[36] In New York as well, narratives about homelessness and the foreclosure crisis reinforced one another. Efforts to address foreclosure in Brooklyn's East New York neighborhood, for example, involved members of the Occupy Movement partnering with local community organizations, including VOCAL-NY, formerly the NYC AIDS Housing Network, Union Healthcare Workers East, Picture the Homeless, and City Council members Charles Barron and Ydanis Rodriquez, installing families made homeless by foreclosure back in their Brooklyn homes and defending the rights of homeless persons to occupy foreclosed properties.[37]

At the same time that Occupy identified sacrifices that had been disavowed, its rhetoric and practices performed some of the same disavowal. Many women and African Americans were critical of white male participants for their unwillingness to acknowledge their own privileges even as they identified other forms of systemic injustice. In a piece published in the *Black Scholar* entitled "A Critique of the Occupy Movement from a Black Occupier," Emahunn Raheem Ali Campbell argues that the Occupy sites were not safe spaces to raise the issue of white privilege. Campbell writes:

> ". . . it is without question a *white-led movement* that primarily deals with the concerns of *white middle-class youths*. Occupy Wall Street does not have enough people of color to raise important questions of white privilege and its operation within Occupy. Without support in numbers to protect Occupiers of color from acts of alienation, Occupiers of color cannot carve out important space for a serious dialogue about white privilege (and, indeed, racism), nor can they fully expect white Occupiers to create this space."[38]

The first example of white protestors' tone deafness to the experience of nonwhites was their attempt to appeal to the police by chanting, "We are the 99 percent! So are you!" For Campbell, the chant is evidence of the gulf that separates how whites relate to state security forces and how

African-Americans and Latinos relate to the police. The death-row execution of Troy Davis in Georgia on September 21, 2011, and the deaths of Sean Bell, Trey Joyner, and Oscar Grant at the hands of police officers earlier in the year, were reminders that for African-Americans, especially men, their interactions with police as a group were determined by racial discrimination and that individual officers would have to earn their trust. Referring to Occupy's appeals to the police and to protestors to "take back your country," Kenyon Farrow writes that the frequency of police harassment and violence directed toward African-American males makes it "hard to believe that the government is just broken—it seems pretty insistent and hell-bent on your demise."[39] Campbell also points to Occupy the Hood, which split from Occupy Boston, for its failure to address "racism and white privilege" while, at the same time, noting that independent and progressive news sources that enthusiastically covered Occupy barely registered the break or the activities of Occupy the Hood activists in Boston, Baltimore, and New York. According to Campbell, Occupy and those who covered it were reluctant or unable to examine white privilege, which had the consequence of marginalizing nonwhites who were sympathetic to its concerns.

According to Campbell, the distancing begins with the choice to label the movement Occupy, observing that for much of its history in North America the term occupation has referred to occupations of indigenous lands by white settlers. In his "Open Letter to the Occupy Wall Street Activists," Anishinaabe writer John Paul Montano indicates how the language of "occupy" unintentionally excludes indigenous peoples. Although he makes clear he is sympathetic to the movement's critique of capitalism and desire to do the "right" thing, writing that he thinks the protestors' hearts are in the right place, Montano argues that the members of the movement have failed to acknowledge how they have and continue to benefit from colonialism. Montano criticizes the group for claiming to act in the name of equality and justice without acknowledging the legacy of colonialism. He writes:

> Hoping and believing that you enlightened folks fighting for justice and equality and an end to imperialism, etc., etc., would make mention of the fact that the very land upon which you are protesting

> does not belong to you—that you are guests upon that stolen indigenous land. I had hoped mention would be made of the indigenous nation whose land that is. I had hoped that you would address the centuries-long history that we indigenous peoples of this continent have endured being subject to the countless "-isms" of do-gooders claiming to be building a "more just society," a "better world," a "land of freedom" *on top of our indigenous societies, on our indigenous lands, while destroying and/or ignoring our ways of life.* I had hoped that you would acknowledge that, since you are settlers on indigenous land, you need and want our indigenous consent to your building *anything* on our land—never mind an entire society. See where I'm going with this? I hope you're still smiling. We're still friends, so don't sweat it. I believe your hearts are in the right place. I know that this whole genocide and colonization thing causes all of us lots of confusion sometimes. It just seems to me that you're *unknowingly* doing the same thing to us that all the colonizers before you have done: you want to do stuff on our land without asking our permission.[40]

The issue was not just the movement's obtuseness around how indigenous communities understood the term "occupy"; it extended to representations of Native Americans in posters posted online featuring the words "Decolonize Wall Street" and "Decolonize the 99%" placed above and below an image of a Native warrior. Analyzing the poster on the *Native Appropriations* blog, Adrienne Keene argues that the poster's portrayal of Native Americans is deeply misinformed. It features a Plains warrior, a buffalo, and the outline of a red fist within a arrowhead along with the words "Wall St. is on Occupied Algonquin Land" even though Lower Manhattan is Lenape and was never home to buffalo. [41]

Occupy in the context of the movement also refers to the idea of filling a particular intersection of space and time. But as Campbell observes, filling space with direct action implies either filling an empty space or displacing another group or object.[42] He uses the example of a call for action on December 6, 2011, issued by the Brooklyn-based anti-foreclosure group Take Back the Land, entitled "Occupy Our Homes," wondering whether groups of color like Take Back the Land would have received any coverage of their activities if it were not for their alliances with white Occupiers. Campbell voices a critique of Occupy among local activists, especially those working in and with communities of color: their sense that Occupy emerged with a sense of entitlement to name issues that other groups had been working on for years, if not decades, without first consulting them or learning of their activities. He quotes activists from Washington, DC who objected to Occupy for assuming that the city lacked grassroots organizations, something they found almost incredulous given the city's lack of congressional representation. These activists also rankled at what earlier generations of activists had termed "John Brown syndrome" to refer to a form of well-intentioned white paternalism in which whites are "crowned heroes and rescuers of those who cannot do it themselves."[43]

Though it is true that much of Occupy's rhetoric did alienate people of color, its participatory character did allow some of the concerns raised by Campbell to be addressed during meetings of its General Assembly. In a video published on the news website *Colorlines*, people of color involved in Occupy Wall Street (OWS) are asked whether diversity is leading to a shift in the agenda that OWS has embraced. The first response comes from a young man who says, "There are a lot of movements that are very white. There is not space to enter and change them. OWS is a break from some of that. It feels like an opening in time and space that three weeks ago I had no idea could happen. . . ." The second interviewee rates whites involved in OWS as doing better than average "struggling not to be what we are already," but notes that their concern about student loans does not register with neighbors who have not had access to education.[44] A member of the OWS People of Color Working Group reports that she and other members were able to change the post-racial language in the initial draft of the "Declaration to Occupy New York." Writing elsewhere about this experience, Manissa McCleave Maharawal reports that blocking the initial draft required that,

> There in that circle, on that street-corner we did a crash course on racism, white privilege, structural racism, oppression. We did a

> course on history and the declaration of independence and colonialism and slavery. It was hard. It was real. It hurt. But people listened. We had to fight for it. I'm going to say that again: we had to fight for it. But it felt worth it. It felt worth it to sit down on the on a street corner in the Financial District at 11:30 pm on a Thursday night, after working all day long and argue for the changing of the first line of Occupy Wall Street's official Declaration of the Occupation of New York City. It felt worth it not only because we got the line changed but also because while standing in a circle of 20, mostly white men, and explaining racism in front of them: carefully and slowly spelling out that I as a woman of color experience the world way differently than the author of the Declaration, a white man, that this was not about him being personally racist but about relations of power, that he needed to, he urgently needed to listen and believe me about this, this moment felt like a victory for the movement on its own.[45]

Keene notes examples of local Occupy sites where participants were also able to respond and change in response to criticism from within and outside the movement. She lauds Occupy Oakland for making it clear that the issue of colonialization remains current. Contrasting an Occupy Oakland poster sharing its slogan "Decolonize the 99%, Defend Mother Earth" with the offending OWS example, she argues that the juxtaposition of the city's skyline with an image of a member of the local Ohlone tribe appropriately acknowledges the sacrifices of the local indigenous community.[46] Likewise, she praises Occupy Denver for acknowledging settler colonialism in its statement of purpose.[47]

In other words, there is evidence to indicate that Occupy was able to raise questions of sacrifice such as, who has sacrificed? and for what and whom?, even if imperfectly and that the admission of these sacrifices enabled participants and observers to undermine the circuit linking sovereign individuals to actions taken to uphold the sovereignty of the state and its interests. That is because sacrifice is rarely part of the dominant narratives around sovereignty and because acknowledging sacrifice means recognizing the relationships of interdependence upon which sovereignty depends. Yet Occupy provided citizens contexts in which they could examine the fact and appropriateness of sacrifice together. Maharawal's account and the experience of the Occupy Eugene assembly suggests that participants were able to develop greater awareness of their own limited perspective, sacrifices made by others, and the sacrifices yet to be acknowledged. Such dialogue represents practices of citizenship that extend far beyond institutional duties like voting. Indeed, as Maharawal's recollection suggests, being heard by others in the context of taking action in common can contribute a sense of vitality to citizens who have primarily known the experience of being silenced or voiceless.

Vitality is cultivated within and through associational movement practices; it is less available through individual reflection. The "We Are the 99 Percent" Tumblr page may have been participatory, but the nature of this participation can be judged thin. Viewing, reposting, and commenting on entries may generate deep empathy and identification, but it hardly represents the robust exercise of creative, world-making powers. This tells us two things about mutual vulnerability and vitality. First, they are not always present together. Second, they point to the limits of personal reflection. It is not that practices of self-reflection are unable to generate a more generous disposition toward difference and a deeper appreciation of contingency. Connolly is right that they can. But they are less likely to awaken a deep sense of vitality in citizens who are not already sensitive to and on the lookout for vitality in the world. Public philosophy is an associational practice that can help create openings that enable citizens to experience vitality and be transformed by that experience.

CONCLUSION

Wendy Brown concludes her recent book on neoliberalism's stealth revolution by observing how the language of "shared sacrifice" has crept into in popular discourse as both citizens and workers are called on to "take one for the team." Drawing on the work of Moishe Hallbertal, Brown distinguishes between religious sacrifice and what might be termed secular sacrifice. In the former instance, sacrifices are offered to the divine on behalf of the collective. An animal or individual is publicly and ritualistically sacrificed to the religious body in order to recommit the community to its authority

In the latter case, individuals must sacrifice part or all of themselves for the good of the larger collective. Secular sacrifice affirms the ideal of the free, autonomous, consenting member of the political community, but Brown notes that both forms of sacrifice call on "noneconomistic and non-marketized forms of exchange" and are thus supplemental to neoliberal reason.[48]

The forms of shared sacrifice particular to austerity measures are both secular and religious in character. Insofar as they are, like Harper's justification for the annulment of Section 35, framed in terms of sacrifices for the common good, they appeal to self-interest. But these sacrifices also have a religious character because those who are sacrificed or are asked to sacrifice are not rewarded for their sacrifices. As Brown puts it, referring to the sacrifices documented in Occupy's micro-narratives of suffering,

> Thus we are returned to the religious valence of sacrifice. In shared sacrifice for economic restoration, we sacrifice "to," rather than "for," and make an offering to a supreme power on which we are radically dependent, but that owes us nothing.[49]

Brown considers how the religious aspects of this sacrifice invite consideration of objects which might be substituted for the sacrifice of citizens and concludes by suggesting that Occupy's call to prosecute the investment banks reflected an effort at this kind of substitution. Similarly, she suggests that public contemplation of exactly the sort of restorative work their sacrifices are performing might lead citizens to hesitate and possibly refuse these sacrifices.[50]

I think Brown's interpretation of sacrifice is correct, even if she does not pursue how to break the seeming necessity of emergency measures and economic powers "on which we are radically dependent, but that owes us nothing." In this chapter, I have suggested it might involve undermining the link between the sovereign state that undertakes those emergency measures and the sovereign self that is patterned after it. My argument has been that acknowledging sacrifice is the first step to democratizing sovereignty and contesting emergency politics under conditions in which citizen sacrifices had been determined necessary to preserve economic growth and security.

The difficulty of acknowledging sacrifice is due in part to the legacy of American individualism, which celebrates self-reliance and individual initiative. This tradition idealizes the sovereign individual who is responsible for his own achievement and failure, obscuring the societal factors that play into how individuals live out and the degree to which individuals actually experience sovereignty in their lifetimes. The resulting understanding of sovereignty obscures how national and individual sovereignty is built on sacrifices small and large.

Occupy's documentary practices contributed to undermining the image of the self-reliant sovereign individual by generating micro-narratives of suffering that indicated how citizens had sacrificed their sovereignty for economic stability. The admission of personal vulnerability in these posts took their sacrifices from out of the realm of personal experience and made them public. The resulting publicity created the possibility for citizens to identify with one another around their shared vulnerabilities and form counterpublics to contest the necessity of their personal sacrifices.

Yet while Occupy sites proved an effective forum for the acknowledgement of some forms of sacrifice, its rhetoric made it difficult for members of the polity who had long been made to sacrifice for the sovereignty of settler citizens to fully participate in that dialogue. The economic hardship and personal suffering articulated in the Occupy encampments and archived in Occupy's online videos, websites, and documents, often stopped short of exploring or acknowledging the sacrifices made to secure the vitality and agency that protestors experienced through their participation. Occupy's rhetoric and actions were a mark of privilege that one commentator summed up by asking whether the police would have stood by had five thousand young black men decided to occupy Zuccotti Park.[51]

Some women reported being intimidated and harassed by shirtless men drumming and dancing around them and marginalized by a leadership that was dominated by white males. Similarly, well-intentioned but post-racial rhetoric was insensitive to the experiences of men and women of color just as the focus on rising student debt alienated those who had been shut out of higher education to begin with.

At the same time, Occupy enabled citizens to name individual and collective sacrifices that had rarely been acknowledged as sacrifices. The degree to which local Occupy groups in cities like Albuquerque, Denver, Eugene, and Oakland, responded to the concerns of participants who felt marginalized at first by the movement's rhetoric and practices contributed to the vitality that these citizens reported and which arguably drew them to Occupy in the first place. Occupy thus enabled citizens to acknowledge sacrifice and experiment with forms of associational life unavailable to them under emergency conditions. These new associations disrupted the circuits of sovereignty linking individuals to the state in relationships of acquiescence. This disruption was the product of examining sacrifices citizens had been forced to make together and the vitality that accompanied those discoveries. It was also the consequence of citizens trusting one another to reveal their personal vulnerabilities to strangers.

Brown sees the public occupation of privately owned properties like Zuccotti Park as part of "efforts to revive the image of the nation as *res publica*" in contrast to the relentless market orientation that characterizes neoliberalism. I have argued that Occupy's documentary practices played an important role in facilitating this revival, but what of the other citizen practices that were animating the protests? Theorists like Danielle Allen and Judith Butler argue that sharing these vulnerabilities is an important component of democratic life, but exactly how important is mutual vulnerability and what role does it in play in democratizing sovereignty? What about the DIY ethos prominent in the Idle No More flash mobs and Occupy encampments? The next chapter examines the limits of mutual vulnerability through the lens of the 2011 Egyptian Revolution, while the one after that weighs the potential of DIY models of democracy.

3

Inspiring Solidarity

Some, but not all, of the protestors who occupied Cairo's Tahrir Square during the eighteen-day effort to remove President Hosni Mubarak from office lived there round the clock: preparing and eating their meals together, sleeping, cleaning toilets, coordinating the delivery of water and removal of trash, protecting one another from raids by informal and secret police, tending to those injured in clashes with Mubarak's forces, keeping spirits up, and mediating the conflicts that arise among people who share close quarters with little personal space. They were helped by a larger number of protestors who traded off these responsibilities or simply lent the movement the support of their bodies, shouldering part of the risk those living in the square had taken on. The idea of "occupying" Tahrir would not only inspire direct citizen actions elsewhere, those actions would also take the form of occupations.

From the occupation of the Wisconsin State Capitol by those seeking to recall Wisconsin Governor Scott Walker in February 2011 to the occupation of Zuccotti Park that fall and even the occupation of Hong Kong's Central District at the end of 2014, the idea of citizens protesting by living for days out in these public spaces was different from the idea of citizens marching in the streets. Occupying these spaces seemed to put the focus on survival and endurance under bodily duress and, often, threat of removal by state forces. In each case, citizens seemed to be committed to their democratic actions by virtue of, not in spite of, an acknowledgment of their shared vulnerability and dependence on one another to sustain the biological needs of their bodies. In other words, they seemed to be carried by a commitment to the more generous ethos that Connolly and Judith Butler have argued is necessary to the practice of democracy.

In the context of her widely distributed remarks about the occupation of Tahrir Square entitled "Bodies in Alliance," Butler has argued that when bodies that are meant to be uncounted gather together and insist on public visibility through the performance of acts of mutual care and maintenance, they produce the solidarity observed among the protestors. Butler's lecture, which includes her reflections upon the Egyptian protests as well as her participation in a march with transgender individuals in Ankara, Turkey, is situated within a larger argument she has made about how the violent reassertion of state sovereignty is premised upon the denial of what she calls precarity or "the problem of our primary vulnerability to others" that I argued in the last chapter should be seen as one of Occupy's achievements for making visible.[1] "Bodies in Alliance" is the centerpiece of Butler's 2015 volume entitled *Notes Toward a Performative Theory of Assembly*. The essay appears in that volume in a revised form, though the body of her claims remains intact.[2] Butler's most recent work extends the direction and themes of her scholarship since the September 11, 2001 attacks.

Butler's response to the invasions of Afghanistan and Iraq, *Precarious Life,* identifies in US foreign policy, media reports, and moral support for the wars in Afghanistan and Iraq that came from some corners of the Left and feminists, a collective and individual desire for security, autonomy, and the disavowal of shared vulnerability and mutuality in the wake of the attacks on New York and Washington. Media coverage of the War on Terrorism, Butler contends, worked to frame nonviolent responses to the 9/11 attacks that acknowledged mutual vulnerability as signs of weakness at a moment when strength was called for, misplaced and misinformed sympathy with terrorists, and, ultimately, un-American.

Butler charts the means by which the media produce a public sphere in which American lives are grievable, those killed in the War on Terror are not and efforts to re-evaluate US foreign policy following the attacks are silenced as unpatriotic. Butler notes that the speed with which Americans were urged to get over the trauma of the attacks and take action foreclosed other possible responses. The alternative she sketches is a form of ethical responsibility that responds to violent action not in kind but produces a commitment to direct, nonviolent action among protestors originating in the recognition of their mutual bodily vulnerability. For Butler, this radical democratic solidarity is politically incompatible with and opposed to the sovereign self and the sovereign state.

Yet a closer look at the occupation of Tahrir Square suggests that while protestors were keen to remove Mubarak from power by actively resisting his efforts to clear them from the square, reforms to democratize the country's constitution, specifically by eliminating the emergency laws that had allowed Mubarak almost limitless powers,[3] and thus secure the gains of the revolution were the ultimate purpose of their protests. Moreover, evidence suggests that many Egyptians, especially the large percentage of ordinary Egyptians forced to live and find work in the nation's informal economy, following neoliberal policies which privatized state industries leaving many jobless and shrinking the social safety net, shared a prior sense of bodily vulnerability. The start of the protests on January 25, 2011, on a national holiday honoring the police, as well as the prominence of the "We Are All Khaled Said" Facebook group sparked by a video capturing the 2010 murder of a young man at the hands of police, point to the prior existence of a widely felt but passive sense of bodily vulnerability among Egyptians.[4]

My argument is that these feelings had to be activated and transformed through inspirational spectacles of interfaith cooperation in order to generate forms of mutual trust lacking among Egyptians. Mubarak had secured his three-decade rule by, in part, furthering sectarian divisions and distrust among Muslims and the country's Coptic Christian and secular minorities and by offering citizens a tradeoff: accept the rule of a strongman in exchange for the freedom to pursue economic self-interest. I examine features of the Islamic congregational prayers performed on Fridays during the occupation of Tahrir Square. I argue that along with the public performance of the five daily prayers, special prayers for those killed, and the Christian Masses held on the following Sundays, these prayers helped generate significant political and moral resources not only to preempt and resist the possibility of breaking down along sectarian and religious/secular lines but also to carry out the mundane aspects of occupying the square such as cooking and cleaning there. The repeated spectacle of tens then hundreds of thousands of Muslims bowing in prayers, guarded by Coptic Christians and secularists, represented a collective, albeit nonverbal statement of the norms of inclusiveness, reciprocity, nonviolence, and equality among a diverse public that Egyptians aspired to cultivate in the wake of Mubarak's departure.

Each of these prayers were "rational rituals" that coordinated real and symbolic forms of trust that signaled to those gathered and those watching that their protests could succeed and generated forms of solidarity that could be felt.[5] My suggestion is that these prayers introduced among subjects what Aletta Norval calls an "aspect change": seeing "something in a different context: one that enables one to make new sense of it."[6] In this case, the aspect change allowed Egyptians to see themselves not as rivals but as potential collaborators. This argument joins the work of other scholars critical of Butler's attempt to define democracy in opposition to practices of state sovereignty by identifying the limits of understanding democracy in terms of ethical practices alone.

DEMOCRACY WITHOUT SOVEREIGNTY: PRECARITY AND THE POLITICS OF THE STREET

In order to understand Butler's reading of the protests in Cairo, it is first necessary to appreciate how it fits in with her earlier contributions to a broader conversation about sovereignty, mourning, vulnerability, and ethics that has emerged in response to the September 11, 2001, attacks. Butler's remarks on Tahrir Square are in line with her larger claim about moving away from the practices of sovereignty and cultivating instead a non-violent ethic of vulnerability. For her, the September 11, 2001, attacks represented a "missed opportunity" for the United States to redefine its role in the global community. The attacks, according to Butler, exposed an "unbearable vulnerability" in American security, selfhood, and entitlement that the nation worked hastily to shore up. Instead of considering non-responses to the attacks, Butler writes that fear and mourning were channeled into efforts to overcome the undeniable dependence and interconnections that link humans. Response to the attacks took the form of efforts to reestablish sovereignty by exerting control over national territory in the face of terrorist threats and by restoring normalcy for citizens on the home front. As Sheldon Wolin observes, President Bush defined normalcy not in terms of duty or sacrifice but personal sovereignty, suggesting the best thing Americans could do to affirm their freedoms would be to live as if untouched by global events. He writes, "President Bush's first words to the citizenry after 9/11 were not an appeal for sacrifice in a common cause but 'unite, consume, fly.'"[7] Butler sees journalists, feminists, and public intellectuals as complicit in the War on Terror and the invocation of national security to justify domestic surveillance, having folded their commitments to justice and critical inquiry. Her own writing then stands as a statement and example of public philosophy under circumstances where political dissent and criticism of US foreign policy are popularly viewed as unpatriotic.

The wars in Afghanistan and Iraq and the passage of the US Patriot Act, which curtailed civil liberties and expanded the power of the government to spy on its own citizens, represent efforts to shore up sovereign power at a moment in history when an older notion of undivided sovereignty has become anachronistic. Butler terms this a resurgent but spectral sovereignty that has emerged through the expansion of discretionary powers.[8] This is best seen, according to Butler, through the judgment over who the US government considers "dangerous" and therefore can justifiably and indefinitely detain without trial.[9] She describes how judgments that enable the power of the nation-state to detain and hold "enemy combatants" at Guantanamo Bay turn on the suspension of US and international law: "sovereignty is reintroduced in the very acts by which the state suspends law or contorts law to its own uses."[10] The decisions of administration and military officials, Butler writes, do not conform to the traditional idea of a monolithic sovereignty that is identical to itself. Nonetheless, the diverse actions and motivations of so-called "petty sovereign" decision makers within the administration call into being a unified concept of sovereignty as "a self-grounding and unconditional basis for decision that has self-preservation as its primary aim."[11]

Butler believes that the 9/11 attacks might have instead prompted reflection on our primary vulnerability as socially constituted bodies. For her, the concept of sovereignty denies the fact that we are socially constituted. Individual selves are constituted through norms that they themselves do not author but nonetheless take on, add to, and contest through their actions. As Butler explains, as social norms, "neither gender nor sexuality is precisely a possession, but rather is a mode of being dispossessed, a way of being for another or by virtue of another."[12] Efforts to shore up sovereignty deny this primary sociality and vulnerability, but they remain resources for alternative visions of community founded on recognition of this common, pre-discursive vulnerability or precarity.[13] In her remarks about the protests in Tahrir Square, Butler contends that this vulnerability represents the basis of "a different social ontology" and it explains why she connects the recognition of mutual vulnerability to moments of grief and practices of mourning.

Butler emphasizes that acts of mutual recognition may not occur and, secondly, because these acts of recognition are idiosyncratic "vulnerability is fundamentally dependent on different norms of recognition if it is to be attributed to any human subject."[14] Because recognition is performed iteratively, its shape is not universal but contingent.[15] The variability and openness of recognition hint at what for Butler are its radically democratic possibilities that are contrasted with the closures associated with practices of state sovereignty. As Butler puts it, "I am not bound to established forms of subject formation or, indeed, to established conventions of relating to myself, but I am bound to the sociality of any of those possible relations."[16] The iterative character of recognition opens up the possibility of greater freedom for the subject. The origins of that freedom are revealed in the contingency and performativity of the norm and as the subject becomes aware of her inherent embeddedness in a network of social relations. According to Butler, the moments of address in which subjects recognize one another as public, mutually dependent selves, invite the self to reflect on her place in those social relations. For Butler, the resulting ethos of nonviolence contrasts with the circuit linking the sovereignty of modern states and subjects, though critics have questioned whether Butler has really dispensed with the idea of sovereignty. David McIvor notes that Butler endorses a form of "enraged non-violence" that seems to rely on "a superego-like figure to facilitate a less violent politics" by restraining the subject's anger from turning violent.[17]

In "Bodies in Alliance," Butler identifies the source of solidarity among the protestors in the stubborn materiality of their bodies. By gathering together and claiming the right to occupy Tahrir Square, by making public the fulfillment of bodily needs for food, rest, safety, and health and by exposing themselves to the threat of physical violence, she argues that the protestors used their bodies to challenge the legitimacy of the state. Even more than speech, Butler claims, the appearance of bodies on the square is what advanced the claim to political rights and undermined the moral legitimacy of the state. The power of this claim was not reducible to any single individual but was sustained by individuals acting together. The claim emerged through the rotation of responsibilities for preparing meals, keeping the sleeping areas tidy, cleaning toilets, and providing medical care and security; together, these activities worked to create horizontal relationships of equality among the protestors. Here is Butler:

> In other words, it is not that bodily action and gesture have to be transplanted into language, but that both action and gesture signify and speak, as action and claim, and that the one is not finally extricable from the other. Whereas the legitimacy of the state is brought into question precisely by that way of appearing in public, the body itself exercises a right that is no right; in other words, it exercises a right that is being actively contested and destroyed by military force, and which, in its resistance to force, articulates its persistence, and its right to persistence. This right is codified nowhere. It is not granted from elsewhere or by existing law, even if it sometimes finds support precisely there. It is, in fact, the right to have rights, not as natural

> law or metaphysical stipulation, but as the persistence of the body against those forces that seek to monopolize legitimacy . . . action in alliance happens precisely between those who participate, and this is not an ideal or empty space—it is the space of support itself—of durable and livable material environments and of interdependency among living beings.[18]

Butler suggests that solidarity among the protestors was a product of occupying space and collectively taking on the risks of physical violence associated with doing so. This is especially evident in the concluding section of her essay, which deals with the relationship between these bodily alliances and state police. She relates her participation in a march organized to protest police harassment of transgendered persons and a failure to protect transgendered persons from violence directed toward them in Ankara, Turkey. Reflecting on the public march, Butler writes that the presence of living bodies and the centrality of their material needs to politics suggests the body is the source of a "different social ontology." This ontology begins from the "presumption that there is a shared condition of precarity that situates our political lives." In her revised volume, Butler at times moves away from thinking about vulnerability in terms of ontology. Butler's language of "exposure" is a reminder that those appearing in the streets are risking injury by being there at that moment, which suggests that shared vulnerability is historically contingent rather than ontological.[19] Yet she also writes that "susceptibility and vulnerability [to others] constitutes me at the most fundamental level," a condition which makes mutual vulnerability prior to ethical responsiveness.[20]

Butler's move to link bodily appearance to police violence draws from the work of Michel Foucault, who identified the police as a central instrument in the modern state's ability to govern its population and maintain order.[21] According to Foucault, the police, being concerned with "little things," serves to regulate and discipline members of the population, bringing their individual conduct in line with the purposes of the regime. As Salwa Ismail observes, the breadth of activities covered by the Egyptian police under Mubarak, which included management of markets for food, electricity, and gas, as well as responsibility for public morality and taxation on top of public security, suggests that the daily needs of ordinary citizens brought them into regular contact with Egyptian police forces. The frequency of these contacts increased, she argues, with the growth of Egypt's informal economy and housing as government employment and social services shrank during the 1980s and 1990s, leaving more residents to live their lives on the public streets of Egypt's large cities and bringing them into more regular contact with police.[22]

Asef Bayat's research confirms that active use of public spaces by the subalterns of the neoliberal city brings this population into regular contact with state police. Examples of the active appropriation of public spaces include not only squatter settlements and vendors who set up stalls and workshops on sidewalks and alleys but also the visible practices of living life in public spaces: sitting, conversing, arguing, eating, sleeping, praying, and so on. Activities belonging to what he calls the quiet encroachment of ordinary spaces draw the attention of authorities who view them as a threat to "state prerogatives, including the meaning of order, control of public space, of public and private goods, and the relevance of modernity."[23] Taken together, he sees in the embodied actions by non-collective actors seeking to better their individual life circumstances the basis of political claims for autonomy and recognition from state authorities, but these do not begin as self-conscious acts of resistance. Moreover, most of these efforts are defensive. They involve holding on to spaces that have already been appropriated, not about gaining new ones. For example, Bayat observes that the common response to police raids is to scatter, to return to homes and businesses once police have left. In other words, the tactics tend to be evasive rather than confrontational; they represent micro-practices of coping and survival that permit macro-level practices of state sovereignty to remain intact.

Increasing contact between ordinary citizens and police forces and greater exposure to aggressive police tactics partly explains the significance of the start of the protests on January 25, 2011. January 25, Ismail notes, is a national holiday in Egypt, "Police Day," held to commemorate the role of the police forces in the independence movement against British colonial forces. Anti-police sentiment, and specifically, indignation over regular police harassment and abuse, she argues, was a strong component of the revolution. The organizers of the "Kulina Khaled Said" ("We Are All Khaled Said") Facebook group had chosen the January 25 date for the protests because Khaled Said had been a victim of police violence. Bystanders had filmed his death, at the hands of policemen who had pulled him from an Internet café in Alexandria in June 2010 on falsified drug charges. The images of police brutality had angered many Egyptians, who identified the abuse as commonplace, just as the 2010 death of Muhammad Bouazzi, whose act of self-immolation after police had confiscated his fruit cart and publicly humiliated him had incited many Tunisians to rise up against the Ben Ali regime. Finally, viewing the revolution as a response to police violence also explains why more than ninety-nine police stations across the nation were attacked and burned in the opening days of the uprising and crowds released prisoners from police cells.[24]

This story presents a problem for Butler, though, because it suggests that in their ordinary spaces and everyday lives many Egyptians already shared a sense of passive solidarity originating in the entwined intercorporeal experiences of economic precarity and exposure to the threat of police violence. Luca Mavelli argues that by publicizing images of tortured bodies, Egyptian bloggers made that knowledge a source of resistance. He suggests that knowledge of torture and collective indignation became the basis of a post-secular unity that bridged the divisions that the Mubarak regime had actively nurtured among secularists, Islamists, and Coptic Christians.[25] While Mavelli demonstrates that anger over police brutality and torture were historical constructions, this knowledge was broadly distributed among a public composed of non-collective actors. Bayat compares knowledge distributed via online networks to the solidarity that is formed among passive non-collective actors on the street. As he explains, intercorporeal visibility is a central feature of quiet encroachment, where solidarities are formed primarily in public spaces through members of a "passive network" engaged in ordinary life on the street. He writes, "poor street vendors would recognize their common predicaments by noticing one another on street corners on a daily basis, even though they may never know or speak to one another."[26] Similarly, the work by bloggers to publicize images of tortured bodies extended knowledge of abusive police practices to literate, well-off, and younger members of the Egyptian public. For Bayat, the emergence of a common threat is what turns these passive networks into "active communication and organized resistance," but again he emphasizes such resistance is most often in defense of gains already won through quiet encroachment rather than in the advancement of new demands.[27]

But the protests in Tahrir Square boldly sought the end of the regime and emergency law. In the words of Mohamed Elshahed, "An uprising was long coming in Egypt, but Egyptians could not break the fear barrier created by the state." According to Elshahed that fear was the product of not only aggressive policing but also the regime's efforts to create a false dichotomy between itself and the Muslim Brotherhood, rhetoric that was aimed at garnering support from Coptic Christians as well as moderate Muslims and secular Egyptians. As Elshahed notes, the government was even suspected of having bombed one of Alexandria's largest churches only months before the revolution began in an effort to further antagonize relations among Coptic Christians and Muslims. "The regime used the incident to highlight the need for its suffocating security and intelligence and the threat from 'Palestinian' elements and fundamentalist Islam."[28]

How then did activists confront mutual fear and distrust? How, to put it differently, did Egyptians actively organize solidarity around knowledge of police aggression? How did they incite one another to move on this knowledge and to overcome their fears of the state and one another? My suggestion in the next section is that the prayers in Tahrir Square inspired protestors to act courageously and in solidarity to hold the square as a condition of removing Mubarak from office. The initial Friday prayer was likely spontaneously organized and, in the spirit of the moment, non-Muslims protestors formed a human chain around those praying. But from that first event, the prayers grew in size and symbolism, helping to inspire future actions, cooperation, and trust among a diverse body of Egyptians during the eighteen days of the Revolution that added to the shared knowledges and desires for regime change Elshahed mentions in his report.

SPECTACLES OF INTERFAITH COOPERATION

There is no question that holding the square was the cornerstone of the protestors' strategy as well as the Mubarak regime's effort to put an end to the uprising. The regime made great efforts to clear the protestors from the square.[29] During the opening days of the occupation of Tahrir Square, plainclothes policemen attacked protestors with tear gas, rubber bullets, water cannons, broken bottles, and ultimately live ammunition. According to David D. Kirkpatrick of the *New York Times*, on January 28, 2011, Mubarak dispatched more than one thousand riot police to central locations in Cairo, in addition to cutting communication networks, in an effort to keep protestors from reaching Tahrir Square and to restore order. More than nine hundred protestors were injured as they clashed with police attempting to hold the Kasr al-Nil bridge. Another four hundred were critically injured in the adjacent Giza district and a total of six individuals were killed during the protests in Cairo and Giza, along with thirteen killed in Suez.[30]

Faced with open revolt, Mubarak dispatched uniformed and secret police to remove protestors from the city's public squares and to enforce a 6:00 p.m. curfew. Uniformed policemen fought open battles with the protestors during the first days of the revolution, aided by the more aggressive tactics of the secret police. In addition to infiltrating the ranks of protestors, members of the secret police organized themselves along with those paid by the ruling party as pro-Mubarak supporters in an effort to balance the otherwise one-sided picture of discontent with the Egyptian leader among the general population. These pro-Mubarak groups were meant to suggest uncoerced support for the president, but in practice their "independence" gave them free license to respond with greater violence while the government could claim no control over their actions.

The so-called Battle of the Camels, which took place on February 2, 2011, the day after Mubarak had pledged to step down from power, is representative of the regime's desperate efforts to regain control over Tahrir Square and disperse antigovernment protestors as they continued to grow in numbers and strength. Eyewitness accounts report that pro-Mubarak supporters acted according to a violent, predetermined script. Arriving en mass on buses, members of the pro-Mubarak faction were outfitted with identically printed signage along with a range of crude weapons—pliers, cleavers, clubs, knives, chains—and, it appears, concealed guns. Reports indicate that at exactly 2:15 p.m. the pro-Mubarak forces who had been shouting their support for the president, calling him the "father" of the country, began to attack the antigovernment protestors, who tried to resist responding to the provocation with violence. Later that afternoon, men on camel and horseback wielding chains, whips, and clubs attacked antigovernment crowds.[31]

Mubarak's use of the police to keep order lends the performance of the Islamic congregational prayers in Tahrir Square special political resonance because before the January 25 protests Mubarak had policed religious expression in Egypt in order to minimize threats to his rule. By trying to regulate the expression of Islamic identity and practice in Egypt, Mubarak exemplifies the exclusive and jealous character of sovereignty that concerns Butler. Mubarak had gained international support for his regime and latitude to exercise broad power to maintain his position by representing himself as necessary to stop the spread of more radical versions of Islam like the Muslim Brotherhood. Like Nasser and Sadat before him, Mubarak tried to incorporate Islam into and identify it with state institutions and, in doing so, to produce legitimate and illegitimate versions of Islam. Having a legitimate version of Islam also meant having legitimate and illegitimate places to worship, and legitimate and illegitimate subjects for the *khutba*, or sermon, that is the centerpiece of the *Salat-al-Juma* or Friday congregational prayer.

Mubarak's Ministry of Religion turned Islamic clerics and imams into government employees responsible for crafting, through their sermons, a version of Islam that was supportive of his rule.[32] The creation of an official

Islam compatible with, at least formally speaking, Western-style constitutional rule allowed Mubarak to preemptively cast rival versions like the Muslim Brotherhood as extreme and undemocratic. As Alaa Al-Aswany notes, Mubarak permitted the visibility of conservative Salafist clerics, especially on satellite television, so long as they emphasized the virtue of obedience to (his) authority, in order to outflank the appeal of the Muslim Brotherhood among conservative-leaning Muslims.[33] Having a legitimate version of Islam also allowed Mubarak to fix blame for sectarian violence directed toward Egypt's Coptic minority onto more "radical" Islamist groups, casting his regime as defender of minority rights and antagonizing the possibilities for coalitions across sectarian/secular lines.[34] In other words, Mubarak secured his rule by generating mutual fear and suspicion among competing sectors of Egyptian society, playing one group against the others.

Against this backdrop, for Egyptian Muslims, Copts, and secularists to independently organize the juma prayers during successive Fridays and mass on the following Sundays during the revolution were political acts of resistance. The performance of the prayers were real and symbolic acts of cooperation and trust that were important in inspiring further action because they demonstrated that the anti-Mubarak protestors and not the government were in control of Tahrir Square. As many reports observed, the crowds in Tahrir Square grew larger and more diverse over the three weeks of the revolution. By the Day of Departure on February 4, news reports portrayed the protests as drawing participants from all walks of Egyptian society including young and old, women and men, secular and religious, educated and illiterate, wealthy and poor. Initially though, the protestors were composed largely of men, many of whom were affiliated with Egypt's football clubs and were comparatively experienced with street fighting and confrontation.[35] Together, this suggests that Egyptians grew more confident in their ability to join those protesting in public squares around the nation. My argument is that this confidence can be partly be explained by considering the impact that the spectacle of the prayers had on viewers and participants. Specifically, the performance of the Islamic Friday prayers in Tahrir Square inspired viewers and participants to continue their struggle in the face of violence and intimidation because they were public spectacles of cooperation that generated widely distributed knowledge and feelings of commonality, trust, and solidarity among diverse Egyptians.

The *Salat-al-Juma* that marked the Fridays of Rage (January 28), Departure (February 4), and Victory (February 18) were enormous events that grew in size and spectacle. On February 11, 2011, an estimated 300,000 were gathered for the *Salat-al-Juma* prayers in Tahrir Square. In a televised address to the nation the night before, Mubarak had handed over authority to Omar Sueliman but had not given up the presidency. Now they had gathered to demand he step down completely. Many observers cited the growth of the crowds in Tahrir Square as a reason for a rising sense of safety and confidence among the protesters.[36] By the second Friday of the occupation of Tahrir Square—called the Day of the Martyrs to mark those who lost their lives and were injured during the bloody confrontation with state police forces and pro-Mubarak militia earlier in the week—several participants identified the *Salat-al-Juma* held on that day in the square as something special. Activist Gigi Ibrahim tweeted a photo of hundreds prostrating in prayer, writing that the scene had given her goosebumps. The popular blogger Sandmonkey tweeted: "The scene in Tahrir right now is incredible. Millions of people praying. Reverence. It looks like Mecca in haj." Another tweeted a plea, "Please please understand that mass prayers are a form of protest, not necessarily a display of religiosity, but unity."[37] In *Associated Press* photos of the prayers from Ben Curtis and Tara Todas-Whitehill taken on this day, those praying fill every corner of Tahrir Square, situating themselves between tents and tanks. Soldiers are seen praying alongside antigovernment protestors. Searching for any clear space, they stand atop tanks and army vehicles, shoulder to shoulder in prayer, surrounded by a ring of Coptic Christians. According to a photo caption, Yusef al-Qaradawi, returned from exile in Qatar but well known to Egyptians as a regular presence on Al-Jazeera, addressed the protestors. He told them, "Don't let anyone steal this revolution from you, [especially] those hypocrites who will put on a new face that suits them," speaking to over three hundred thousand peaceful demonstrators who gathered after Friday prayers in Tahrir Square. "The revolution isn't over. It has just started to build! Egypt, guard your revolution!"[38]

These prayers were remarkable at many levels. Not only did the scale of the prayers rival only the Hajj or annual pilgrimage to Mecca in numbers and visual impact, but also these prayers were unique in how inclusive and pluralistic they were. Egyptians had few points of reference to comprehend the presence of non-Muslims participating in the prayers and Muslims participating in a Coptic Mass for Martyrs of the Revolution the previous Sunday.[39] Nor did they have experience with men and women standing, in some cases, next to one another, shoulder to shoulder in prayer rather than in segregated areas. Set against the backdrop of the hierarchically organized public sphere of the Mubarak regime, where most women had a marginal public presence, and the fact that relations among Muslims, Coptic Christians, and secularists had been tense, the *Salat-al-Juma* on these dates emphasized mutual care and equality among citizens rather than differences. Coptic Christians and secularists stood forming a human barrier around Muslim worshippers, securing the safety of those praying the *Salat-al-Juma* on the Friday of Rage and the Friday of Departure. Muslims in the square performed the same task during Christian services on the following Sunday mornings.

Those leading each of the prayers emphasized the shared dependence and struggle linking the members of the two faiths as Egyptians, with Christian clergy addressing Muslims on Friday and Imams reciprocating on Sunday.[40] Here is al-Qaradawi at the start of his February 18, 2011, *khutba* addressing an audience of several hundred thousand that had gathered to celebrate Mubarak's departure one week before:[41] "The usage of preachers, for their sermons, is to say "O Muslims!" but me, I say in this Square, 'O Muslims and Copts! O children of Egypt! This is the day of the children of Egypt all together. It is not the day of the Muslims alone.' "[42] Al-Qaradawi continues by comparing Mubarak to Pharaoh in a story familiar to many of his listeners. Referring to Surah *Taha* (Q. 20), al-Qaradawi proclaimed:

> That Pharaoh had said to the Egyptians: "Do you believe in Him before I give you permission?" (Q. 20:71). Similarly *this Pharaoh*

> said: "Do you make a revolution before I give you permission to make a revolution?" It is not allowed to the minds to be convinced, nor to the hearts to believe, nor to the limbs to move except with an authorization from Pharaoh! "You are making a revolution before I give you permission to make a revolution?" "You are believing in Him before I give you permission?" The children of Egypt, once they believed, said to Pharaoh, defiantly: "We will not prefer you to what has come to us of clear proofs and to Him Who made us; therefore, decide what you are going to decide" (Q. 20:72). Observe the human being when he believes and the human being before he believes! The magicians whom Pharaoh had brought together from all the regions of Egypt threw their cords and their rods and said: "By Pharaoh's might, we will surely be the winners" (Q. 26:44). And "they said to Pharaoh: 'Will there surely be a reward for us if we are the winners?' (Q. 26:41)—'Is there money?'—"He said: 'Yes, and surely you will then be of those who are made near.'" (Q. 26:42).—"There is money, positions, and many benefits!"—And what did these authentic Egyptians say once they believed, the truth having appeared to them? "We will not prefer you to what has come to us of clear proofs and to Him Who made us; therefore, decide what you are going to decide; you can only decide about this world's life. Surely we believe in our Lord that He may forgive us our sins and the magic to which you compelled us; and God is better and more lasting" (Q. 20:72-73).

Patrick Gaffney explains that since the earliest *khutbas* delivered by Prophet Muhammad, the *khutba* had served as the formal setting for major decisions in addition to educating believers in interpreting and practicing the faith. As Islam grew and the task of proclaiming the *khutba* was assigned to persons who were not the caliphate, the *khutba* and *Salat al-Juma* became a crucial arena in which power struggles were witnessed and waged. According to Gaffney, "in times of crisis, such as a siege, an insurrection, an interregnum, or an invasion, a sermon might provide the occasion for a signal to muster in a mass uprising or it could serve notice of shifting loyalties by means of the preacher's naming of some emerging aspirant to the throne instead of its current disputed occupant."[43]

Asghar Fathi has studied the role of the *minbar*, from which the *khutba* is delivered, as a mode of political communication during the Abbasid Caliphate, the Ottoman Empire, and during the more recent anti-colonial movements in Iran and North Africa. He argues that whether tethered to state interests, as in the Ottoman era, or directed against them, the institutional character of the *minbar* made it an especially effective forum for face-to-face communications and coordinating information. He notes that the message delivered from the *minbar* could have a wide reach since mosques neither had regular congregations nor were associated with a particular class. The audience of the *khutba*, he writes, was distinguished by "anonymity and heterogeneity" and the *khutba* itself was a highly political form of public address: "The *minbar* not only played an active role in the development of public issues, but on certain occasions it also was used to oppose the established authorities."[44]

Qaradawi's effort to make the *Salat-al-Juma* inclusive was reinforced by the popularity of handheld signs and graffiti that portrayed the crescent and cross together as signs of national unity. The cross and crescent symbol hails from the 1919 Revolution in which Muslims and Copts organized mass protests against British occupiers and is therefore a reminder of successful interfaith cooperation in the past. The visibility of these signs as well as the images of thousands of bodies moving in prayer together beamed onto television screens and the Internet created shared points of reference and affective identification for those watching and participating. Michael Chwe has argued that such "rational rituals" play an important role in coordinating social action and producing common knowledge in complex societies. The visibility of these rituals and the circulation of such images, he argues, allow viewers to confirm that they are not alone in witnessing what they are seeing even if they may draw different conclusions about its meaning or significance.[45] Such rituals, in other words, can inaugurate new public understandings among those who are witnesses to such events.

In this case, one of the underlying messages generated in the spectacle of the prayer was the emergence of trust among members of groups that, during the period of Mubarak's rule, had regarded one another with suspicion. Although the language of Qaradawi's *khutba* and the signs carried by protestors testified to new forms of trust and cooperation that had taken hold among protestors in Tahrir Square, it is arguable that this trust and its capacity to inspire further action became legible in the embodied spectacle of the prayer as worshippers stood and prostrated together, protected by a human chain of fellow Egyptians standing watch over them. In other words, in coordinating the Friday prayers and Sunday masses, the protestors were enacting trust in order to generate it among the larger public. Butler is, broadly speaking, correct about the importance of bodily acts over speech in generating a shared sense of solidarity. It is arguable that the force of this emerging trust was felt affectively for Egyptians who witnessed and participated in the prayers. William McNeill has noted that participants in coordinated bodily movements such as ritual prayer or military drills often experience a sense of togetherness, solidarity, and mutual attachment as a result of their participation.[46]

The significance of this affective, bodily experience is what might explain the shift from passive forms of solidarity, such as Bayat's networks and known opposition to Mubarak's rule, into more animated forms of solidarity. That is because viewers of the prayer and the protests at large, whether present in person or watching from a distance through a screen, were engaged with a moment that invited judgment. As public spectacle, the prayers demanded response from viewers who had to negotiate whether or not they identified with the worshippers and protestors. The prayers constituted an event that had the potential to bind the viewers and participants into a public with shared concerns and aspirations. The repetition of these prayers over successive Fridays enabled participants and viewers to consider the inspirational content and significance of this ritual not once, but repeatedly in the company of those who had also likely witnessed or heard about the prayers. The repetition allows viewers to revise, refine, and sharpen their shared understandings of the event and what it meant for the other parts of the protests. The growth of the prayers also transmitted growing trust among Egyptians over the duration of the occupation.

The prayers can be interpreted as an effort to move the larger mass of Egyptian citizens from their passive identification with the knowledge that Mubarak was disliked to an animated knowledge that enabled them to confront their fears of the state and mutual suspicions. That is, recognizing the prayers as an event that included them entailed acting on the knowledge that Mubarak had to be removed from power while at the same time underlined that this could not be possible without the trust that had given them the courage to act together. After all, shared intercorporeal precarity had been a near constant feature of daily life for most Egyptians. That explanation alone appears insufficient to explain the solidarity required for protestors to overcome their fears of one another and reprisals from Mubarak's police.

But if the prayers are seen as efforts protestors made to inspire trust and courage in one another through heroic acts of interfaith cooperation, they also previewed the habits of citizenship that a post-Mubarak, democratic Egypt would require. Citizens of this new Egypt would carry forward the affects and dispositions that had made the revolution possible, especially the highly participatory practices of mutual attentiveness that forged new attachments among diverse Egyptians. These include the examples of mutual tending to bodily needs and safety that Butler highlights as well as an appreciation of the physical and psychic sacrifices others had made to the revolution, not just during the eighteen-day occupation but also during the years leading up to it. As Elshahed points out many communities paid the cost of challenging Mubarak even if they challenged Mubarak simply by insisting on the right to live as they pleased: "Mubarak has been a ruthless dictator who has cracked down on everyone from secular political opposition and the Muslim Brotherhood to heavy metal fans and gays."[47]

To idealize the episodic democracy of citizen assemblies and acts of mutual generosity in contrast to the experience of limited freedom particular to the exercise of spectral sovereignty offers little comfort to those who must keep living in the months and years after the revolution. In particular, it does not acknowledge how the shared experience of the revolution generated attachments among Egyptians as well as to experiences of mutual cooperation, trust, and action that serve as surfaces to which future actions could attach. In this sense, Butler is right to see the acknowledgment of loss as central to the project of founding and sustaining democratic communities. The acknowledgment of loss and sacrifice are crucial to fortifying the mutual trust generated through rituals like the *Salat-al-Juma*, but they require citizens to initiate additional rituals that can sustain and augment the trust necessary for citizens to go on together. The state and its laws and institutions are important sites for the recognition of these sacrifices, and for building trust among citizens—in Egypt, where religious differences, and also in America, where the realities of racial sovereignty, represent barriers to full citizenship.

The notion that the experience of the Friday prayer could produce new understandings amongst the collective body politic and, ultimately, a body politic that understands itself and its possibilities differently is grounded in the spiritual purpose of the Islamic prayer or *salat*. For Muslims, the *Salat-al-Juma* is an embodied practice of cultivating conduct and the self that works from the outside in. Anthropologist Saba Mahmood connects *salat* to what Pierre Hadot, in his reflections on ancient Greek philosophy and ethics, called "spiritual exercises."[48] Such exercises, she explains, proceed from the "outside in" following an Aristotelian model of ethical pedagogy in which moral virtues are learned through habitual repetition. She traces the reception of Aristotelian concepts of moral formation now popular among contemporary virtue ethicists like Alasdair MacIntyre by Islamic thinkers and theologians, which she uses, along with her field work, to sketch the role of *salat* in facilitating and realizing a desired ethical regime.[49]

For the women Mahmood studied, *salat* was among the most important rituals where the moral character of the self is shaped over time into something approaching a second nature.[50] Moreover, Mahmood notes the moral training and conduct addressed during the performance of the *salat* is understood to extend to the sphere of ordinary conduct: "This understanding of ritual prayer posits an ineluctable relationship between conventional or rule-governed action and routine and practical conduct... ritual prayer is conjoined and interdependent with pragmatic and utilitarian activities of daily life, actions that must be monitored and honed as conditions for the performance of the ritual itself."[51] Mahmood's research suggests that prayers like those that took place in Tahrir Square were not regarded as separate from everyday life but informed and guided ordinary conduct. Butler notes that the protestors chanted "silmiyya," meaning "peaceful," in order to restrain themselves from responding to provocation with violence. Silmiyya comes from the Arabic root *silm*, which also appears in words like salaam and Islam.

Khaled El Fadl argues that Coptic Christians were responsive to the Islamically rooted rituals and discourses of the revolution. He notes that Coptic Christians were drawn toward efforts to frame Mubarak's removal as a righteous *jihad* or struggle against injustice, corruption, and despotism.[52] Likewise, Charles Hirschkind points to social commentator Tariq al-Bishri's claim that Coptic Christians are bound to a larger Egyptian public through Islamic institutions, discourses, and rituals since Islam represents an important constitutive component of Egypt's social and political life.[53] On this point, Gaffney writes "the traditional symbols of Islam and the modern Egyptian nation-state [have been brought] into such close conjunction that they not only overlap, but to many observers, they seem in many circumstances to virtually coincide."[54]

The Friday prayers were real and symbolic acts of interfaith trust and cooperation that viscerally and visually forged a sense of solidarity among Egyptians. As spectacle, the prayers were enormous gatherings and noticeably inclusive rituals. For participants witnessing them firsthand and on screen, the prayers were recognizably different from those that took place in the space of the state-monitored and sponsored mosques. Against the backdrop of mutual suspicion, division, and hostility cultivated by the Mubarak regime, the prayers in Tahrir Square were statements of autonomy by a diversely constituted Egyptian public committed to pluralism and indifferent to old sectarian divisions. Although this message is heard in statements like Qaradawi's *khutba* and seen in signs that combined the crescent and the cross, it was primarily felt. The active solidarity that allowed Egyptians to believe they could remove Mubarak from office, I have argued, was communicated in the spectacle of the prayers. Of course the activities of routine care and maintenance that Butler cites and which were essential to holding Tahrir Square were important sources of solidarity, but they drew upon passive forms of solidarity originating in exposure to police violence. The congregational prayers were significant sources of inspiration and moral support that made those other activities and the risks they entailed more endurable. As a spectacle of interfaith cooperation, the prayers helped animate passive forms of solidarity among Egyptians who had long harbored suspicions of one another that broke down along sectarian lines. The prayers were embodied spectacles involving thousands of diverse Egyptians that allowed them to believe that they could act together to remove Mubarak. Spaced over three weeks, they were decisive moments that inspired courage, allowing Egyptians to turn passive solidarity around opposition to Mubarak and police violence into open opposition.

CONCLUSION

Butler concludes her lecture with a concrete example of how bodies can act in alliance to claim a right to the public. She relates her participation in a walk organized in support of the rights of transgendered to appear in public in Ankara, Turkey, where transgendered persons have been fined by the police, beaten, and murdered in recent years. She emphasizes that the alliance that assembled in support of this community and its rights was appealing because it brought together local activists with European representatives who were split into camps over the question of transgendered persons, on the one hand, and the rights of Muslim women living in Europe to wear the *burqa* or *niqab* there, on the other. She states that the participants in this walk claimed this right not just for those present, but any transgendered person or supporter who wishes to walk on the street without worry of police harassment or bodily injury. Their shared precarity is born in the conditions of their corporeal appearance and interdependence.

But her example also makes visible the very different sources of that shared precarity. Although they may share a common thread of violence and vulnerability, not all practices of organizing the public are alike or draw upon the same resources in shaping a shared condition of precarity. These vary with the identity of those participating, the status of their visibility in society, and what traditions and experiences they share among them.[55] So while Butler is right to be critical of Hannah Arendt's simplified concepts of public space and action, the sources of trust and cooperation necessary for Egyptians to occupy Tahrir Square were not simply the products of their assembly. Rather, I have argued trust was generated through acts of interfaith and sectarian cooperation that inspired participants and viewers watching from a distance.

The examples also illuminate the character of Butler's style of public philosophy. There is no disputing that her work fills an important gap in the public debate over the resurgence of state sovereignty and the increasing precarity experienced by the majority and minority world. Hers is an influential and a rare critical voice. However, Butler's second goal of developing a post-foundational ethic out of her analysis of examples of precarity, because it feels abstract and strangely separate from the texture of those accounts, runs the risk of appearing to turn to political events to validate and build a theory. Although she cautions against reading universalist aspirations in her work, and her conception of recognition as an iterative process goes some way to minimize these charges, the fact the debates that Butler intervenes in form the backdrop to the emergence of her theory of ethical responsibility suggests that, for Butler, vulnerability constitutes a universal political imperative that is prior to politics. As Moya Lloyd has argued, the result is paradoxical. For Butler, ethical vulnerability is simultaneously prior to politics yet can do political work in contexts that are graded by power.[56] Butler's effort to save democracy by recasting it with a "different ontology" seems to mirror arguments by US officials justifying measures that shortcut democratic processes and freedoms in the name of preserving the nation's freedoms and way of life. George Shulman has written that efforts to define democracy in terms of ethics reflect either a lack of confidence or wariness about the possibilities of democratic mobilizations.[57]

Like the Idle No More activists, the protestors in Tahrir Square faced a general public lacking confidence and agency, wary and doubtful of their abilities to change the status quo. In Egypt, the barriers to citizens joining the protests included fear of the state and mutual distrust. The prayers in Tahrir Square were spectacles of cooperation that addressed these barriers by generating real and symbolic trust among viewers. The size and publicity of the prayers made them spectacles of animated solidarity that was felt and communicated in the shared movements of the bodies prostrating in prayer and in the human chain protecting them. Such cooperation was inspiring and spaced over consecutive Fridays of the revolution; the growth in the size of the prayers and demonstrators served to not only renew the protestors' resolve to hold the square and to do the mundane work required to perform this important task but also rearticulated the norms of equality that they hoped their revolution would bring into post-Mubarak Egypt.

But as the Oscar-nominated documentary *The Square* (2013) argues, the recognition of equality among diverse Egyptians that made the occupation in Tahrir Square possible was only the start of the revolution.[58] The activists profiled in the documentary are insistent that their democratic revolution will not be complete until constitutional reforms protecting the freedoms they had experienced while removing Mubarak from power are extended beyond the space of the square. In contrast to Butler, they suggest that democracy and the extra-juridical forms of sovereignty that removed Mubarak from office need juridical protections. Scholar Nathan J. Brown echoes this point in a recent essay:

> Yes, they wanted jobs and better wages. But both leaders and the foot soldiers of the massive uprising were startlingly quick to render their desires in constitutional form. They demanded diminution of the powers of the presidency, the repeal of attempts to enshrine emergency measures as normal constitutional procedures, judicial monitoring of elections, and term limitations for the head of state.[59]

They need, in other words, laws and institutions that protect and nurture these extra-juridical forms of sovereignty.

Of course, the path of Egypt since the 2011 Revolution has been neither straight nor democratic. The army's removal and trial of Mohammed Morsi, just ten months after he won the first open election in Egypt's history, as well as Morsi's attempt to rewrite the constitution to give himself more discretionary power, have cast shadows on the legacy of the revolution and the extraordinary acts of courage and cooperation that gave birth to it. While it is tempting to call the Egyptian revolution a failure because the army remains an entrenched power and holds a firm grip on state affairs, and the nation's economy has been in free fall since Mubarak was removed from office, such a conclusion assumes that the action that began in Tahrir Square and many other public sites around the country has come to an end.

However, the afterlife of the action and sensibility that began in the 2011 Revolution can still be seen in the Egyptian people. Many, of course, do wish for a return of normalcy, by which they mean economic and political stability, and they are willing to endure the tradeoffs in their freedoms that the army demands in exchange for delivering this security. Yet citizens also continue in their direct actions and calls for juridical reforms and the end of emergency laws. Egyptians rallied in Tahrir Square to protest the army's proposed postponement of elections until 2013 and its refusal to lift the country's emergency laws.[60] They rallied in Tahrir Square to call for the removal of the country's democratically elected president Mohammed Morsi,[61] just as his supporters in the Muslim Brotherhood rallied there to protest his overthrow by the army. Egyptians of many colors continue to take to Tahrir Square and to engage in a range of confrontational strategies in order to demand public accountability and to protest efforts to silence and exclude them. The demand that General el-Sisi address the prevalence of sexual violence against Egyptian women after a video showing a woman being stripped and beaten by security forces in Tahrir Square surfaced on the eve of his inauguration, prompted el-Sisi to apologize to the victim in a televised visit to her hospital bedside.[62]

Four years on, they continue to commemorate the revolution, challenging the state's effort to silence and intimidate its citizens. On January 24, 2015, masked policemen shot and killed thirty-one-year old Shaimaa el-Sabbagh, who had travelled from Alexandria to Tahrir Square to lay flowers with other activists in Tahrir Square. A poet, mother, and left-leaning activist, el-Sabbagh's killing was captured on video as she marched with others. Police also shot and killed seventeen-year old Sondos Reda, who was attending an Islamist rally in Alexandria on the same day, and they killed more than twenty Egyptians in protests the next day, the anniversary of the January 25 uprising.[63] These Egyptians understand that they do not have a democracy today, but they are aware that it exists as a possibility for them. They are evidence that the events in Tahrir Square have vitalized citizens to continue the efforts to contest and democratize sovereignty.

4

Democracy and the State

Occupy Sandy is the name of the mutual aid and disaster relief network that sprang up in the hours after Hurricane Sandy hit the New York and New Jersey coastline on October 29, 2012, causing major destruction and bringing life in the region to a standstill for weeks. The *New York Times* marveled at the diversity of citizens who contributed to and found purpose in the improvised mutual aid network. They included stay-at-home mothers from Manhattan, members of a motorcycle gang who combined gruffness and a can-do spirit, Brooklyn hipsters, labor activists, community groups, for-profit recovery companies, private contractors, and representatives from the city's Sikh Cultural Society, who all made their way to Far Rockaway, Queens, a barrier-island community that sustained some of the most severe damage during the storm.

Occupy Sandy earned widespread praise from the general public for the speed with which it acted and the extent of its aid efforts, which ranged from supplying safe drinking water and generators to residents in the days after the storm, to coordinating cleanup efforts weeks and months later. Occupy Sandy volunteers were often on the ground in the hardest hit neighborhoods days before representatives from the Federal Emergency Management Agency (FEMA), the American Red Cross, and city and state emergency services. This meant that storm victims often had their initial contact with other citizens mobilized by the desire to extend mutual aid to their neighbors rather than with government or agency representatives.

Many thousands benefitted from Occupy Sandy and the group in turn attracted many thousands of volunteers. This chapter turns to this recent episode in order to consider what kinds of democratic goods were generated through mutual aid and self-initiative given that Alexis de Tocqueville had identified self-initiative and mutual aid as signs of self-rule and democratic culture in the United States. Coming from France, he was struck by how Americans responded to problems by rolling up their sleeves and joining together to remove obstacles in their path. More recently, theorists have pointed to the citizen-initiated mutual aid following Hurricane Katrina as evidence of democratic intuitions and practices that have survived even as decision-making powers have become more concentrated and remote from citizens. In the words of theorist Sheldon Wolin, citizen initiative and mutual aid were examples of democratic light in an era otherwise defined by darkness.[1]

For authors like Connolly who see the cultivation of generosity and pluralism as essential to the task of weakening the defensive ethos that supports arguments for the necessity of state sovereignty, it is hard not to find encouragement in developments like Occupy Sandy. Likewise, there are theorists like Lauren Berlant for whom mutual aid represents a chance for citizens to exercise desires for public agency and attachment without the pressures of competition found in the workplace and market. Berlant's work charts how, on the one side, public life has become monopolized by what she calls post-political forms of belonging. Similar to Anker's concept of felt legitimacy, these depoliticized forms of identification are exemplified by invocations of shared consensus during moments of crisis and emergency that bolster support for unilateral sovereign authority. On the other side, Berlant sees citizens discouraged by the closures associated with these calls to state action because they reinforce feelings of devitalized agency. They give rise, in her analysis, to a sense of impasse and cynicism that characterizes what she terms the "cruel optimism" of political life that causes subjects to seek agency in outlets lateral to politics. According to Berlant, these lateral outlets are appealing because they offer glimpses of reciprocity and mutuality. Citizens want but cannot find relationality and mutuality within the marketplace. The competition there leaves them feeling frayed and vulnerable, reduced to "desperate doggy paddling" and worried about just getting by.

Against this backdrop, Occupy Sandy's mutual aid network represents an alternative in which citizens are not merely responding to crisis with a shrug that registers both their frustration and lack of confidence but by creating positive attachments. For Berlant, the ability to resist the directives of state sovereignty as well as its dissembling consequences lies in assemblies and affective attachments that can emerge through experiences of agency in areas outside of formal political institutions, especially those that are imbued with and are the product of do-it-yourself (DIY) practices.

The DIY ethos, which has animated anticapitalist and antihierarchical movements ranging from punk to anarchists to squatters, is part of a tradition that has tried to reimagine the attachments that modern subjects have to ideas like private property and wages through experiments in cooperation and sharing that try to build a better world within the shell of the existing one. In her history of DIY culture, Amy Spencer identifies DIY as part of an effort to form community with like-minded individuals that took root among queers, punks, and feminists. She notes that zines or self-published newsletters played an important role in the development of each of these communities. Authors were attracted by the freedom that zines offered since they were relatively free from censorship as well as the idea that anyone could become an author or contributor.[2] Participation and creativity were central to the ethos of DIY and DIY was crucial to the development of networks that could support micro-practices that were free expressions of one's identity.

Spencer describes DIY as requiring the creation of a community around values opposed to the mainstream, a point that echoes Michael Warner's concept of the counterpublic. Warner defines counterpublics as associations and attachments that are formed by virtue of their "conflict with the norms and contexts of their cultural environment" and which are indebted to practices of display and circulation.[3] Both self-transformation and the transformation of the larger culture are the goals of counterpublics, according to Warner. Referring to the formation of queer counterpublics, Warner writes:

> And they were elaborating not only new shared worlds and critical languages but also new privacies, new individuals, new bodies, new intimacies, and new citizenships . . . Styles of embodiment are learned and cultivated, and the affects of shame and disgust that surround them can be tested, in some cases revalued. Visceral private meaning is not easy to alter by oneself, by free act of will. It can only be altered through exchanges that go beyond self-expression to the making of a collective scene of disclosure.[4]

Understood in terms of counterpublics, DIY can be understood as an ambitious project to remake the terms of the ordinary world within the existing world through the cultivation of potentially transformative micro-practices. It is for this reason that Berlant and others are clearly drawn to DIY as a way of thinking through the predicament that neoliberalism represents.

Even more recently HIV/AIDS activists embraced DIY techniques to advocate for increased funding for research and treatment with success, yet I argue in the case of Occupy Sandy, its DIY ethos was linked to anti-statist discourses similar to those on the right advocating limited government. The association means that Occupy Sandy's DIY practices reinforce the set of entrepreneurial practices workers navigating the flexible economy must cultivate. The resemblance between Occupy Sandy's DIY practices and the habits of workers who are encouraged to think of themselves as human capital help shore up support for the "necessity" of neoliberal reforms that serve the interest of capital. These include privatization efforts that are undertaken in the name of efficiency, competitiveness, and cutting waste.

The homology between DIY practices and the set of skills that define what sociologists Luc Boltanski and Eve Chiapello call "the new spirit of capitalism" suggests that the experiences of agency and cooperation that enlarge the capacity of citizens to act via participation in mutual aid networks like Occupy Sandy may be in tension with elements that undermine a commitment to democratic governance or which intensify existing patterns of distrust among citizens. The growth of distrust in democratic governance is especially damaging to a citizenry whose members are separated from one another according to their status as economically "productive" members of society and, frequently, racial difference. The new spirit of capitalism refers to the set of promises that affectively draw and commit workers to capitalism despite the exploitation at its heart. With these commitments in mind, I conclude by examining another aspect of the interactions among citizens made possible by Hurricane Sandy. I focus on the desire of those who lost their homes to rebuild in the same communities, suggesting that this decision illuminates the desire for stability and community that are also part of the new spirit of capitalism. I argue that challenging macro-practices of sovereignty associated with neoliberalism must involve augmenting associational micro-practices among citizens in conjunction with reclaiming the state.

OCCUPY SANDY, DIY CITIZENSHIP, AND THE STATE

Lauren Berlant's interest in DIY citizenship reflects her reading of devitalized agency under conditions of contemporary capitalism that increasingly leave citizens caught between postwar dreams of the good life and the reality of just trying to get by. Cruel optimism is Berlant's shorthand for this experience. As she explains, these attachments are cruel insofar as they are out of reach and remain out of reach for many. Workers stretched to work longer and longer hours; the educated but under or unemployed; inner-city youths who have grown up cut off from surrounding neighborhoods and access to jobs; their visions of the good life are increasingly out of view and unattainable. According to Berlant, this makes those visions cruel as far as they remain the horizon around which citizens organize their aspirations, desires, and actions.

Berlant describes the individual experiences of vulnerability and crumbling confidence and agency collected in the micro-narratives of suffering in the "We Are the 99 Percent" Tumblr as "crisis ordinary." The term conveys the normalization of crisis, a development that has blunted the sharp edges of crisis making it more difficult for citizens to muster a response. To claim crisis has become ordinary is to grasp how crisis has lost what made it distinctive. Derived from the Greek word, *krino*, crisis means to separate, to choose, to decide, or to judge. In other words, crisis characterizes an event that demands judgment and, with it, action that marks off the period before and after the crisis event. *Krino* denoted a turning point in the expression of disease where the patient's life or death hung in the balance.[5] To propose that crisis has become ordinary suggests two related phenomena. First, it conveys the degree to which the current moment has become defined by the lack of citizen response to small and large crises, or their inability to respond. Second, crisis ordinary explains why so many citizens identify with the necessity of state actions to protect what remains of their sovereign powers from the perceived threats of terrorists, immigrants, and others who make claims on state resources and challenge sovereignty.

Berlant argues that the normalization of crisis and the experience of cruel optimism have reduced many citizens to the demands of bare survival and battered their confidence. Drawing on a diverse archive of film and literature, Berlant sees evidence of citizens living at a political impasse: feeling either that they cannot change the present and therefore should not even bother trying or experiencing frustration and anger as their efforts are blocked and fall short. Political impasse has diverted desires for agency and self-making to unexpected venues like diet and exercise that offer subjects semblances of the sovereign powers they once enjoyed through political participation. These lateral outlets for agency represent a means of coping with the stresses of crisis ordinary and political impasse. Combined with the energy devoted to survival and the increasingly nonpolitical ways of being together invoked by sovereign powers, citizens are left with both little experience of acting with others and, because conditions of diminished sovereignty have compelled so many to defend what remains by relating to citizens as competitors, they have grown wary of cultivating attachments to others.

This does not mean that the desires for attachment and agency have been entirely extinguished. Berlant discovers that these desires persist despite being battered by the anxiety of trying to survive, with citizens desperate to find any forms of steadiness that might lend them strength. She sees in Liza Johnson's short film, *South of Ten*, traces of ambient citizenship and "the ambient noise of ongoing life."[6] The film is set in post-Katrina Mississippi, in the stretch of land that runs from the south of Interstate 10 to the Gulf Coast that received little attention from the national media despite sustaining tremendous storm damage. *South of Ten* depicts citizens without sentimentalizing them or the past. Instead, it focuses on how they are adjusting to the present within "a kind of loose solidarity."[7] Berlant emphasizes that the film portrays everyone in "survival" mode, re-establishing the conditions for living again. Scenes of adults scavenging and tending to the recovery are merged with bodies at rest, surveying the damage. Berlant sees the film's silence and its lack of dramatic expressiveness as key features of the ambient citizenship it portrays.

Although facing impasse means accepting that no action will change the historical present, Berlant argues that the business of going on together depicted in *South of Ten* as "a stubborn collective refusal to give out, wear out, or admit defeat" might be "the bare minimum evidence of not having given up on social change as such."[8] For her, embodied practices of making solidarity without predetermined ends, what she summarizes as "an attachment to the process of maintaining attachment" represents an ideal form of resistance to the conditions of crisis ordinary.[9] She argues that this potential solidarity, which also emanates from "outrage at not mattering," should follow "the model of anarchist/DIY performativity" because it generates the desire for public attachments. These new bodies, she suggests, offer the "hope that changing the white noise of politics into something focused but polymorphous can magnetize people to a project of inducing images of the good life that emerge from the sense of loose solidarity in the political that now occupies the ordinary amidst the exhausting pragmatics of the everyday."[10]

But there is no single model of DIY and its origins can be traced back to multiple starting points. Spencer's history of DIY centers on zines, self-published pamphlets and newsletters that circulated among feminists and fans of punk music in the early 1990s. George McKay traces a similar concentration of DIY energy among members of the British dance club and rave scene during the same period, but finds DIY also animating efforts among English animal rights activists, environmentalists, urban squatter communities, and anti-nuclear activists stretching back to the early 1980s.[11] For Chris Carlsson and Kyle Bravo, DIY describes the activities of self-organized urban gardeners, bicycle workshops, knitters and crafters, and even the Burning Man festival. Or as the subtitle to Bravo's *Making Stuff and Doing Things* puts it, DIY applies to doing just about everything.[12]

For these authors, the appeal of DIY is its emphasis on direct action, which for Bravo is synonymous with autonomy, or "not waiting for requests to pass through established channels" only to bog down in paperwork and endless negotiations.[13] According to Bravo, DIYers do not need to wait for permission from outside authorities to address problems that are waiting for solutions. Instead they act independently, seeking out other people with similar goals and shared projects.[14] Likewise, Elaine Brass and Sophie Poklewski Koziell pitch DIY in terms of "radical action for those tired of waiting" in the subtitle to their book on DIY culture, *Gathering Force*. They observe that in Britain during the 1990s, the DIY label spanned individuals and groups tired of feeling fed up with the lack of response from the government and who "decided to take matters into their own hands."[15]

Brass and Koziell identify government centralization and privatization as the causes necessitating direct action to "bypass institutions," but the end or goal of DIY direct action can vary.[16] Carlsson describes DIY as a "Nowtopia," understood as "a new politics of work" that promises to liberate participants from market life through practices of self-reliance and mutual aid. DIY cooperatives represent an alternative to conventional political and economic structures that allow citizens to extract and separate themselves from what Carlsson regards as increasingly commodified forms of life and the ritualized spectacle of electoral democracy in the United States.[17] Like Carlsson, Brass, Koziell, and Spencer, McKay observes that DIYers generate a vibrant culture that binds them together and gives their activities purpose, but, for him at least, DIY resistance to the status quo in Britain during the 1990s was everywhere *but* the workplace. McKay believes that the DIY movements in Britain were "lifestyle" movements that left in place the basic structure of capitalism, unlike the earlier class-based resistance of trade unionism which made working conditions central to their demands. DIY groups and what McKay calls their "intuitive liberal anarchism" sprang up in response to trade unionism, which, because it was seen as accommodationist and hierarchical, was viewed along with government as obstacles to change.[18]

In Fred Turner's history of American counterculture, DIY practices took shape not in opposition to market capitalism but in line with it. According to Turner, DIY emerged from the shadows of domestic conflict and the Vietnam War during the 1960s to emphasize the benefits of social change through collaboration and harmony. An influential segment of the counterculture was especially drawn to the ideas and technologies emerging from American research culture. During the Cold War and Space Race, engineers, scientists, and administrators had flattened bureaucracies in order to collaborate and innovate, developing sophisticated information and network communication systems.

Turner argues that Stewart Brand is the figure that bridged and joined counterculture and technology circles by organizing meetings, conferences, and publications, which enabled members of these two communities to share ideas. In 1968, Brand published the first *Whole Earth Catalog* which catered to the needs of those aspiring to head back to the land and found communes. Along with reports submitted by members of these communes, the *Catalog* also featured articles written by researchers and network pioneers such as Norbert Weiner, suggesting a strong parallel between the attempts to improve social relations through technological innovations and the actions of young, idealistic DIYers. Brand was a key figure in identifying the countercultural potential of technology, especially as personal computers and online publishing became more affordable and common. In 1985, Brand gathered members of this network through the Whole Earth 'Lectronic Link, or the WELL, and together they shaped and advanced the countercultural dream of the Internet as a space of freedom and collaboration. The vision of networked workplaces and revolutionary technologies that would unleash new levels of economic growth and productivity was elaborated in the pages of *Wired* magazine, which Brand founded with other members of WELL in 1993. Turner argues that

American counterculture's opposition to hierarchy and bureaucracy, to nuclear weapons, and consumer culture actually gave rise to the "free-wheeling, interdisciplinary, and highly entrepreneurial style of work" that defines what the editors of *Wired* labeled the New Economy.[19]

It is clear that the profile of DIY is diverse. This diversity begs several questions. Given the elements of state skepticism and entrepreneurial culture that developed with DIY citizenship practices, how does DIY citizenship inflect the practices of state sovereignty and the pattern of idle citizenship associated with the liberal-democratic state? Does DIY citizenship challenge the distribution of power between state institutions and citizens or leave them in place? Certainly, DIY represents an accessible starting place for citizens to act when there are no forms of institutional support for political action in common. Second, DIY can harness the agency that had been diverted to areas outside of politics to address the feelings of political impasse and impassivity that characterize crisis ordinary. Finally, DIY practices have the potential to join citizens together in fellow feeling and solidarity as Berlant suggests. Trust, confidence, and attitudes of self-reliance are all important democratic goods that can form in these associations. Yet, I am suggesting it also matters what kinds of state-level practices these solidarities are formed around.

DIY was absolutely necessary to the work of the HIV activists who stand in the background of Berlant's scholarship, even if they did not articulate their activities in the language of DIY as it was developing in the 1980s and 1990s. Just as with women and members of minority groups, HIV activists were effectively shut out of the culturally dominant public sphere.[20] In the context of the early decades of the HIV crisis, gays, lesbians, and queers were turned out of their families, fired by their employers, and denied health care and other services by the state. They had no choice but to invent networks of mutual care, support, and advocacy. As Deborah Gould argues the stakes for doing so were literally life and death. With many thousands dying each year, gays and lesbians had to improvise networks of support to keep one another alive and to demand that the state take action rather than ignore their deaths. Gould is clear that while organizations like ACT UP offered participants chances to participate in meaningful action that engendered a powerful sense of belonging, the erotics of togetherness that drew many to ACT UP were directed toward a "powerful critique against the state and its dominant institutions."[21] ACT UP held die-ins at the National Institutes of Health to demand funding for HIV research, at city health agencies to demand health insurance and medical care. ACT UP's actions were an angry response to the unilateral character of state sovereignty and bureaucratic indifference, but not an abandonment of state institutions.

The point of ACT UP's DIY practices was to put pressure on the state and its institutions, not to supplant or replace them. That this was the direction of ACT UP and that confrontational tactics were central to its ability to have its demands heard have not been preserved in popular memory underscores how the story of not just this group but also other activists has been told. If activism is framed in terms of inclusion and enlarging political rights, it gives the impression that these are always available, minimizing the power and necessity of anger and unrest. Sarah Schulman refers to this dynamic as the gentrification of memory, one that has its specific roots in the deaths of thousands of gays and lesbians to HIV/AIDS. The history of HIV activism, she observes, has been rewritten as a result of these deaths so that it now validates dominant norms and institutions. Schulman's memoir validates Berlant's insight into the dynamics of appropriation by the dominant public sphere and need for sustained counterpublics capable of preserving memory.[22]

Independent DIY institutions that can tell the stories of marginalized groups who are shut out from the mainstream or only admitted on assimilatory terms, as we saw with Idle No More, are absolutely necessary. Most often they perform a politics of refusal. Like Bartleby, they refuse to participate in order to maintain their independence and integrity and, ultimately, to endure during periods of low-intensity activism. That endurance is important, but to valorize endurance-as-resistance within the conditions of crisis ordinary is to mistake how much the freedom to resist is protected and tolerated because it is recognized as one of many possible lifestyles. Though it is an overstatement to suggest that individuals or small groups who act differently in the name of resistance are no different from individuals with other idiosyncratic lifestyles, the groups and bodies that have the monopoly on sovereignty today do not consider all resistance equally. They are chiefly concerned by movements attempting to democratize sovereignty by addressing the conditions of daily life that tilt power away from ordinary citizens. My suggestion is that refusal represents the start but not the end of enlarging the sphere of agency and that the state must be the focal point if citizen counter conduct is to address the larger structures that contribute to feelings of impasse and unfreedom.

ACT UP is a reminder that on its own terms DIY can feed into and even intensify an anti-statism that is dangerous and destructive, at least in the context of the neoliberal rollback of the very idea of the state as the provisioner of public goods and protector of public rights. Though it is worth noting that how this state-skepticism signifies likely depends on the race and class of the skeptic in question. Affluent, white kids' DIY may translate more easily into libertarianism, while poor or working-class black kids' attitude of self reliance may reflect a more understandable and justified suspicion of state power as we saw in the second chapter.

In the case of Occupy Sandy, its DIY practices were central to its more generous ethos of cooperation, but mutual aid also identified with a strong current of anti-statism. Sarah Corbin, an organizer featured in Josh Fox's documentary film *Occupy Sandy*, explains the group's mutual aid work in terms of a larger commitment to pluralism by emphasizing how volunteers were able to form attachments to one another and to victims: "Aside from simply being anti-racist, anti-sexist, anti-homophobic, anti-classist, etc., we believe that in the work that we do, we have to be actively undermining those structures that separate us and keep some people down and elevate others."[23] (8:34–8:46). Among the core democratic goods Occupy Sandy generated was trust among volunteers and trust among volunteers and storm victims (who were, in many cases, also volunteers). For Corbin, that trust was given immediately and affirmed through common actions. Although she does not frame her comments in terms of agency, it is not hard to pick up an attention to growing agency within her words. She describes Occupy Sandy's operational ethos as entrepreneurial, stating that the group is receptive to volunteer initiative. Or as she put it, "If you recognize there is a gap, fill it" (9:29).

But the group's entrepreneurial micro-practices also resonated with anti-statist discourse within the movement. In an article published in *Tidal: A Journal of Occupy Theory*, organizer Nastaran Mohrit celebrates the care that the Occupy Sandy-affiliated YANA (You Are Never Alone) Medical Clinic was able to provide residents left homeless and marginalized by the storm, while at the same time attributing YANA's success to its entrepreneurial and anti-statist culture. She writes:

> Void of the constraints, bureaucracy and red tape of agencies and organizations who clumsily attempted to navigate the post-disaster landscape, volunteers structured a disaster response that served the needs of the community first and asked questions later. Within days, we discovered with shock and numbness that both FEMA and the American Red Cross were referring residents to YANA ... No longer hamstrung by the same bureaucracy and red-tape of their own professions, volunteers were able to serve the needs of patients above all other considerations ... They felt a sense of pride and purpose in their work that had long been stolen from them by a system that refuses by its nature to acknowledge barbaric ineptitude.[24]

Mohrit's words suggest that the trust and solidarity that emerged among YANA volunteers were mixed with a larger distrust of government entities, though not for the same reasons that victims who benefitted from the aid distributed by Occupy Sandy were inclined to distrust government. As storm victims Colleen Dalton and Jeff Vielandi told reporter Nick Pinto: "The government didn't come ... The Red Cross stinks. All that money, they should have been here. I don't think anyone in my family will donate to them again ... LIPA (Long Island Power Authority) has no excuse ... Our local governments have failed us greatly. From major loss, the gain of volunteers and people we've met have been invaluable. But I am not going to say I'm glad this happened."[25]

Because she valorizes the efficiency of private sector actors at the expense of calling for a strengthening of the government's ability to respond, Mohrit is strangely in line with the antigovernment, antiregulatory corporate positions that the Occupy Wall Street protestors had identified as the cause of much of the economic misery and suffering since the 2008 financial crisis. Mohrit's understanding of DIY and direct mutual aid seems consistent with the desire to circumvent the give and take, disagreement, and time required for democratic politics that informs the arguments for the "necessity" of swift action by unaccountable bodies ("asked questions later"). In this case, DIY organizations like Occupy Sandy feel they strengthen rather than work against the micro-practices that align and reinforce unilateral practices of state sovereignty. As I demonstrate in the next section, that is because volunteers are encouraged to think of themselves as human capital, just as they are encouraged to think of themselves as human capital in the modern workplace.

THE NEW SPIRIT OF CAPITALISM AND THE DANGER OF DIY CITIZENSHIP

Luc Boltanski and Eve Chiapello investigate the transformation of ordinary life under contemporary conditions of capitalism in *The New Spirit of Capitalism*. Their work offers something missing from Berlant's scholarship: an explanation of how crisis and anxiety have become routine. Their analysis is instructive, furthermore, for identifying how Occupy Sandy's DIY organizational model aligns with micro-practices that support neoliberal rollbacks of government social safety programs and privatization. Their study is drawn from an analysis of working conditions in France, and they are careful to emphasize that neoliberalism is an ongoing historical process characterized by regional differences. Nonetheless, their findings are helpful for understanding how neoliberal ideology has made such deep inroads into society and why the invocation of crisis now struggles to provoke social critique and change.

Their research focuses on management discourse, reasoning that capitalism must appeal to and attract support from managers if it is to enjoy legitimacy, because the management class is responsible for sustaining capitalism as a system. This is what they call, following Max Weber, the spirit of capitalism: the ideology that justifies their participation in the workforce and animates their complementary actions and dispositions. The new management literature they examine arose in response to the limitations of the organization or the firm. The large firm or organization of the post-Second World War period was viewed as the apogee of expertise, progress, and bureaucratic efficiency, which made it attractive to ambitious graduates whose academic credentials were valued by the firm. The large organization depended on long-term planning and coordination and its success was identified with the common good. The idea that organizations served a civic purpose is heard in the adage: what is good for General Motors is good for America. Achievement of this common good demanded a high level of institutional discipline, a sacrifice for which workers were promised job security. According to Boltanski and Chiapello, this period was marked by a minimization of class struggle as well as an increasing distinction between ownership and management. The latter trend has accelerated and the demands of shareholders for higher returns on investment have diminished job security, pensions, and benefits for workers.[26]

Managers are positioned in the middle of this changing landscape. As wage earners, they do not directly benefit from capital accumulation, but they are nonetheless charged with justifying the purpose and legitimacy of capitalism to their subordinates and one another. Managers, in other words, identify with concerns about security, autonomy, and the common good, but the relationship among the three has recalibrated as workers and firms have moved toward more flexible forms of employment. With less job security available, the emphasis has shifted toward calls for greater workplace autonomy and freedom. As the authors explain, demand for jobs that offer flexibility, opportunities for creativity, and innovation have their origins in what they term the artistic critique of capitalism and which the authors identify in the May 1968 protests.[27] Since 1968, the belief that private enterprise generates and contributes to the common good and is where the freedom once associated with the vitality of citizenship can be best experienced have gathered support. As Harper's pipeline construction proposal demonstrates, increasingly government's function is to support freedom and the common good, by minimizing the barriers to economic growth and guaranteeing the nation's security.[28]

Modeled after the freedom and independence of the bohemian artist, this critique of capitalism is opposed to the loss of authenticity and beauty implied by the commodification and standardization associated with mass-produced goods and the alienation of the workers who must labor under such conditions.[29] Boltanski and Chiapello explain that firms were inclined to accommodate the demands for greater freedom, creativity, and inclusion of difference (for women and underrepresented minorities, in particular) in the workplace in the form of flexible working schedules and greater independence over their work responsibilities because, together, these lowered the cost of labor by enlarging the labor pool. With the pressures for job security (the implicit tradeoff with autonomy) reduced, firms responded by offering workers greater autonomy, the capacity to multitask (as opposed to insisting on the specialization of labor); encouraging novelty, spontaneity, and out-of-the-box thinking; making workplaces less formal, less hierarchical, and more convivial (in the form of office parties and casual dress); and valorizing entrepreneurial visionaries (*kaizan*, the Toyota workplace empowerment model, Steve Jobs, etc.).

However, the authors argue, workplace autonomy and flexibility are best measured by the rise in projects, which have had significant consequences for how workers consider arguments about justice, equality, and mutual responsibility. Projects originate and reflect a highly networked set of social relationships among workers. Projects are short-term working groups assembled to complete specific assignments, composed of workers from the same organization or workers contracted to produce a "pocket of accumulation" by bringing certain goods or services into being.[30] The transition to projects offers workers freedom but, because they require varying degrees of mobility and flexibility to meet the demands of the short-term project schedule, this freedom comes at the cost of security and steadiness. Workers in a project-based economy have become habituated to dislocation and grasp, at least tacitly, that their own advancement depends on being mobile and avoiding attachments to persons and places that cannot be unbroken. The normalization of dislocation is one reason that crisis does not register with the same significance and becomes part of ordinary life.

At the same time, though, projects are the products of connections among workers in an extended network. Ambitious workers initiate projects and seek to be staffed on projects, in turn. An invitation to participate on a project is a reflection on the resources the worker can contribute and a skilled project coordinator recruits staff by offering them work that appeals to their desire to improve their future employability. In an environment with fewer sources of security, employability is linked to the worker's skill in making and leveraging connections. Projects permit workers "ownership" over the products and services they generate, while also placing greater responsibility for the success or failure of their endeavors directly on workers.

In other words, projects transform workers into entrepreneurs in two ways. First, projects represent opportunities to develop as human capital: to acquire the skills and know-how that will increase the prospects of their future employment, skills which make them more desirable to project managers, in turn. Second, because participation on projects is the function of individual ability to attract interest from peers and hiring managers by cultivating a strong reputation for likeability, trust, and prior success, projects reduce the distinctions between private conduct and forms of conduct formerly restricted to the marketplace or workplace. Workers in a highly networked economy are, according to the authors, owners of themselves, responsible for their own bodies, images, successes, and destiny.[31] One significant consequence of being responsible for oneself is a reduction of solidarity among workers. A second consequence is that winning and losing positions can be explained in terms of one's ability to navigate the network. The notion of being responsible for oneself obscures any larger shared sense of social responsibility associated with the idea of crisis.

Boltanski and Chiapello argue that an important result of the shift toward a network economy organized by projects and the development of human capital is to undermine the force of "exclusion" as a critical concept and basis for social action.[32] The term gained ground because it captured the injustice of both *de jure* and *de facto* forms of societal discrimination based on race, gender, and/or physical handicap. The authors note that the language of exclusion versus inclusion "was able to take the place previously assigned to social classes in the representation of social misery and the means of remedying it."[33] Humanitarian groups made the rhetoric of exclusion the basis of their efforts, but at the same time this sector was also reorganized along the lines of the network, composed of nongovernmental organizations that worked together on projects to provide patchwork solutions. As Boltanski and Chiapello explain, not only were these groups acting in a vacuum of government action, their activities were often explicitly contrasted with those of established political organizations like labor groups and government agencies.

Mohrit's praise for YANA emphasises that volunteers created immediate and intense mutual bonds, thanks in part to the freedom they were permitted to define the organization's priorities and activities. She explicitly distinguishes this freedom by saying that it was "unavailable" in their own professions since they tended to be tied up in bureaucratic red tape. Mohrit's description of YANA echoes the artistic critique of capitalism. Specifically, she names the desire for self-ownership, authenticity, and unalienating work as the reasons why so many volunteered and, like her, were deeply moved by their experiences.

Groups like YANA that are shaped by the artistic critique of capitalism are meant to fulfill the desire for attachment since they tend to be smaller than the large firms and government agencies they replace. Networked workplaces are comparatively non-hierarchical. They privilege face-to-face interactions since these were viewed as more authentic (and less dehumanizing) working conditions. They are also more ideologically plural than the larger, rigid organizations they replaced. These smaller groups work with corporate, nongovernmental, and even government partners in an extended network on campaigns, making membership and participation more fluid and flexible.

Rebuild and Recovery reflects Occupy Sandy's DIY ethos as well as the larger shift toward a more flexible and project-oriented economy. Started by friends who had volunteered in Haiti after the 2010 earthquake there, the group continued to hone their expertise in coordinating logistics by volunteering in other disaster areas. The group had put itself in charge of operations in Far Rockaway by virtue of its experience. Its members trained less-experienced volunteers on how to pump out flooded basements and clean damaged floors and walls, using homes located next to the Occupy Sandy Rockaway beach headquarters as training sites. According to a November 21, 2012, article in the *Village Voice*, Respond and Rebuild had "already brought in mold-remediation experts and other specialists to train Occupy Sandy team leaders for the next phase of recovery."[34]

Together with an anti-statist message, Occupy's DIY practices were in tension with the associational goods and solidarities it produced. Given how closely, in this case, DIY resembled the logics of the networked economy and its emphasis on the development of human capital, there is some question about how transformative micro-practices of mutual cooperation and the new publics that they inaugurated could be. On balance, I am suggesting, it is possible that without the kind of claim on state power seen in ACT UP, DIY practices can deepen rather than work against the grain of neoliberal reforms that further devitalize the demos and its capacity for political action. The specific worry is that the micro-practices of mutual aid found in Occupy Sandy strengthen the logic of emergency politics. Together, these micro-practices support actions to consolidate state sovereignty by trimming "unnecessary" functions so that the state's powers over the remaining areas are sharpened and made more efficient.

THE LIMIT OF HUMAN CAPITAL

There are two aspects of Josh Fox's *Occupy Sandy* documentary that point to an alternative critique even though most of the film is dedicated to arguing that the hurricane is another, unavoidable sign of climate change. The venue chosen for the first screening of the film is the first indication of the film's critique and target. On November 29, 2012, less than one month after Hurricane Sandy hit the New York metropolitan region, an audience of about one hundred people gathered to watch a guerilla projection of the film onto the walls of an Exxon-Mobil gas station at 2nd Street and Avenue C in Lower Manhattan. The film opens with a radar image of Hurricane Sandy, tracking along the eastern seaboard. A song entitled "Bizness," written and sung by the Tuneyards, begins to play. Images of the storm damage begin to scroll to the sound of the song's chorus, which repeatedly pleads, "Don't take my life away." Scenes of sand and debris, homes posted with signs warning "Restricted Access" and "Unsafe," boats tossed out of the water and onto city streets, fill the screen. The final introductory shot of a fence spray-painted with the words "Global Warming" previews the arc of the film's argument.

A large fraction of the documentary is devoted to an interview with 350.org activist and climate scientist Bill McKibbin. Fox, McKibbin, along with Naomi Klein and Andrew Ross, have turned to climate change as evidence of the unsustainability of capitalism, on the one hand, and, on the other, to criticize neoliberal policies that have weakened government regulations to the point that they are unable to protect public goods like the environment.[35] In *Occupy Sandy*, McKibbin makes this point by claiming that naming storms after "innocent little girls" obscures the storm's ultimate cause and misdirects political response. He suggests that the public would be better served if, instead of Sandy, the hurricane had been named "Hurricane Exxon" to underline the role that fossil fuel emissions had played in warming the environment and ocean temperatures. He concludes, "there is really no normal anymore."[36] According to McKibben, rising temperatures and ocean levels make it so that even "normal storms" are capable of inflicting greater damage. Neither McKibben nor Fox explicitly link Exxon's economic clout to government policies that support exploitative capitalism. The film's closing messages seem aimed at challenging the public's deep skepticism about global warming.[37] They do, however, push for a systemic analysis and response since individual effort alone will not reverse increasing greenhouse gas emissions. By inferring a role for the government, the film strikes a clear contrast with Occupy Sandy's antigovernmental narrative.

Fox's film also creates a spectacle of out of mutual aid that resists the normalization of volunteer efforts back into the project-based network economy. The film leverages the techniques of documentary to present its audience, many of whom at the first screening were both victims of the storm and volunteers engaged in the storm cleanup, with a collective mirror on its activities. The film pushes viewers to move beyond the immediacy of the storm damage by styling the response to the storm as an independent *event*. In focusing on the response to the storm and not the storm directly, Fox asks the viewers to pass judgment on the response, both in terms the antecedents to the response and the appropriateness of that response. Moving the focus from the immediacy of the storm damage and the volunteers' DIY response, Fox spotlights not the visible crisis, but circumstances that require more lasting and ongoing forms of attachment to address. To challenge the silence on climate change, the film suggests, will require not just strengthening connections among citizens but also the connections that citizens have to state institutions.[38] By naming Exxon as a cause of these violations, or as a stand-in for the beneficiaries of exploitative capitalism, the film also suggests that increasing perceived and actual levels of security and the common good will call for strengthening government regulation over corporations like Exxon which underprice the cost of climate change and pass those costs on to the public. Without meaningful attachment to the state, the laws needed to compel reduced emissions will not be forthcoming. Identifying climate change as the ultimate cause of the storm reveals the inadequacy of notions of democracy that, in the interest of separating democracy from entrenched hierarchies of power, eschew any relationship to the state altogether.

There is a second aspect of the film that competes with its attempt to craft a critique of unregulated corporate power, environmental exploitation, and government capture resulting in the abdication of its role in protecting public goods. By depicting citizens the storm rendered homeless, the film offers a portrait of human capital at its limit. It suggests that the storm's victims are not liberated by virtue of dislocation. Instead, they want to reestablish the community bonds that had nurtured them and offered them security even if this means, perversely, rebuilding on sites that will leave them vulnerable to similar storms. Rather than embrace a level of network mobility and freedom that only most corporations enjoy, the rebuilding effort suggests an unwillingness to pursue to these opportunities. Complete dislocation cuts the tension between security, autonomy, and the common good, which Boltanski and Chiapello had identified as the three constitutive elements of the new spirit of capitalism, so that only autonomy remains.

Viewers who are chilled by the image of complete autonomy portrayed in the documentary have to build pressure to recalibrate the relationship between security, autonomy, and the common good. At one level, this appeal to the common good is filtered though how the common good is experienced or, in the case of the film witnessed, locally. Insofar as the documentary depicts a violation of the common good and security, it rebukes a network economy that prioritizes autonomy and revolves around the augmentation of human capital. To reject thinking of oneself and others as human capital is to refuse the circuit linking the desires for sovereignty to support for "necessary" emergency measures that have been the cause of widespread social anxiety and worry over job security. It is a critique that is grounded in the desire for meaningful attachments with others, but which begins to address the conditions under which it is possible to form and sustain such relationships.

A critique based on a *desire not to be human capital* questions a fundamental assumption about the subject's attachment to late capitalism and the form of freedom it offers.[39] Solidarity based on this immanent critique of neoliberalism resists, rather than carries forward, the entrepreneurial norms that Occupy Sandy's DIY ethos shares with the project-based economy and which align with the exercise of state sovereignty.[40] It is not hard to imagine, for instance, citizens responding positively to arguments for the "necessity" of climate change action even if that change is initiated unilaterally and without democratic oversight. Philip Mirowski demonstrates how much of the climate change discourse is couched in the language of competition, entrepreneurship, and economic growth.[41]

A critique based on a rejection of human capital is distinct from Boltanski and Chiapello's argument for critiques that foreground exploitation within the network. Instead of the exclusion critique which aims to generate indignation at poverty but falls short of doing more than making that condition more tolerable (for both the poor and those who pity the poor), Boltanski and Chiapello recommend a social critique based on exploitation within the network which identifies opportunistic behavior that represents an abuse of position. Although individuals and firms gain profit and status within the network by multiplying their links to others, finding ways to distribute resources to the greatest number at the lowest personal cost, the network functions only as far as it is perceived to offer benefits to all participating parties. The network does not function when an opportunistic participant has not reciprocated contributions to the network. Boltanski and Chiapello define such opportunistic behavior in terms that recall actions taken by individuals who think of themselves as self-sovereigns: "consisting in not acknowledging debts contracted with other persons, either individual or collective."[42] As they note, if participants only withdrew resources without making contributions, the network would collapse.[43]

CONCLUSION

I have argued here that the solidarities and lateral agency that emerge through the DIY ethos that Berlant associates with ambient citizenship is animated by and gives rise to a misplaced critique. That critique, instead of scrutinizing how neoliberal policies and governance intensified the damaged caused by Hurricane Sandy, was in harmony with the entrepreneurial, antigovernment views advocated by neoliberals. Occupy Sandy's DIY ethos complemented anti-statist arguments for freedom from government regulation and oversight in the markets made by neoliberals. Occupy Sandy celebrated the achievements of ambient citizenship as an example of democratic renewal. On this view, however, democracy embodied in practices of ambient citizenship is bound to the "authenticity" of face-to-face, ultimately fugitive moments. Or as Berlant puts it, "This locates politics in a commitment to the present activity of the senses. It sees the work of citizenship as a dense sensual activity of performative belonging to the now in which potentiality is affirmed."[44] But if sensual togetherness and potential are affirmed on the back of a critique of bureaucratic inefficiency and state failure, they concede a broader critique of the forces that necessitate citizen-led mutual aid in the first place. While such gatherings may provide temporary relief and affirm joyous forms of togetherness and cooperation that are welcome breaks from the anxieties of competition in the network economy, as forms of resistance they are tolerated by neoliberal powers because they do not unsettle the basic relationship: that government is to serve the interests of capital rather than citizens.

Yet the daily experiences of impasse, in the form of economic precarity and political powerlessness, that, according to Berlant, characterizes neoliberalism in its ordinary as well as traumatic guises, cannot be addressed without the state. There is nothing illegal about the dislocations caused by neoliberal policies or governance. Indeed, Boltanski and Chiapello suggest the degree to which the precepts of neoliberal political economy have become commonplace is an indication of how well it satisfies the desires workers have for work that affords them freedom, flexibility, and creativity. Popular movements that wish to meaningfully gain a handle on the myriad of unaccountable powers organizing daily life will need the state to enact new laws that change the rules to place limits on exploitation and strengthen provisions for the common good.

Berlant is right to note that, even for all of its harms, detachment from the present and identification of futures more worthy of attachment will be challenging. Berlant and others believe that the imagination necessary to support such a transition may emerge from new forms of being together anchored in the experience of crisis ordinariness. To the degree that occupations of public spaces have been an almost defining feature of mass political movements in recent years, Berlant may be right. She imagines the resulting solidarity to be a product of the shared experience of meeting the demands of bare survival. Her work suggests a politics of the ordinary and movements that are committed to politicizing the circumstances of everyday life based on satisfying needs of the body that are common to everyone, regardless of identity or history.

Movements that aim to transform the present impasse by highlighting its abuses need to cultivate sources and practices that inspire courage in everyday contexts. Just as they must work to identify sources of resistance that are commonly accessible, they must also nurture sources that inspire the courage necessary to detach from the present and believe in the possibility of something better. To emphasize the mundane sources of solidarity minimizes the courage, and the fact that courage must be inspired, required for us to let go of our current attachments, even if they are cruel. Cultivating a sense of the extraordinary through the performance of courageous acts in the midst of the mundane gives each more weight. Insofar as what we come to regard as extraordinary relies on mundane acts of repair and maintenance, those tasks are infused with greater purpose and respect. At the same time, the extraordinary and the window it opens to possibilities beyond the present are embedded in everyday experience, breaking down the longstanding opposition between reform and radical critique. The merging of these two helps address the feeling of impasse that Berlant sees as characterizing the experience of neoliberal subjects. It addresses the feeling of resignation that either fatalistically accepts the present as something to be suffered or looks to external sources for salvation and it is the subject of the next chapter.

5

Debt and Sacrifice

I began this work by observing the increasingly legitimacy of emergency measures in response to threats to the nation-state from terrorism and greater economic competitiveness. Terrorism and capital represent non-state actors that compete with states and which have compelled the reassertion of state sovereignty even has they have revealed the limits of sovereignty. Though capital has no national borders, the demands of capital, including laws and investments to ensure the conditions necessary for stability and growth, increasingly drive decision-making in many nations. Capital directives can partly explain the Harper legislation that provoked Idle No More activists. Harper had tied national security to development of the energy sector and enlarging his country's trade with China. The observation of capital's ability not just to influence but in practice to limit the scope of decisions that governments consider viable has led Wendy Brown to suggest that capital possesses something approximating political sovereignty, although without a central body patterned after a monotheistic god. Nonetheless, she describes capital's ascendency in terms that rival the divine: "almighty, limitless, and uncontrollable."[1]

Brown is deeply ambivalent about the prospects for democracy at this moment in history given how capital dominates the lives of citizens while remaining outside of their collective grasp. She argues that the difficulty of democratizing the economy is rooted in capital's lack of a unified sovereign body toward which citizens might direct their efforts or which would enable them to recognize one another as members of a shared community. She writes:

> In sum, apart from state power, both capital and a range of less forthrightly economic normative powers must be reckoned with when considering prospects for redemocratization today. History features no success, or even sustained experiments, with democratizing either. So continued belief in political democracy as the realization of human freedom depends upon literally averting our glance from powers immune to democratization, powers that also give the lie to the autonomy and primacy of the political upon which so much of the history and present of democratic theory has depended.[2]

Democracy has to be reinvented; it cannot be meaningfully invoked to the extent that it does not address capital's sovereign status, according to Brown.

Other theorists, examining the same situation are less ambivalent. Jodi Dean argues that capitalism and liberal democracy are so entwined and mutually reinforcing that only post-democratic political formations have any hope of overturning neoliberal hegemony. That is because for Dean democracy and democratic values of inclusion, deliberation, spontaneity, and participation are illusory values. Dean argues that because these values take material form in network communications technologies and in the market, what she calls "communicative capitalism," they contribute to a form of *interpassivity*. Along with consumerism, Dean argues citizens are attached to forms of communication that allow them the *illusion* of constant participation but the reassurance that nothing will change. The Internet embodies the paradox of open access to dialogue and participation yet political disempowerment because communication there is individualistic and does not require commitment. To argue that more democracy can solve the problems of neoliberal democracy is naïve and even self-deceptive, according to Dean. This belief is summed up in the title of Dean's recent *Democracy and Other Neoliberal Fantasies*.

Dean believes that Occupy and other movements have in common an opposition to capitalism and therefore herald the return of Communism. Although she sees Occupy's inability to sustain itself as evidence of its lack of discipline and need for a party structure, she claims its insistence on naming a class division between the 1 percent who profit from neoliberalism and the 99 percent who grow increasingly impoverished is absolutely necessary. For Dean, the Occupy protests, the demonstrations in Istanbul's Gezi Park, and the 2013 riots in Brazil represent ruptural events that inaugurate a new political subject which identifies as a member of a collective body that has suffered exploitation and dispossession under neoliberalism. This subject is intent on *breaking completely with* and overcoming the impasse represented by both capitalism and democracy.

Yet to claim the arrival of a new political subject through a ruptural event is to minimize the strength of the affective bonds citizens have to the both the market and the forms of devitalizing state sovereignty that Dean recognizes hold them in place and keep them from joining a communist movement (until now). Dean's announcement of a Communist Horizon in her book-length writing speaks to her desire for purity and her impatience with the uncertainty of democratic practice and messiness of citizenship, but does not match the tone of more occasional writing found online, on her blog, and even her social media accounts.[3] There Dean appears to be looking for evidence of its emergence across a wide field of political activities organized around enlarging the powers of democratic citizens. My suggestion is that while Dean may be off the mark in her calls for a post-democratic subject and politics, her analysis of communicative capitalism and her criticism of the Left's rejection of state power represent exactly the type of reckoning that Brown is calling for. Dean's analysis of the entwinement of capitalism and liberal democracy illuminates how the sub-constitutional habits of democratic citizens have been transformed. Citizens have been worn down by the rhythms of crisis ordinary and left with fewer connections and resources to draw on to challenge emergency politics.

My argument across the preceding chapters has been that democratizing the unilateral exercise of state sovereignty in response to emergency and crisis requires addressing the micro- and subject-level affects and dispositions that support and affirm devitalizing articulations of sovereignty. In brief, movements have focused on practices that generate vitality and solidarity among citizens by disrupting the routinized physical and mental circulations that enforce passivity and idle citizenship. In this chapter, I extend this argument to the economy more directly, focusing on how the activities of the Strike Debt movement are attempting to reconfigure the moral economy that makes debt a source of shame and guilt and codes debt repayment as obligatory.

Strike Debt is a nascent debt-resistance movement that is actively trying to loosen the "necessity" of debt by rewiring the attachments that subjects have to debt through several initiatives, including organizing a Rolling Jubilee to purchase and retire medical debt; instructing citizens on how to minimize the accumulation of debt and avoid repayment; holding parties that make debt a source of pleasure rather than shame; and advocating debt forgiveness in the form of a biblical-style debtors jubilee. Noting that debt forgiveness was once a condition of democracy and democratic citizenship, Strike Debt has tied the future of democratic practice and government to challenging the legitimacy of austerity measures in Southern Europe and in US cities like Detroit. Strike Debt casts doubt on Dean's claim about the ability or even need for subjects to break with present values. In particular, I show how Strike Debt identifies resources for change from within rather than from outside, as Dean imagines, the existing political and economic order. Its focus on debt as a defining condition of ordinary life is combined with an explicitly radical attempt to organize a different imagination of the future that would be unrecognizable from the present. Strike Debt's attention to the conditions of ordinary experience—how, on the one hand, debt constrains choice, and how, on the other hand, it can be resisted and negotiated—is what invites citizens to think, hope, and believe in the possibilities for democratizing the quasi-sovereignty of capital.[4]

Although Strike Debt is aimed at a critique of neoliberalism and is alert to the role an aspirational horizon can serve, its *Operations Manual* and Jubilee are rooted in the everyday experience of indebtedness. By offering readers guidance on how to minimize, avoid, and resist personal debt, along with new spaces and practices of association, the *Operations Manual* acknowledges the shame and guilt associated with indebtedness that must be addressed if citizens are to organize not only a debt resistance movement, but to have the time and ability to join other citizens in political action. Strike Debt recognizes that debt tethers citizens in place by narrowing their sense of the future. Its activities around the *Operations Manual*, the Jubilee, and Rolling Jubilee are intended to affectively reorient citizens by helping them see debt not in personal terms but as the basis of a collective movement that offers pleasure in the company of others as well as the pleasure of forgiveness. I focus on the Jubilee through the lens of Friedrich Nietzsche's *On the Genealogy of Morality*, arguing that it represents an effort to retrain the subject's affective investments from a moral economy that links credit with the pleasure of punishment and shame to one that seeks pleasure in forgiveness and, in doing so, represent a subject-centered critique of neoliberalism based on the desire not to be human capital. I conclude by suggesting that Strike Debt represents the basis of a more elaborate version of the critique of human capital that is the heart of neoliberal governance that I identified at the end of the last chapter, but one that could be further strengthened if framed within the bounds of existing political or economic institutions.

JODI DEAN: DEMOCRACY AND OTHER NEOLIBERAL FANTASIES

Dean's advocacy of a communist alternative to neoliberalism is squarely placed in a conversation about Left politics and critique. She argues that the Left's attachment to the ideals of democracy like deliberation, participation, and inclusion and the turn to micropolitical and ethical practices of mutual vulnerability and generosity by those like Judith Butler who wish to rework notions of the sovereign self and responses to nation-state sovereignty are both mistaken. To begin, she argues, they underestimate the degree to which these democratic values are identical to those celebrated and more accessible in the market and hence they must acknowledge their conservative origins. Secondly, because they define democracy in terms that are opposed to sovereignty, Dean contends that they are unable to confront the fundamental class conflict that defines political life. According to Dean, Butler's theory of ethical vulnerability and responsibility neither accounts for the will to power identified by Nietzsche nor concepts of the sovereign self animated by the will to power.[5] Whether conceived as participatory deliberation or micropolitical acts of vulnerability and generosity, these definitions of democratic practice cannot support the acts of condemnation that are necessary to name neoliberal capitalism as a wrong and to unite individuals around challenging this injustice.

Advocates of democracy misunderstand how the values of inclusion, participation, creativity, and change are in line with the principles of communicative capitalism they are meant to correct, Dean writes. Dean identifies the contemporary subject's experience of communicative capitalism and free trade as their primary sources of attachment to neoliberal governance. Communicative capitalism is Dean's term for the neoliberal configuration of liberal democracy, which leverages the accessibility of new communications technologies to hold open the promise of popular sovereignty while ensuring that participation remains largely at the level of individuals expressing their opinions rather than deliberating with one another.

As Dean explains, blogs and social media offer an unparalleled opportunity for ordinary citizens to have their voices heard. Yet the networked structure of the Internet, where corporate media and entertainment websites that enjoy the greatest popularity drive the search algorithms that make information on the Web accessible, means that the majority of these opinions are never accessed and never contribute to dialogue. Thus, they offer the appearance of citizen participation. Clicking and forwarding links, signing online petitions, and contributing to online forums offer the appearance of hyperactivity, but as Dean notes these forms of communication are largely responsive, expressive, and segmented.

The left-of-center MoveOn.org embodies this style of participation, argues Dean. MoveOn is a professionally run organization that emails its followers invitations to participate in online petitions, virtual sit-ins, and, of course, contribute money on behalf of left-leaning causes and candidates. The MoveOn community, Dean writes, offers busy people the sense of satisfaction that they are participating in political life, "alleviating their guilt, while assuring them that nothing will change too much."[6] This style of participation is convenient and meshes seamlessly with the lifestyle of networked individuals. Dean uses the term interpassivity to express the paradox of feeling virtually connected and active, but at the same time knowing that this participation is inconsequential. Interpassivity belies the truth of devitalized agency for Dean.

Free trade represents the second source of subjects' attachment to neoliberalism. Free trade offers subjects the fantasy of fair competition and, by amassing enormous wealth, winning this competition. Subjects look to the market to satisfy their desires for enjoyment and pleasure. The idea that the market is fair, accessible, and works perfectly to match buyers and sellers invites the belief that the subject will be able to satisfy all of her desires. Understanding the market through the lens of desire explains overindulgence and debt as well as the regret that might accompany such acts. Writing of those who gambled and lost, Dean writes, "At the very least, they failed to achieve the proper balance necessary for the promised, inevitable market success."[7] Dean's analysis of the apparent openness of free trade explains how the notion of individualized, self-responsibilization has taken hold in popular culture.

The belief in the perfect market drives the faith that participants can crack its code but also that they might have succeeded if either market constraints were removed or the market were properly supported. The first licenses government deregulation and privatization of markets while the second calls on governments to open new markets for trade and enforce free trade rules. Like communicative capitalism, free trade offers subjects the fantasy that everyone could win as well as underlines the need to strengthen support for free trade so that everyone could win.[8]

The subject's affective attachment to communicative capitalism and free trade make appeals to democracy ineffective in addressing neoliberalism, in Dean's view. First, communicative capitalism, given the way it produces interpassivity, renders calls for more democracy nonsensical. With their emphasis on inclusion, participation, and deliberation, contemporary democratic theorists skirt politicizing the fundamental division between the 1 percent who benefit from neoliberalism and the overwhelming majority who do not. She concludes that such efforts reflect the acceptance of capitalism and aspirations for, at best, reforms or more ethical forms of capitalism rather than communism's unequivocal opposition to capitalism.

As for the specific values, Dean implies that a focus on deliberation and dialogue are out-of-step with the temporality of neoliberalism. To pursue "discussions and find ethical spaces for decision . . . in a world where one bond trader can bring down a bank in a matter of minutes," appears naïve.[9] Faith in deliberation is also an artifact of the university seminar room that has little standing outside of it.[10] Dean points to the decision to go to war in Iraq as an example of how debate, dialogue, discussion, and criticism on the Left failed to deter the Bush Administration's resolve to go to war. The example illustrates how normative and descriptive accounts of deliberation within democratic theory justify the legitimacy of democratic procedures. Yet, Dean observes, the administration referenced this dissent as evidence that it had arrived at its decision democratically even as it chose to ignore the criticism directed toward it. Because deliberative democrats regard deliberative procedures already in place as the means of redressing wrongs, Dean believes that theories of deliberative democracy "brings utopia inside, eliminating it as an external space of hope."[11]

Appeals to deliberation are, in other words, trapped in the gap between legal rights to participate promised to citizens of the liberal democratic state and their actual, devitalizing experience of state-sovereignty as one of passive spectatorship and impasse. Under communicative capitalism, these citizens are able to participate in dialogue and deliberation at greater levels than any point in history, while they are simultaneously more distant from the decision-making process than ever before. For Dean, their inability to reconcile this experience is an indication of how empty the term democracy has become and how Bush was able to include spreading democracy among his reasons for invading Iraq.

The injunction to remake oneself through consumer purchase constitutes the barrier to efforts to reconceive democracy in terms of local, micropolitical practices. Taking Butler's theory of ethical responsibility examined in the third chapter as representative of this shift, Dean writes that Butler's "general avoidance of the economy" blinds her to how contemporary subjects relate to the market.[12] According to Dean, the market provides "nuggets of enjoyment providing momentary, fleeting sites of attachment" that compete with the desire for attachment that Berlant observed and offer immediate, if ultimately hollow, satisfaction. Dean argues that theories of ethical self-care and refashioning like Butler's or Connolly's are drowned out by messages in the marketplace that encourage subjects to think of themselves as flexible and open to change. Dean writes:

> We are bombarded with messages telling us that the purchase of a given item will deliver that extra special something missing in our lives. Yet even as no item ever really has that "extra something," capitalist subjects continue to shop and strive, and capitalism continues to intensify and expand, subjecting ever more aspects of life to its inexorable processes.[13]

According to Dean, the marketplace is able to relentlessly commodify and channel dissent by posing lifestyle choices as radical and reducing critique to easy political expressions like Pride Flags and Malcolm X T-shirts.[14]

But for Dean the opposition to sovereignty animating these practices is indicative of a more serious error: the Left's abdication of the state, closely linked to its failure to cultivate a vision of social solidarity. Against the backdrop of identity politics, and its emphasis on pluralism, inclusion, and diversity, which segmented the Left, Dean suggests that the embrace of local, micropolitical practices means that the Left no longer has the resources to communicate a vision or experience of solidarity. This lack accelerated both the retreat from the state and acceptance of the inevitability of capitalism, which contributes to a loss of political agency—the sense that "we can't do anything about anything."[15]

Moreover, just as Dean believes deliberative democrats have brought utopia inside, she suggests that theorists who point to the potential of democratic renewal by citing on-going democratic practices are ultimately conservative. These practices remain attached to the "present values" that trap criticism of neoliberalism in a reinforcing circle and must therefore be completely jettisoned.[16] Dean views Occupy and the Arab Spring as evidence of a radical break with present values and a shift from individual to mass struggle. Dean's enthusiasm for the Occupy Movement is premised upon seeing it not as a continuation with the terms of the regnant experience of the ordinary world encompassed by communicative capitalism, but a break with those political conditions. To support this claim, she argues that the occupation of public sites represents the rejection of convenience "in a society ideologically committed to it," its opposition to Wall Street, and its rejection of the fundamental link between capitalism and the people.[17] Dean instead views Occupy as the enactment of capitalism's fundamental antagonism: class struggle. According to Dean, Occupy reflects a new political imaginary and "new possibilities for the [Communist] party form" inasmuch as it claims to represent the interests of the 99 percent and, in doing so, names the gap separating the wealthiest 1 percent and the rest as a wrong.[18]

At the same time, she observes that Occupy was limited by its emphasis on inclusive decision-making, democratic procedures, and its anti-hierarchical, horizontal structure. This generated confusion and disillusionment about the "fact of hierarchy" within the organization, that Occupiers witnessed, and failed to effectively bind them into a collective political subject, as should have occurred.[19] The problem with allowing every person to participate in a structureless organization, according to Dean, is that "they continuously confront one another's particularities as differences that must be expressed rather than, say, disciplined, repressed, redirected, sacrificed, or ignored as not relevant for this struggle."[20] Because neoliberalism is committed to freedom and opposed to planning, according to Dean, opposing neoliberalism requires a resilient organizational structure. Dean argues that members of these emerging movements should effectively attach themselves to the Communist Party for three reasons. First, opposition to capitalism defines the Communist Party. Second, it offers members of the class exploited under neoliberalism a sense of collective identity.[21] Finally, under Communism "the sovereignty of the people points to a view of the state as what *we* use to govern for *us* as a collectivity."[22] In short, a reimagined Communist Party can provide a horizon for movements contesting neoliberalism.

Dean refers to "specific histories and struggles whose successes and failures can continue to inspire, that can—but may not—incite a desire to look at our present differently, to see it in light of the communist horizon."[23] Dean names three sources that suggest the emergence of a new Communist Party. In her introduction, she refers briefly to the declaration that, "The general horizon of the era is communist," made by Alvaro Garcia Linera, following the election to power of his party, the Bolivian Movement for Socialism—Political Instrument for the Sovereignty of the Peoples.[24] Next, she cites an academic conference On the Idea of Communism held in 2009 in London where organizers had to accommodate an overflow of audience members, as well as conferences organized subsequently.[25] But the primary evidence to support her claim about the emergence of a new Communist Horizon is Occupy Wall Street.

Dean, however, does not expend much effort listening to the substance of the Occupier's claims beyond their opposition to inequality and Wall Street. The claim that "This is what democracy looks like!" was carried on signs and heard at many Occupy events.[26] Occupiers conceived of democracy as the ability of ordinary citizens to come together to solve common problems. This definition of democracy is a recurring feature of Occupy narratives and media. It is the thesis of Keith Gesson's essay "Laundry Day," which revolves around the General Assembly's discussion on the mundane task of washing laundry after rain fell on the encampment. The mutual care and diversity that characterizes relations among Occupiers in Zuccotti Park and the indifference that many of them faced from fellow citizens of the liberal-democratic state is a central theme of the essay. Gesson is intent on clarifying misunderstandings of the Occupiers circulating in the public, and he does so by celebrating acts of cooperative listening, kindness, and work necessary for the occupation of Zuccotti Park to maintain its operations. The essay highlights the ability of Occupiers to patiently endure discussions about how they should do their laundry when they would rather discuss ending patriarchy or white privilege because these mundane acts of maintenance are part of the business of going on together that make those higher-stakes discussions possible.[27]

At the same time, Dean finds evidence of emergent resistance in diverse locations and activities. On her blog and in social media, she highlights on-going mobilizations by students against rising fees and tuition and activists in New York's Finger Lakes region against fracking. It is Dean who seems eager to collect them into a new, already formed political subject acting under the banner of communism. But there is little evidence to support her claim, because these movements remain attached to the language and practice of democracy, which inspire both their extra-juridical activities and their hopes for reforming laws and legal institutions. The activism profiled in Dean's online presence is in tension with her strident insistence on an institutionally disciplined party. In the former engagements, she appears more tolerant and even hopeful about these diverse, experimental approaches.

Yet because the economic and political impasse that Dean observes so smartly is undoubtedly real and serious, the suggestion in her academic work that it may be fully overcome without democratic struggle is both wrong and dangerous. Its appeal leverages the fact that most citizens today are estranged from traditions of democratic practice and experience. Dean's interpretation of Occupy as the enactment of a fundamental division that inaugurates a new political subjectivity exploits devitalized citizens who are estranged from democratic traditions and one another and who have little confidence in their own capabilities to engage in common action by offering to substitute one unilateral sovereign authority for another, more beneficent one. Dean's *Communist Horizon* holds out the fantasy of instantaneous change suited to the habits of citizens accustomed to the rapid tempos of the market by suggesting to these frustrated and beaten citizens that a Party will change everything for them upon its arrival. Her totalizing vision of political change is, furthermore, suited to readers who have little first-hand experience or patience with negotiating with difference. By rejecting the state and economy in their current iterations, *Communist Horizon* represents a desire for purity in politics that Weber identified with a prophetic commitment to ultimate ends and that Jean-Paul Sartre suggested was, for humans, ultimately destructive.[28]

Additionally, imagining such a radical transformation minimizes the affective attachments that most contemporary subjects have to the present, which, however, limits their ability to think and act collectively about the future. Although Dean perceptively notes how the paucity of experience with collective life represents a barrier to collective action as well as how the widespread of experience of debt "privatizes the future" in her analysis, she skips right over them with her declaration of a new political subject. Calling this an instantaneous transformation relieves Dean of having to specify affective practices by which this transformation might proceed. Dean is right that democratic theorists do not adequately consider the degree to which contemporary subjects are drawn into and internalize neoliberal ideology through their participation in the credit markets or how the experience of indebtedness naturalizes the subject's uneventful experience of neoliberalism, but neither does she.

Maurizio Lazzarrato, author of *The Making of the Indebted Man*, argues the demand of repayment is what indexes the contemporary political subject to the neoliberal economy.[29] Access to credit represents a necessary condition for entrepreneurial risk for most individuals and, as an obligation, it teaches them to become future-calculating subjects.[30] That is, credit marks the shift from an older model of market behavior patterned after the model of exchange and interest described by Adam Smith to one that realigns the measurement of all kinds of human activity according to rational self-investment. In the next section, I briefly summarize Nietzsche's analysis of debt in order to foreground how Strike Debt's practices attempt to rewire the attachments subjects have to debt that keep the obligation of repayment and, therefore the necessity of austerity, in place.

TRANSFORMING THE MORAL ECONOMY OF DEBT

The introduction to *The Debt Resistors' Operations Manual*, a 115-page document authored anonymously and available on Strike Debt's website, does not try to create a division among the people. Instead of advancing class-antagonism by pitting the 99 percent against the wealthiest 1 percent, per Dean's recommendation, it claims that debt affects all citizens, regardless of their position in the economy, because debt drives the economy to which all belong. It begins:

> *Everyone is affected by debt*, from recent graduates paying hundreds of dollars of interest on their student loans every month, to working families bankrupted by medical bills, to elders living in "underwater" homes, to those taking out payday loans at 400% interest to cover basic living costs, to the teachers and firefighters forced to take pay cuts because their cities are broke, to countries pushed into austerity and poverty by structural adjustment programs.[31]

Debt, the authors note, is an invisible but ever-present part of daily life for most Americans. Its invisibility is due to the fact that debt has long been regarded as a private matter, closely tied to personal morality, although this has not always the case.[32]

According to Nietzsche, debt represents the basis for an entire moral economy in which subjects have deep psychic investments. As Nietzsche puts it, when presented with alternatives, human beings enmeshed in this moral economy are defined by "an active desire not to let go, a desire to keep on desiring what has been, on some occasion, desire."[33] Nietzsche explains the persistence of this attachment in terms of a feeling of guilt between creditors and debtors that is prior to "the beginnings of any social form of organization or association."[34] He notes that the desire to enforce contracts between creditors and debtors and to enforce punishment for failure to repay is what motivates the invention of "legal society." He writes that this system of punishments involved sacrifice; initially sacrifice to the ancestors and the gods in the form of flesh and blood but later in terms of habits of self-sacrifice and asceticism that were instrumental to the formation of reason and which made those sacrifices appear reasonable.[35] The connection between sacrifice and reason has consequences for how we view the appropriateness of sacrifice on the part of debtors, according to Nietzsche, because we view progress in terms of how much has been sacrificed in its name. Just as we saw in the first chapter that the sacrifice of indigenous groups was formative to the development of the modern constitutional state, the sacrifice of debtors is fundamental to seeing the credit economy as modern and progressive.[36] This moral and legal code places boundaries around what is permissible and forbidden, holding the repayment of debt as the highest value for the individual.[37] Thus, debt (and punishment) is a means of making humans more predictable and therefore more governable.[38] Practically speaking, the moral obligation to repay a loan works to narrow the choices and decisions individuals can make about their futures and whether they have the resources to act politically.

Debt connects not only guilt and punishment, according to Nietzsche, but is also the source of multiple pleasures: the pleasure of forgiving but mainly withholding forgiveness, the pleasure taken in the cruelty of punishment, the pleasure of shame and suffering but also the empowerment of victimhood, and the pleasure of *ressentiment*.[39] Debt is a form of social control, the "social straitjacket" Nietzsche calls it,[40] and that is exactly why we like and do not wish to detach from it. The "bad conscience" of guilt associated with indebtedness relieves humans of the responsibility for their freedom. This is the late, ripe bitter and sour fruit that hangs in the tree, unpicked, according to Nietzsche.[41] Bad conscience was learned through punishment and these festivals of cruelty remain vital forms of entertainment that Nietzsche argues humans enjoy too much to give up: "Through punishment of the debtor, the creditor takes part in the *rights of the masters*: at last he, too, shares the elevated feeling of being in a position to despise and maltreat someone as an 'inferior'—or at least, when the actual power of punishment, of exacting punishment is already transferred to the 'authorities,' of *seeing* the debtor despised and mistreated."[42] Contemporary dramas of indebted cities and nations offer the same pleasures of superiority, shame, punishment, and cruelty.

At least for most Americans, debt is also a product of the pleasure taken in outsized consumption. From conspicuous consumption to positional goods, debt fuels envy and desire for status, enabling the many to imitate the spending habits of the few, the rich. Debt resistance will mean addressing the shame and pleasure (and shameful pleasure) associated with individual indebtedness.[43] Without debt-driven consumption, social esteem and self-worth will have to be drawn from and find expression in other outlets. Nietzsche's examination of debt suggests the need to cultivate new economic subject positions, whose desires and pleasures are oriented away from fulfillment in the marketplace.[44]

Strike Debt has initiated a Rolling Jubilee to begin the work of transforming the subject's affective attachment to debt from perpetuating the cycle of cruel punishment to taking pleasure in forgiveness. Rolling Jubilee buys and retires debt at discount prices, staging "direct actions across the country, ranging from debt burnings to targeted shutdowns of predatory lenders of all kinds," and campaigning for fair wages, adequate housing, and access to affordable health care.[45] The group has already been successful in raising funds to retire debt, exceeding its initial drive to raise $50,000 for the purpose more than eightfold.[46] The money was raised through donations and fund-raising concerts, where attendees were invited to identify themselves by the number representing their total level of personal debt on "My Name is . . ." nametags. The purpose of these public practices has been to ease the stigma associated with indebtedness, to inject indebtedness with some fun, and to create solidarity around that pleasure.[47] The Rolling Jubilee events have been a symbolic preview of the carnival-like relief that is the promise of the ultimate Jubilee.

With this money Strike Debt has purchased in bulk medical debt valued at more than $15 million for $400,000 in the secondary debt market. Without knowing the identity of individual debtors beforehand, it contacted nearly twenty-seven hundred debtors to inform them that their debts had been retired and repayment obligations fulfilled.[48] These purchases are largely symbolic, but this does not mean that they have been inconsequential for those whose debts have been cancelled or those involved in the movement. The Rolling Jubilee is an attempt to inaugurate an alternative moral and political economy that prioritizes the virtues and pleasures of giving and receiving unexpected gifts. The Rolling Jubilee is an acknowledgment of a radical aspiration for those working to address debt's role in shaping the terms of ordinary political life, even as they are constrained by the realities of living with debt.

The Rolling Jubilee is one example of how Strike Debt is creating new attachments among citizens that run counter to the hegemonic norms enforcing individual and collective debt repayment. Members of Strike Debt's Bay Area chapter have nurtured a diverse array of associations that identify them to themselves and others as an emerging public broadly committed to reclaiming agency and contesting the sovereignty of private capital. At their core, all of these associations offer participants pleasure in being together that helps to break down the subject-level micro-practices, such as investments in defensive and positional goods, that complement the logic of emergency measures. The associations include reading groups on the role of debt in the economy that meet over tacos and drinks and parties held in conjunction with the release and distribution of printed editions of the *Debt Resistors' Operations Manual*.

A flyer for such an event held on March 23, 2014, depicts a silhouette of concertgoers beneath an image of a giant golden nugget that threatens to crush them (Fig. 5.1). A man in a hat wearing shorts and a blue colored top can be seen on the right side straining to hold back the massive boulder beneath the words "Strike Debt!" printed to resemble the script for the "Star Wars" films. Partygoers at the March 23 event (Fig. 5.2) can be seen in photos posted to the group's Facebook page laughing while taking turns to strike a piñata shaped like the giant golden nugget (Fig. 5.3). The party atmosphere, the physical act of striking the piñata, and the chance to experience pleasure together all work to rewire the attachments that attendees have toward debt. The subtext of such practices is that debt need not be private or shameful but that the practices that enforce the hold that debt has over citizens can be broken just like the symbolic piñata. Secondly, the ecstatic moment of release that those gathered can be seen enjoying together in the photos is importantly the product of their shared

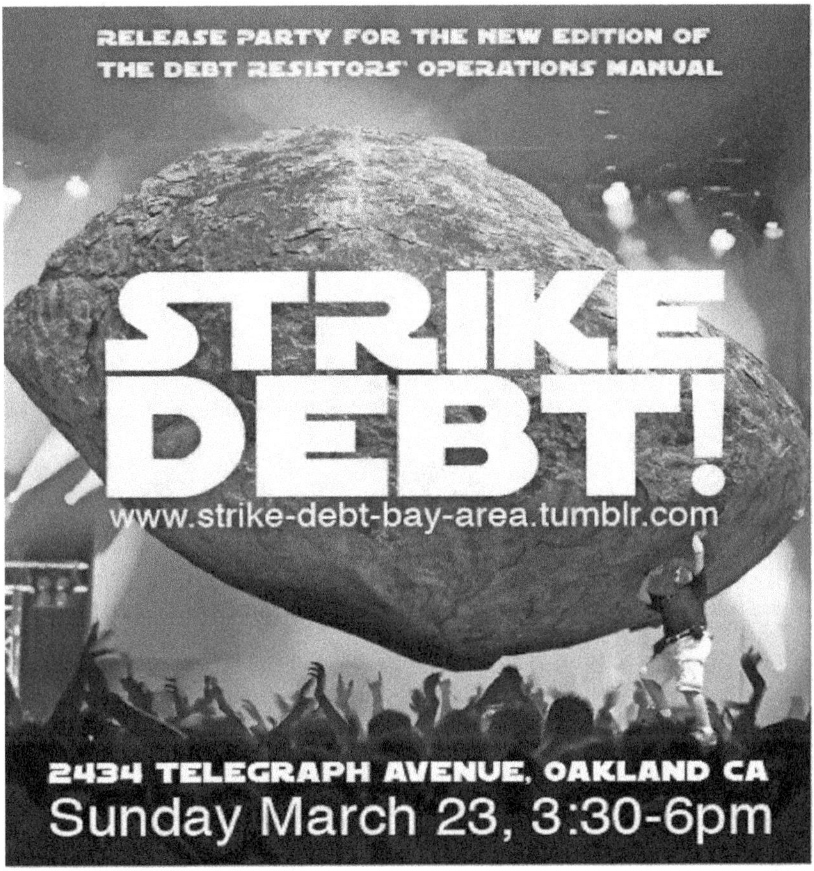

Figure 5.1 Flyer for Strike Debt Resistor's Operations Manual Release Party. Reprinted with permission of Strike Debt Bay Area group.

labors. The piñata breaks—debt can be broken—only through a series of concerted actions taken by citizens acting together (Fig. 5.4).

The *Operations Manual* includes advice on how to resist debt collectors and how to negotiate with lenders. Its authors do not pretend that many readers will find it possible to live in a world "as if" its economy does not revolve around credit and acknowledges that such negotiations are always tilted in favor of those who write the rules. The *Operations Manual* does not only focus on negotiation, it combines advice on how to cope and live within those limits with an attempt to think beyond the rules and

Figure 5.2 Party-goers gather at a Bay Area Strike Debt event, with giant, golden-colored piñata symbolizing individual and collective debt visible on right side of photo. Reprinted with permission of Strike Debt Bay Area group.

Figure 5.3 Party-goers take turns striking the piñata as others look on and cheer. Reprinted with permission of Strike Debt Bay Area group.

Figure 5.4 Ecstatic moment of release as a party-goer smashes the piñata o pen to the accompaniment of a rock band. Reprinted with permission of Strike Debt Bay Area group.

possibilities of the current economy. Strike Debt suggests that challenging neoliberal governance will require more than appeals to democratic justice or fairness—after all, Dean is right that the rules in question are the products of democratic processes and remain open to modification by those processes. But neither will identifying an alternative to neoliberalism require a radical break with the terms of ordinary life or democracy, as Dean insists it does.

Strike Debt's goal is to create solidarity around debt as a means of articulating a critique of neoliberalism and the consequences of the credit-driven economy. This starts with identifying debt as pervasive and then educating citizens about the necessity of debt and repayment to the stability and maintenance of the neoliberal economy. The purpose is to indicate how debt resistance might slow and ultimately weaken its operation as well as to illustrate the forms debt resistance might take. Varying from using cash only to minimizing reliance on credit or renegotiating outstanding loans, these forms of resistance represent alternatives that citizens can experiment with on their way to fuller participation in the movement.

Strike Debt's goal to publicize and politicize indebtedness today is evident in one of its earliest slogans: *You are not alone/You are not a loan*. The first part of the slogan is intended to discount the prevailing idea that debt represents a personal failure by alluding to the prevalence of indebtedness in society today. To publicize debt is to attempt to remove the shame that keeps it from being avowed and that Nietzsche argued allows guilt to hold in place the obligation of repayment. To this end, the *Operations Manual* paints a portrait of indebtedness, at all levels of American society, which is overwhelming. The purpose of its statistical snapshot is to establish that debt is an undeniable fact of daily life that Americans have in common even if debt is currently understood as a private and individual obligation. Seventy-six percent of Americans are debtors and in 2008 the total value of household debt as a share of income exceeded 100 percent. The average American household with at least one credit card owed almost $16,000 in credit card debt, contributing to an aggregate amount of credit card debt that topped $1 trillion dollars, a number rivaled by only by the more than $1 trillion dollar tally of outstanding student loans (in 2012). Two-thirds of students earning four-year degrees owe more than $25,000 and 1 in 10 owe more than $54,000;[49] repayment delinquency rates have increased from 12.4 percent during 2005–2007 to 15.1 percent in 2012.[50] The foreclosure crisis has affected more than 5 million homeowners, 30 percent of all US mortgages are "underwater" (i.e., in negative equity), and nearly 11 percent of all homes in the United States are believed to be empty today.[51] Underlying this mountain of personal debt, the authors explain, are America's indebted municipalities, which threaten to drag everyone, even those who have managed to steer clear of personal indebtedness, under if and when they default on their debts.[52]

Affirming the idea that "you are not alone" is also the purpose of the solidarity-building exercises undertaken in conjunction with Strike Debt's release of the *Operations Manual*. For instance, Strike Debt Bay Area's members have responded to the proposed sale of Berkeley's historic Post Office building, which is part of a national campaign to sell off historic properties in order to close the Post Office's budget shortfall, by regularly tending to the trees and plants on the property (dubbed the "Garden of Common Good") as well as tenting on its front lawn. The practice was meant to highlight the building and their own activity as part of the same *res publica*, thereby questioning the legitimacy of the sale and its underlying "necessity." The tending represents an effort to reestablish the habits of democratic citizenship and, in turn, to reshape the proper scope of juridical sovereignty. Here, juridical sovereignty refers to the idea of an accessible Post Office whose mail services are affordable and whose spaces are ones that literally anchor the public's sense of civic identity. In a post entitled "Hello to All Who Love Gardens and Post Offices" on the group's website inviting others to join in the action is written:

> This garden is yours if you want it, just as our public postal service is yours if you want it. So many things on Earth have been handed over to become private possessions for increasing personal wealth. The people of Berkeley have shown that we want to keep the post office for our collective use and this garden is an act of commitment to the concept of common good . . .
>
> From the beginning, our public postal service has been such a part of our communal lives, and we haven't had to think of being without it. It has endured so long and so well by using profits from the sale of its services to keep the cost of those services as low as possible while using some to build post offices everywhere they're needed and to carry mail to the doorstep of everyone in the country. The USPS hasn't made millionaires out of its executives, nor has it divvied up its profits amongst speculators. From the beginning, our post office has honored its mission to provide services that are of value to all of us—not just a group of shareholders, not just those able to leave their homes to collect and send mail from a remote location, not just those who can afford postage rates set to maximize dividends, not just those who live in densely populated areas, and not just those who live on the rich side of the tracks.[53]

The group's defense of the Berkeley Post Office has been a defense of the public and publicly minded corporation but, more generally, tending its gardens should be understood as a way of nurturing the conditions and habits that enable citizens to overcome the experience of impasse. These efforts include a regular half-hour radio show on station KPFA explaining how the economy works and the production of a Strike Debt-themed rap celebrating the group's purpose.[54] Strike Debt's diverse efforts are at once embedded in and aimed at ameliorating the indebtedness that defines ordinary life for many Americans but also point to possibilities of democratizing the sovereignty of debt presently beyond the fold.

The radio program, the rap, and the *Operations Manual* instruct readers on how their loans fit into the operation of a larger credit-based economy, naming the key players and connections that link credit card and medical debt; student debt; payday loans and so-called "fringe finance transaction" products aimed at those who do not have access to traditional banks; and mortgages, especially the category of subprime mortgages which played a prominent role in the 2008 financial meltdown. It not only includes advice on how to minimize debt but also how to fight debt collectors, renegotiate repayment and manage bankruptcy, and even resist debt repayment. The appendices includes sample letters for those interested in obtaining or disputing their credit scores, challenging false or inaccurate reporting of their credit history, or validating the amount of debt that they owe. The *Operations Manual* also highlights efforts by some local communities to fight the terms and conditions of the payment obligations attached to the cost of servicing municipal bonds.

The final chapter of the *Operations Manual* articulates the group's mission to shift the feelings about debt from shame and isolation to public outrage and action.[55] It cites a growing resistance to debt and the conditions that compel the growth of individual and collective indebtedness, such as the popular actions against austerity measures in Greece and Spain, where the *los indignados* movement has named the global financial system, not government corruption or unemployment, as its target.[56] Mexico's El Barzon, which took the government and banks to task for the devaluation of the peso in 1994, an action that drove interest rates on loans and mortgages dramatically upward and made the cost of repayment exorbitant, is cited as precedent for contesting personal debt. The movement successfully claimed that debtors should not be held responsible for the action of the government and banks and forced the government to provide relief to many debtors.[57]

But the authors reserve special attention for the rising costs associated with neoliberal policies that have starved public institutions of higher education, passing the costs onto students. Referring to the high payments associated with loans taken to finance the cost of higher education by many students as a modern form of "debt bondage," the *Operations Manual* points to the wave of student-led protests in Chile and Quebec against the neoliberal policies that have reduced funding for universities and university students. They point out that the symbol of the 2012 student protests in Quebec—the red square—is meant to "signify being financially 'squarely in the red' amid tuition hikes, cuts in social entitlements and the specter of spiraling student and consumer debt."[58] These protests are part of a chain of student-led actions that includes the 2010 and 2011 student-led strikes against Governor Louis Furtuno's plans to privatize the University of Puerto Rico and raise tuition for students at its campuses,[59] and Cooper Union's announcement that it would begin charging tuition for students in violation of its founding charter.[60]

The purpose of citing existing and recent debt resistance movements is to underline that these possibilities already exist in the world. Strike Debt, however, augments its case for practices of debt resistance and renegotiation along with its call for a "debt jubilee" to cancel all outstanding debts. Borrowed from David Graeber's *Debt: The First 5,000 Years,* the idea of the jubilee has its roots in Biblical accounts of debt forgiveness.[61] Leviticus refers to a Jubilee Year to be held every fifty years during which the Israelites were "to proclaim liberty through out the land to all its inhabitants" (25:10). The jubilee would erase previous debts and begin them anew: "When you buy from your neighbor, you shall pay only for the number of years since the jubilee" (25:15). In invoking the biblical jubilee, Strike Debt makes a link to religious traditions that have a long legacy of moral and political commitments to extending both democracy and equality in the United States and around the world.[62] In answer to Dean's criticism that efforts to politicize ordinary matters are inherently conservative because they accept the terms of the status quo, Strike Debt does more than work within the terms of the credit economy. Its jubilee lends a utopic horizon to practices that are meant to help subjects cope with the difficulty of separating themselves from the credit economy.

With its Rolling Jubilee, *Operations Manual* release parties, and common gardening, Strike Debt takes a step in the direction of organizing a popular movement aimed at disrupting the neoliberal economy with the eventual goal of transforming it completely. Although its *Operation Manual* contains guidance on how to resist debt collectors and how to negotiate with lenders alongside its calls for a transformative jubilee, its authors do not pretend that many readers will find it possible to live in a world "as if" its economy did not revolve around credit. They highlight the danger of such action, by warning readers that they should probably consult a lawyer, or if they cannot afford one, speak with staff at one of the several legal assistance agencies whose addresses are included in the *Operations Manual*, before committing to any course of action. They do not pretend that acting "as if" will not have traumatic consequences but at the same time that it offers practical advice for dealing with the indebtedness many struggle with day to day and year to year, the *Operations Manual* also encourages them to imagine the terms of their lives as more than a present and future organized by the demands of repayment: *You are not a loan.*

By insisting upon speaking of its aspirations for debt forgiveness in the same breath as its concerns for navigating and negotiating the indebtedness that presses upon so many today, Strike Debt is able to render a portrait of political action that, on the one hand is attentive to the daily struggle in which movement is seemingly imperceptible, whose lesson is not hope but the "best we can do," and on the other, recognizes that the daily struggle needs to be sustained by possibilities that are outside of it. It is true that Strike Debt does not offer a detailed portrait of a debt-free world, but this too can be understood as an acknowledgment of real-world constraints: to do so would invite disagreement over the details. By refusing to specify the details of its vision of a debt-free economy, it keeps participants who can agree to this overarching goal in the fold. Or, if they cannot imagine what a debt-free world would look like no matter how much they might wish it to be true, Strike Debt invites participants to consider other forms of generating and cultivating shared wealth. At minimum, the movement underlines the need to end current affective investments in indebtedness and invent new ones.

Although its theoretical architecture will need to be revised as the movement progresses, Strike Debt represents an important start in the effort to address the damages of neoliberalism, and its incompleteness should not be held against it. In this sense Strike Debt is no different from other diverse social movements in how it must negotiate the constraints of political action, yet it offers a striking portrait of what action within these constraints look like on the ground today. In brief, Strike Debt's call for a debt jubilee is not imminent in the structure of the neoliberal political economy, but its promise of transformation is attached to, even parasitic, upon it, and it co-exists within Strike Debt's *Operations Manual*, meetings, and activities. In other words, utopic transformations shadow Strike Debt's micro-political practices. The former support the redirection of our affective and psychic investments away from the shame and pleasures made possible by the current credit-driven economy toward a new organization of pleasure and affect oriented around forgiveness and the giving and receiving of unexpected gifts.

CONCLUSION

Although its message and means are part of the dynamics of communicative capitalism that make it easier for such resistance to be absorbed into the operation of politics-as-usual under neoliberalized political and economic institutions, Strike Debt leverages those technologies in order to demonstrate how difficult it is to pay attention to and address the role of debt in the lives of ordinary Americans. The focus on debt is an attempt to politicize a hidden, yet pervasive, element woven into the fabric of everyday relationships, decisions, and actions.

Strike Debt finds hope in the ability of ordinary citizens to negotiate the rules governing debt and, with it, their capacity for self-government. Its Jubilee lends the practices of debt avoidance, negotiation, and resistance outlined in its *Operations Manual* a utopic horizon. That horizon is not outside the experience of citizens living with the realities of debt, as is the Communist Horizon that Dean believes will be necessary to unseat neoliberalism, nor does it give up on the possibility of democracy as a response to the neoliberalization of daily life. Instead, the possibility of that horizon and the reality of a world in which indebtedness disqualifies citizens from self-rule is linked to efforts to retrain the subject's affective identification of debt with cycles of desire and pleasure in shame, cruelty, and punishment. The events associated with the Rolling Jubilee attempt to transform debt, on the one hand, from a hardship suffered privately to the basis of claiming public solidarity and accountability, and, on the other, from a source of ressentiment to an opportunity for taking pleasure in forgiveness. The authors do not romanticize the risks it will take for citizens to join the movement—much of the *Operations Manual* is focused on identifying strategies of coping with debt—but the authors explicitly connect debt resistance to the practice of democracy, writing: "the campaign to plunge the world into debt is a calculated attack on the very possibility of democracy."[63]

Yet even as its Rolling Jubilee attempts to inaugurate new relationships to credit and solidarity around the demand for debt forgiveness, it does so without specifying governmental or societal institutions that could guide and support individual efforts to reduce indebtedness. There is no question that debt repayment has pushed a reluctant class of consumers to consuming less, bartering, and participating in sharing economies. News reports during the foreclosure crisis documented the return of gleaning from fruit trees and vegetable plots on abandoned properties,[64] farming on abandoned lots, and a rise in time-banks where individuals can exchange time for services.[65] A smaller number may also be experimenting with downshifting. The term refers to a lifestyle change from one that is oriented around consumption and working to satisfy their desire for consumer goods to one that is organized around working, earning, and consuming less but gaining more time to cultivate relationships with family and community.[66] These are all indications that more people today are unwilling or unable to compete in the race to accumulate and develop their human capital. They have decided instead to prioritize stability, even if this means buying less.

But the decisions to withdraw or modify their lifestyles are taken individually, without institutional support, and like any lifestyle choice there is an effort to commoditize and market even simple living.[67] The creation of laws and institutions to limit capital accumulation, competition, and corporate power would signal a public commitment to reigning in the forces that have contributed to feelings of economic and political impasse. The degree to which most regulatory agencies had, nearly three years since the passage of the 2010 Dodd-Frank Wall Street Reform and Consumer Protection Act, missed the timelines for drafting new rules set by Congress and initiated only superficial reforms, is both an indication of the influence of the financial services industry and the weakness of the demos.[68] At the same time, though, the passage of the bill is an acknowledgement of the ability as well as the need for governments to balance its interest in promoting economic growth with its interest in maintaining the public good and fairness. The creation of the Consumer Financial Protection Bureau (CFPB) is a check on the unrestrained market and a statement that affirms that when private markets fail to serve the public interest, they must be corrected.

Institutions with market oversight foreground the relationality that is inherent in market relations, but thanks, in part, to the globalization of production and consumption streams and the larger fraction of wealth generated through abstract financial products, this fact is obscured. The extra-juridical pressure to democratize government institutions and bureaucratic agencies and make them more accountable to the public suggests we understand institutions as marking an on-going set of relationships among the governed and those in power. The emphasis on democratizing these institutions and the number and kinds of bodies that have decision-making power suggests an opportunity to rethink the relationships among freedom, security, and the public good that Boltanski and Chiapello identified as among the purposes of the market.

There is no question that such a process will be slow and inevitably incomplete especially since capital has proven so creative and efficient at reinventing itself and finding new markets to colonize. For this reason, the idea of a debt jubilee to end all debts and to end capitalism is just as much a dream as Dean's desire for a new Communist Horizon. Perhaps in recognition of long road to the jubilee and the patience enduring that wait requires, Strike Debt has focused in a new project titled The Debt Collective that is trying to organize debtors by category to give them leverage in determining the terms of repayment. The Collective's pilot project has been identifying students who had attended the for-profit Everest Colleges affiliated with Corinthian Colleges, Inc. According to an investigation conducted by the *New York Times*, technical colleges operated by Corinthian were found to have made false promises of post-graduation employment to applicants, many of whom were veterans whose retraining costs were financed by private loans made possible by the Workforce Investment Act. The *Times* found that that a lack of regulatory oversight had left students who chose to enroll in for-profit colleges run by private corporations like Corinthian worse off than before they matriculated. Many students did not make it to graduation. Those who did found they were academically unprepared for the careers they had trained for or that positions in those fields did not exist. Most were left deeply indebted and working minimum wage jobs, whether or not they graduated.[69]

During the fall of 2014, members affiliated with the Debt Collective calling themselves the "Everest Avengers," wearing "red square" lapel pins, rallied and testified at Department of Education (DOE) hearings investigating Corinthian's practices. They not only reported how Corinthian, in the words of one Avenger, "profits from poverty . . . sold me a dream and gave me a nightmare," but they also criticized the DOE's attempt to find a buyer for Corinthian.[70] The Debt Collective's activism has already been partly successful. On February 3, 2015, CFPB announced a loan forgiveness program covering a total of $480 million for tens of thousands of Everest students who financed their education with private loans. The program would cover students who were "lured into high cost loans destined to default and then targeted with aggressive loan collection programs" said CFPB Director Richard Corday.[71]

Debt cancellation was once a condition of democracy and Strike Debt suggests that it may once again be a requirement for citizens to experience democracy in terms that are meaningful and respect their powers of self-determination. In ancient Athens, Solon cancelled debts and redistributed property prior to the establishment of democratic laws and institutions. But as *archon*, or sovereign, he possessed the sole authority to introduce such changes.[72] Contemporary citizens lack the matching authority to act decisively, but they are inventing and cultivating attachments and practices that are the basis for democratizing sovereignty in order to challenge the necessity of debt repayment and the quasi-sovereignty of capital in the credit-driven economy.

If democracy really did refer to power in terms of the people's "capacity to do things" in 4th and 5th century B.C.E. Greek discussions of regime types, then the micro- practices of sovereignty I have been describing in this work are chiefly exercises aimed at innovating forms of citizenship and state power that can be said to be democratic.[73] At their most capacious, these movements are democratic insofar as they aspire to transform the experience and understanding ordinary citizens have their own political agency and potential for collective action. By providing opportunities for citizens to experience joyous being together, Strike Debt and other movements profiled in these pages work to generate vitality and solidarity among citizens and undermine the micro-practices of self that affirm the logics of state sovereignty and emergency politics.

Conclusion

On June 15, 2014, Brent Douglas Cole shot a California Highway Patrol officer and Bureau of Land Management agent who were investigating the illegal campsite where Cole had been living in a remote section of Nevada County, California. By some reports, the sixty-year old Cole had been camping in the area around Nevada County for nearly three years by that point. Cole had lived in Nevada County as a young man. He moved there after graduating high school in Idaho Falls, Idaho, married and had a son, before moving away to Texas and then, when his marriage dissolved, to a remote cabin in Alaska, where he lived for the next two decades. According to Court documents filed by Cole in connection with the California shooting, Cole supported himself in Alaska by working in construction and driving a truck.

It was during this period that Cole also found himself drawn into politics; in an interview with *Salon* his brother Marc Cole reflected, "He's frustrated. He'd like to think that his existence matters, like all of us do, and so he gets out there on these controversies thinking he'll be like a beacon for the rest of us. He believes he's going to do the world good. He thinks he's going to save the world." Cole added, "He [Brent] is always looking to champion the little guy and fight the big corporations. In that he is quick to accept any conspiracy theory."[1] Indeed, in a court filing submitted in connection with an earlier gun charge, Cole had alleged that he been the victim of an "unconstitutional" SWAT-style assault, targeted for "exercising my inherent Right by unwitting or unknowing accomplices of a seditious conspiracy against rights instituted by foreign powers inimical to the United States of America."[2]

A survey of Cole's online postings reveals his attraction to conspiracy theories. A common thread of distrust runs through all of his political commitments, which include his deep antipathy toward the federal government, suspicion of President Obama's foreign birth, his strident belief in Second Amendment gun rights, and his anger over the extension of US foreign aid to Israel while the City of Detroit tipped toward bankruptcy. Filings submitted by Cole to the Nevada County Courthouse and Anchorage, Alaska, along with his online activism, identifies Cole as a leader in the so-called "sovereign citizens" movement. In those filings, Cole describes himself as "statutory Attorney General of the United States," an appointment that stems from his belief that

> The judiciary is controled [sic] by a private guild, controled [sic] by foreign powers. That courts of the United States are manifestly unjust is evinced by the fact that the U.S. incarcerates more than any other nation. Purchased votes of "representatives" legislate criminality with presumptions of guilt and crime, and violations of due process. Proceedings in Admiralty divests citizens of their rights and protections, and for profit prisons are filled using treasonous Bills of Pain and Suffering.[3]

For sovereigns like Cole, the government is illegitimate because it is tilted toward foreign powers and commercial interests. Shut out by centralized decision-making concentrated in increasingly powerful government and corporate institutions, Cole expressed his diminishing agency in the melodramatic language of the victim-hero. As Anker suggests, Cole sought to restore his sovereignty by combating the elements he believed responsible for compromising national sovereignty. According to a report on the sovereign movement published on the Southern Poverty Law Center (SPLC) website, sovereigns believe that the current state and legal system is a violation of the original intentions of the American founding fathers. Sovereigns believe citizenship was reserved for only whites and they trace the crossover from this original understanding to passage of the Fourteenth Amendment, which expanded citizenship to include the newly emancipated African American slaves and those born on American soil.[4]

The Cole shooting is part of a string of confrontations between so-called sovereign citizens and law enforcement agents.[5] On June 6, 2014, Dennis Marx attacked the Forsyth County Courthouse in Cumming, Georgia, wearing a bulletproof vest and gas mask, using homemade explosives, grenades, and carrying several guns. He drove up to the courthouse steps in an SUV, exchanging gunfire with court deputies before being killed but his intention had been to enter the building and take hostages. Police discovered Marx had set explosives for them when they entered the hotel room where he had been staying during the week prior to the assault.[6] Like Cole, Marx had been angry over what he believed were "unconstitutional raids" on his property. He had been arrested on drug and weapons charges and had sued the sheriff's department for civil rights violations and use of excessive force. Cole and Marx were motivated by a desire to reclaim the government from "foreign" elements—not just African Americans, but also Jewish financiers and more recent immigrants who were threatening their freedom and, in their eyes, for whom their freedom was being sacrificed.

The desire for freedom under conditions of compromised agency also informs the sovereign movement's analysis of the role capital interests play in contemporary America. The abandonment of the gold standard represents a critical moment for sovereigns. They believe the government's pledge to back currency with "full faith and credit" entails a secret deal with foreign investors in which American citizens—specifically their future earnings potential—are offered as collateral to buyers of American dollars. According to sovereigns, newborns issued birth certificates and social security numbers have secret, shadow accounts—called corporate trust accounts—set up in their names and all other state-issued documents correspond to this account, not the real or sovereign individual to which these rightfully belong. Sovereigns believe that this unrecognized structure of split identity means that many of them are not free under the current state and therefore do not need to follow its laws.

Yet they also believe they are entitled to the money collected in their corporate accounts. That is, they reflect the shift toward human capitalization or at least thinking about government through the lens of capital accumulation while at the same time arguing that they have been wrongfully denied their share of those earnings. Extreme actions like those taken by Cole and Marx excepted, the SPLC report suggests that sovereigns understand political participation mainly in terms of engagement with juridical institutions. It explains that sovereigns believe that their money can be accessed through specially coded legal language taking the form of a complex series of grammatical forms and esoteric references. They have turned to filling such "pseudo legal nonsense" as a means of resistance, drawing out the legal process and overwhelming the court system with mountains of strangely worded briefs for even minor legal infractions like noncompliance with pet licensing laws. The SPLC notes that once only popular with whites, the sovereign movement has picked up African American followers who identify with the group's anti-tax, anti-government rhetoric.[7]

The growth of the sovereign citizens movement is a reminder why democratic activists and theorists should not abandon the language of sovereignty. Left uncontested, sovereigns aspire not to undo government, but to remake the state and citizenship in more exclusive and more racialized terms. Their movement is directly inspired by a belief that their freedom has and is being taken from them by the state since it has become an instrument of "foreign" and commercial elements. Their solution is to limit these elements through alliances with and support for independent militias like the Oath Keepers policing the nation's southern borders and by vocalizing conspiracy theories about President Obama's foreign birth and the September 11, 2001, attacks.

But these movements represent the death throes of devitalized agency. The vulnerability and experience of precarity underlying this distrust are real, but the only way to solve these issues is to democratize sovereignty. The sovereign citizens' loose association is guided by the mistaken belief that individuals acting independently can secure sovereignty for themselves. But such efforts are self-defeating because they can neither change the macro-structure and practice of sovereignty nor generate the vitality to reproduce themselves. *Ordinary Democracy* responds to citizens who have felt some part of Brent Cole's vulnerability, anger, and frustration, by giving them reasons to affirm the possibility of vitality in the company of others and the potential to democratize sovereignty.

The movements profiled in *Ordinary Democracy* are actively responding to the dilemmas of state sovereignty that animate contemporary emergency politics, not by abandoning the concept of sovereignty but by democratizing sovereignty. Fundamentally, by insisting upon the idea that sovereignty is not one-sided, but an on-going relationship that has to be renewed and agreed to, citizens within these movements are challenging the state's monopoly claim over sovereignty. They are doing so by politicizing the habits of citizen acquiescence and idleness that reinforce forms of state sovereignty that trade on and deepen popular political disengagement. They do so through micro-practices that produce alternative forms of associational life and mutual attachment among citizens than those currently available through hegemonic articulations of state power.

Specifically, these movements present the possibility of agency in political associations that are aimed at reclaiming the juridical forms of sovereignty that have crowded out other alternatives. They do so by documenting the precarious circumstances many citizens face that are unacknowledged by dominant narratives of sovereignty and the sovereign, self-responsible individual. These micro-narratives of suffering make visible the conditions of vulnerability and non-sovereignty that define the experiences of many citizens in an attempt to make these ordinary crises the basis for solidarity among them. Within these movements, citizens must address the fear, skepticism, and lack of mutual trust that enforce the sense of impasse which makes them believe that the world is and will be unreceptive to their efforts. The movements pick up on desires for community and agency that had been diverted toward areas outside of politics by presenting politics as more than state actions, beginning instead with the day-to-day concerns of ordinary citizens.

Yet these local actions are connected to and need to be connected to reimagining the citizen and her links to the state from the ground up.

The affective, participatory dimensions of the movements spring from the recognition that citizens must simultaneously unmake their attachments to the state and the contemporary economy if they are to remake state and economic forms of sovereignty in more plural and democratic forms. Unmaking settler-citizens and the habits of idleness, both in terms of consumerism and focus on private freedoms rather than public freedom, was a prominent feature of the Idle No More protests. Similarly, the protestors in Tahrir Square addressed a history of mutual fear and distrust among diverse Egyptians through the performance of interfaith cooperation. Repeated spectacles of cooperation made it possible for Egyptians to overcome not only their fear of police intimidation but also the sectarian violence that Mubarak had long suggested his rule was necessary to prevent. Renegotiating a moral economy that sees debt repayment as the mark of political virtue and a basis for political rights is at the heart of Strike Debt's efforts. Its *Operations Manual* and accompanying release parties as well as its purchases to anonymously retire and forgive debt are attempts to reframe the attachments that subjects have with debt by nurturing new pleasures in forgiveness rather than punishment and removing the personal shame and silence associated with indebtedness. Micro-level practices of rewiring the attachments subjects have to the economy represent important complements to movement efforts to contest imperatives and democratize sovereignty.

These movements are making unacknowledged sacrifices the basis of their collective claims to democratize sovereignty. Acknowledgment of sacrifice reveals the lie of the egotistic sovereign individual that props up and affirms assertions of state sovereignty in response to crisis and emergency. Yet the state remains the focus of these efforts to democratize powers that seem either closed off to citizens or which operate "behind the backs" of citizens—that is, in ways that are inscrutable and unaccountable to them.[8] These citizen movements wish to bring the state's collective resources, laws, and institutions to bear on desires for freedom, agency, community, and the public good, by specifically democratizing these relations. The consistent emphasis on building citizens' desire and capacity to act together and to develop their agency through micro-practices is meant to renew faith in democratic politics and the state by making politics feel closer to the experience and concerns of citizens.

Whether cast as the unmaking of settler-citizens or as the cultivation of *res publica* and care for public goods, the micro-practices witnessed within these movements are aimed at cultivating vitality among citizens and creating spaces for a deeper culture of active citizenship to take root. By presenting the possibilities of pleasure outside the market and in common actions that seek to enlarge the agency that citizens have with the forces that govern their everyday lives, the movements are interrupting patterns of physical and mental circulation that magnetize citizens to the present. These interruptions introduce breaks in the surface of state sovereignty and emergency politics that citizens acting together in an array of different geographies but linked movements are multiplying and enlarging.

These breaks have consequences for the citizens who take part in them and even witness them: they make the possibility of democratizing sovereignty more thinkable and more a part of the texture of everyday life. In this way, these movements make visible the hollowness of the state's felt legitimacy, thus both calling for and lending support to popular forms of legislative power. The focus on the state and sovereignty within these movements suggests the degree to which such popular action is not enough on its own, however. As in Egypt, such assemblies are repeatedly seen as the start, not the end, of democratic action insofar as they make juridical and constitutional reforms their aim.

These movement practices represent a public philosophy that challenges justifications of emergency power while maintaining rather than severing the links among democracy, sovereignty, and the state. Associational at their core, they contrast with the practices of individual reflection or different ontologies that understand democratic politics in terms of ethical practice in which democracy is separate from the state or opposed to the concept of sovereignty. The effort to politicize everyday concerns and the obstacles to active participation within these movements reflects a commitment to the difficult work citizens face in enlarging the sphere of political freedom. Under conditions and within institutions whose legitimacy is measured by the degree to which they promote economic growth and security, citizens within these movements must question the norms and expectations that commit citizens to situations that have also been the cause of their unfreedom from within the desires and attachments that hold them to the present in first place. This means recalibrating the desires for freedom, security, and public good that the shift toward flexible work along with a primarily juridical understanding of democracy have narrowed down to a desire for freedom apart from its constitutive conditions. Only this kind of reconsideration can address structures that encourage subjects to think of themselves as developing their human capital and enhancing their employability, a move that completes the circuit between self-responsible and self-actualizing subjects and their support for the unilateral actions of the sovereign state.

Democratizing sovereignty requires addressing the sacrifices at the center of sovereignty, the modern nation-state, and constitution making. In other words, these movements suggest that efforts to democratize sovereignty and the state must combine practices that challenge the sacrifices that some citizens have had to make to secure the semblance of sovereignty for others. These sacrifices are frequently encoded in the law and this makes juridical reform an important component of democratizing sovereignty, but they are also felt, reproduced, and potentially altered through affects and sites of unfreedom that are believed anterior to political life, including the market and the racial contract that is central to the construction of the modern nation state. Democratizing sovereignty must take on both, given the liberal democratic state's entwinement with both capitalism and racial domination. Movements that illuminate the connections between capitalism and racism can take many different forms across the world, from efforts to contest dam building and land appropriation in India to revolts against the privatization of public resources like clean water and higher education.

In the United States, the Fight for $15 movement is one example of how citizens are stitching together demands for greater vitality with struggles for racial justice and calls for economic and political equality. The movement seeks to unionize America's low-wage fast food workers, though service sector employees working in gas stations, convenience stores, and hospice care as well as airport personnel and Walmart employees have joined them in recent months.[9] The movement has grown from an initial strike in 2012 by several hundred fast food workers in New York City to mass strikes by workers in over one hundred fifty cities across the country on December 4, 2014, and April 15, 2015.

The movement turns on the insight that the workplace represents a daily experience of unfreedom. At one level, work is a form of unfreedom that reflects the fact that for many work is not a choice, but is dictated by the basic demands of survival. But at another, it is an experience of unfreedom that is at the core of what Idle No More had identified as the ethos of idle citizenship that makes emergency politics possible. Cheap labor by those at the bottom end of the racial hierarchy fuels the growth and accessibility of excessive consumerism. By siphoning energy and aspirations for agency away from public life, opportunities to fulfill agency through private consumption help limit the idea of citizenship to the fulfillment of institutional obligations. This idleness is what permits the expansion of settler imperialism domestically and internationally. Harper's abrogation of Section 35 and annulment of treaties with indigenous communities assumed this idleness, just as President George W. Bush's claim about the necessity of the war in Iraq was secured through the acquiescence of the majority of the American people.

The Fight for $15 is a movement that aims to regenerate collective agency which has been worn down by state and corporate power and the rise of an individualist ethos that frames political action in terms of ethical consumerism. It represents an effort to publicize and politicize what Kathi Weeks has called the "privatization of work" or the idea that employment is not a social institution but something that is experienced uniquely by individuals.[10] The movement challenges conventional thinking that views work in terms of choices made by private individuals by reframing working conditions as the product of political decisions that involve sacrifice. At the center of the movement's agenda is the demand for a living wage that assumes abundant resources that have been distributed unequally. The extension of a living wage would ease the sacrifices that poor whites, blacks, and immigrant workers at the bottom of the economy have been forced to make in order to sustain low-priced fast food, consumer goods, and services, whose number, variety, and sophistication are frequently invoked to justify the trade off for low wages. Earning a living wage would allow workers to cease working multiple "part time" jobs under conditions where they are informed of the hours they will work "just in-time"[11] for wages that leave them unable to afford basic necessities like food, rent, health care, and transportation, and which require many to seek public assistance.

These workers are protesting the illegitimacy of their sacrifices and the yet-to-be experienced sovereignty promised to them that is the aspirational horizon for their organizing. They carried signs that read, "We are worth more" to remind the larger public of their sacrifices and to undermine the idea that they had much choice in taking and staying on in multiple low wage jobs. They narrated the larger contexts that have kept many in jobs that have worn them down to almost nothing and effectively identified them as "un-productive" citizens: persistent poverty; insufficient medical care resulting in crippling personal debt; and uncertain family income that drove many to begin working as teenagers, leaving them without the energy to complete high school. These workers are demanding the right to be treated with dignity by publicizing the sacrifices they have been forced to make in an economy where other consumers expect cheap fast food, goods, and services. Their protests have been held in parking lots, stores, and malls, because although they are seeking changes in minimum wage laws, they are building popular support for such legislation by appealing directly to their fellow citizens. The basis of their appeal is straightforward: that their sacrifices have been unjust and will require others to sacrifice in order to improve their status. They see local, state, and federal governments as the ultimate focal point for addressing these sacrifices through legislation.

Though the Fight for $15 has illuminated and sought to address the sacrifices workers have been asked to make through legislation, there are downsides with its organizing structure and with its goals. For Marxists critics, raising the minimum wage through legislation comes at the expense of generating a deeper identification with class struggle even if the movement has revivified the use of the workers' strike. Radical democrats like Jacques Rancière would view the passage of higher minimum wage laws in Los Angeles and New York as the result of democratic actions that reconstitute the order of the "police," a term that is opposed to politics. Rancière identifies politics with conflict and the emergence of a common stage as those who have "no right to be counted as speaking beings make themselves of some account . . . by the fact of placing in common a wrong."[12] The police, on the other hand, reflects the configurations of the visible and sayable that regulates the boundaries of what is recognized as public or private matters.[13] Minimum wage legislation represents a reconstitution of the police order because it breaks up and reorganizes the configuration of the sensible or what citizens recognize as normal. Rancière rarely uses the language of citizenship because it is too closely associated with the state's police order. The consequence of this overdrawn opposition is to render democratic action more extraordinary. In contrast, *Ordinary Democracy* emphasizes the importance of the state as a site of democratic aspirations and action. Elaborating the types of attachments and associations available to citizens within state institutions works against the sense of impasse and acquiescence that support the normalization of emergency politics.

More than the reconstitution of the ordinary, however, to see the Fight for $15 as an example of democratizing sovereignty is to appreciate its emphasis on developing citizens and their ability to see the world as receptive to their efforts. The passage of these laws represent a departure from the unresponsiveness to local conditions that drove citizens like Cole and Marx to violent extremes, but have left many others feeling acquiescent and unfree. Democratizing sovereignty involves making local and national jurisdictions more responsive to promoting citizen initiative, participation, and vitality. Democratizing sovereignty aims to realize the universal promises of liberty and equality at the center of liberal democracy that remain potent draws for citizens whose lived experiences have nonetheless fallen short of these ideals. The push for living wages by Fight for $15 underlines the importance of economic stability to making political participation more routine rather than extraordinary. Another way of putting this is to emphasize how political inclusion without sufficient economic means falls far short, leaving government institutions to the few rather than the many.

Several critics have flagged concerns about the imposition of a top-down organizing model after the Service Employees International Union (SEIU) threw its weight behind the Fight for $15. As Arun Gupta reports, SEIU funding paid for branding and communication consultants to manage and shape a national campaign, leaving workers in local organizations to rubberstamp union-generated proposals at meetings using an up or down vote, without discussion. Gupta quotes one local organizer, who describes local involvement in the SEIU's national level campaign as "going through the motions of getting people to come to the decisions they want them to."[14] To the extent that the SIEU's participation has minimized the development of vitality and may even further the cynicism that low-income workers and their allies have about participation in democratic associations if they feel they are used, movements should be wary of partners like the SEIU.

The worry is that while top-down organization strategies may produce "wins," they may weaken rather than strengthen the confidence that citizens have in the power of their associations. At their best, the movements profiled in *Ordinary Democracy* constitute citizens in new forms of association that help them recognize that the configuration of forces that organize their lives are not natural nor intractable, but the product of decisions that citizens take together. Claiming "We are worth more" reminds citizens that they, not an unseen force in the market, have the power to determine worth and that the market does not merely serve individual interests but that it should also serve the public good. When the market does not enable individuals to live with dignity because it undermines human agency, that configuration of the market constitutes a "wrong."

The moralism of this claim is not framed as a way of purifying political life of its problems by gaining a "solution." Rather it is a moral claim that is being pursued through organizing democratic citizens who are simultaneously claiming their powers over the interconnected web of relations among capital, race, and even taste for cheap fast food that define sacrifice but which, disavowed, allow many Americans to remain innocent of their part in holding in place a low-wage economy that reduces fellow citizens to the edge of survival. The movement has focused attention on the conditions and challenges that routinely define the experiences of unfreedom and unfulfilled agency for many low-wage workers and persons of color in the United States. This explains why some of the protests against the killing of Michael Brown in Ferguson, MO, took place as die-ins at Walmarts around the country. The movement is larger than any single issue affecting low-income workers and people of color; it is trying to address the forms of sovereignty that demand their sacrifice by attempting to reshape subject conduct and action in relation to the economy and state.

In Oakland, CA, protestors marked the 2015 Martin Luther King Jr. holiday by staging a "die-in" in the Walmart parking lot. The "die-in" had a double valence. It dramatized the sacrifice of low-wage workers for low-priced consumer goods and corporate profits at America's largest retailer and employer, Walmart. It was also a reminder of twenty-two-year old John Crawford, who was killed by police in an Ohio Walmart in August 2014 while holding but not pointing a toy BB-gun. The choice of the protests on a national holiday to honor Dr. King suggest the importance of reclaiming the state and state icons as well as the effort to reanimate a critique in which King linked domestic racial injustice to the expansion of American imperialism abroad. More than fifty people participated in the protest at Walmart and another hundred rallied at a nearby mall, singing "Happy Birthday" to Dr. King, calling on other shoppers to refuse to turn his birthday into another consumer holiday, and blocking traffic trying to enter the mall from nearby streets. They chanted "poverty is violence" and "Black Lives Matter," carried photos of Crawford, and called on Walmart to increase pay to $15 an hour.

The Walmart protests were part of a weekend of actions against police violence, racism, and economic injustice. They included protests that disrupted the Friday morning rush-hour commute on the regional BART rail system. Another group of activists chained themselves to the Ronald Dellums Federal Building in Oakland to protest the displacement of the city's African American residents during the recent wave of gentrification.

Protestors also marched to protest aggressive and racist policing practices on both Saturday and Monday evening under the eye of police outfitted in riot gear.[15] These actions disrupted normal patterns of mental and physical circulations and drew attention to the sacrifices African Americans and other minorities in Oakland had been forced to make in order to make the city safe for business and idle citizenship.

The protests are evidence that democratizing sovereignty is taking shape as an emerging but interlocking set of anti-racist, anti-capitalist political movements in the United States whose mature form has yet to be settled. These experimental forms are reasons for hope. They are scratches on the surface of political conditions that have not allowed citizens to attach their actions. They may appear microscopic, but together they roughen the surface for other actions to adhere, take hold, and radiate outward. Public philosophy has an important role to play in preparing these surfaces and citizens to inhabit them. It can profile exemplary actions and practices that can inspire citizens, fortify their courage, and give them the strength to continue the fight to democratize sovereignty and renew the promise of democratic freedom.

NOTES

INTRODUCTION

1. Photographers Joshua Lott and Jake Bacon captured images of the event. These messages are taken from their photographs.
2. John Cassidy, "Wall Street Protests: Signs of the Times," NewYorker.com blog, *New Yorker*, October 6, 2011. Available online: http://www.newyorker.com/news/john-cassidy/wall-street-protests-signs-of-the-times (accessed October 15, 2015).
3. In this book, I will be using the term citizen to refer not to a juridical relationship, but a relationship of governance between powers that organize daily life and subjects who live within those terms but also retain the ability to resist, augment, or otherwise reinvent the terms of those governing arrangements. In this usage, I follow James Tully.
4. On this point see Wendy Brown, *Undoing the Demos* (New York: Zone Books, 2015), 47–78.
5. Bonnie Honig, *Emergency Politics* (Princeton: Princeton University Press, 2009), 1–11. For an analysis of the duration of crisis and emergency see Leonard Feldman, "The Banality of Emergency: On the Time and Space of 'Political Necessity,'" In *Sovereignty, Emergency, Legality*, ed. Austin Sarat (New York: Cambridge University Press, 2010), 136–164.
6. John R. Hibbing and Elizabeth Theiss-Morse, *Stealth Democracy* (New York: Cambridge University Press, 2002).
7. On this point see Brown, *Undoing the Demos*, 79–114.
8. Several authors have observed that crisis has been the occasion for the expansion of neoliberal economic policies and governance. See Naomi Klein, *Shock Doctrine*, (New York: Picador, 2007), 3–26. See also Philip Mirowski, *Never Let a Serious Crisis Go to Waste* (New York: Verso, 2013). I will be addressing neoliberalism in the context of emergency politics in this book.
9. John Locke, "Second Treatise", in *Two Treatises of Government*, ed. Peter Laslett (Cambridge, UK: Cambridge University Press, 1994), Chapter 14, 374-380.
10. Danielle S. Allen, *Talking to Strangers* (Chicago: University of Chicago Press, 2004), 37–38.
11. Ibid., 29.

12. Jean Bodin, *On Sovereignty: Four Chapters from The Six Books of the Commonwealth,* edited and translated by Julian H. Franklin (Cambridge, UK: Cambridge University Press, 1992).
13. The terms devitalized agency and impasse originate in Lauren Berlant's work, *Cruel Optimism* (Chicago: University of Chicago Press, 2011), 1–16.
14. For a rich discussion of this aspect of agency, see Patchen Markell, "The Rule of the People: Arendt, Archê , and Democracy," *American Political Science Review* 100, no. 1 (February 2006): 1–14.
15. Berlant, *Cruel Optimism*, 95–190.
16. Elisabeth R. Anker, *Orgies of Feeling: Melodrama and the Politics of Freedom* (Durham: Duke University Press, 2014). For an analysis of de-politicized attachment similar to the concept of "felt legitimacy" see also Berlant, *Cruel Optimism,* 223-228.
17. Anker, *Orgies of Feeling*, 110–148.
18. Ibid, 40–41.
19. The language of vitality comes from Lauren Berlant's analysis of "devitalized agency" but it has also briefly appeared in William Connolly's recent work, *The Fragility of Things* (Durham: Duke University Press, 2013), 17–18.
20. Stanley Cavell, "The Ordinary as Uneventful," in Stanley Cavell, *Themes Out of School* (Chicago: The University of Chicago Press, 1984): 184. The language of "ordinary" and "uneventful" is drawn from Cavell's work. My choice to approach neoliberalism in terms of the uneventful has been influenced by Thomas Dumm's *A Politics of the Ordinary* (New York: New York University Press, 1999); Dumm's work also builds on Cavell's.
21. Anker, *Orgies of Feeling*, 110–114.
22. Lida Maxwell, *Public Trials* (New York: Oxford University Press, 2015).
23. Jeffrey Stout, *Blessed Are the Organized* (Princeton: Princeton University Press, 2010). See also Romand Coles, *Beyond Gated Politics* (Minneapolis: University of Minneapolis Press, 2005) and Mark Warren, *Dry Bones Rattling* (Princeton: Princeton University Press, 2001). Stout's account of grassroots democracy emphasizes how Industrial Areas Foundation delegates focus on actions that are "winnable," whereas the social movements I am examining take on conditions that feel intractable where the potential for change seems defined by their long, almost impossible odds.
24. Sheldon Wolin, *Politics and Vision, Expanded Edition* (Princeton: Princeton University Press, 2004); Stout, *Blessed are the Organized*; Coles and Hauwerwas, *Christianity, Democracy, and the Radical Ordinary* (Eugene, OR: Cascade Books, 2008); Judith Butler, *Precarious Life* (New York: Verso, 2004).
25. Aziz Rana's account of American freedom is instructional on this point, *The Two Faces of American Freedom* (Cambridge, MA: Harvard University Press, 2010).
26. Chandan Reddy argues that the passage of the National Defense Authorization Act of 2010 (NDAA) secures a link between civil rights and national security. That is because NDAA includes an amendment titled the Matthew Shepard and James Byrd, Jr. Hate Crimes Prevention Act. It is named for the 1998 crimes against Matthew Shepard who was tortured and killed because he was suspected of being gay and James Byrd Jr., an African American man who was tied to and dragged

behind a truck before being murdered by white supremacists in Texas. The amendment enlarges the existing federal hate crime statutes to include crimes against victims based on their perceived or actual gender, sexual orientation, identity, or disability. Reddy observes that almost none of the civil rights organizations celebrating the new legislation commented on how these rights had been explicitly linked to support for American imperialism and predicated on the disposability of lives overseas. Chandan Reddy, *Freedom with Violence* (Durham, NC: Duke University Press, 2011), 1–54.

27. Charles Mills, *The Racial Contract* (Ithaca: Cornell University Press, 1999).
28. James Tully, *Strange Multiplicity* (New York: Cambridge University Press, 1995), 9
29. Claire E. Rasmussen observes the bond between autonomy and political legitimacy in the liberal tradition, writing: "In much of modern political thought, especially liberal theory, the concept of autonomy has been shifted from being used to describe governance at a collective level to being an individual characteristic that determines the parameters of legitimate political authority." Claire E. Rasmussen, *The Autonomous Animal* (Minneapolis: University of Minnesota Press, 2011), xi.
30. Joan Cocks argues the link between freedom and domination at length in her most recent work, *On Sovereignty and Other Political Delusions* (New York: Bloomsbury Academic, 2014).
31. Claudia Rankine has described the legacy of racial sovereignty as the daily experience of a "wrongful ordinary" for African Americans. Rankine, *Citizen: An American Lyric* (Minneapolis: Graywolf Press, 2014).
32. http://www.npr.org/templates/story/story.php?storyId=4833613
33. By juridical I am referring to the laws that outline the formal aspects of a given concept, whether equality, sovereignty, or freedom. My intention is to distinguish laws from the norms, habits, practices, and ethical commitments that contextualize those formal understandings.
34. Charles Louis de Secondat, Baron de Montesquieu, *Spirit of the Laws* (Amherst, NY: Prometheus Books, 2002).
35. Alexis de Tocqueville, *Democracy in America*, edited and translated by Harvey C. Mansfield and Delba Winthrop (Chicago: University of Chicago Press, 2000). .
36. James Tully, *Public Philosophy in a New Key*, Vol. 2, *Imperialism and Civic Freedom*, (Cambridge: Cambridge University Press, 2008), 286.
37. The term counterpublics is borrowed from the work of Michael Warner, *Publics and Counterpublics* (New York: Zone Books, 2002), 56–63.
38. A note on terminology: At various points I use the terms "micro-practices," "citizen practices," and "extra-juridical" interchangeably to refer to the sub-constitutional habits and orders of sovereignty by which I mean how ordinary citizens amplify, modulate, contest, or modify the exercise of sovereign power through their actions. I contrast these terms with the constitutional, juridical, macro-, and state-level expressions of sovereign power understood in terms of law and policy-making through the executive, bureaucracies, and other administrative bodies.
39. According to Connolly, "Citizen participation in the ethos of sovereignty takes place through the micropolitics of sovereignty." William Connolly, *The Ethos of Pluralization* (Durham: Duke University Press, 1995), 143.

40. Ibid., 142.
41. Ibid., 40.
42. Ibid., 112–113.
43. Ibid., 147.
44. Ella Myers, *Worldly Ethics: Democratic Politics and Care for the World* (Durham, NC: Duke University Press, 2013), 15–16.
45. Honig, *Emergency Politics*, 40–64.
46. Bonnie Honig, *Antigone, Interrupted* (New York: Cambridge University Press, 2013), 1–12.
47. Idle No More is part of a string of citizen-centered and citizen-organized challenges to democratize relations with governing institutions. In North America alone, the student protests against tuition increases and cuts in public support for higher education in Puerto Rico, in Quebec, and at New York's Cooper Union; the occupation of the Wisconsin Capitol Building to demand the recall of Governor Scott Walker; and the Occupy movement were all important precedents. Together they created room for citizens to imagine resistance and assured them that they were not alone in their desire to resist. Within these movements, there was special attention to helping fellow citizens identify the possibilities for action in everyday contexts that were initially believed to be unalterable.
48. Sheldon Wolin, *The Presence of Past*, (Baltimore: The Johns Hopkins Press, 1990), 32–46.
49. Judith Butler, "Bodies in Alliance and the Politics of the Street." Availabline online: http://www.eipcp.net/transversal/1011/butler/en, accessed June 7, 2016.
50. Aletta Norval, *Aversive Democracy* (New York: Cambridge University Press, 2007), 15.
51. Michel Feher, "Self-Appreciation; or the Aspirations of Human Capital," *Public Culture* 21, no. 1 (2009): 21–41 and Wendy Brown, *Undoing the Demos*, 175–200.
52. I am holding at arms length works that investigate democratizing the economy through worker cooperatives and similar measures because these tend not to be scalable beyond local communities. I do so, in part, because these works seem to operate with a tacit definition of democracy that privileges local engagements rather than the state and its institutions.
53. See Wendy Brown, "We Are All Democrats Now," in *Democracy in What State?* edited by Amy Allen (New York: Columbia University Press, 2011): 44–57.

CHAPTER 1

1. Stephen Harper and Bob Rubin, "A Conversation with Stephen Harper," Council on Foreign Relations, May 16, 2013. http://www.cfr.org/canada/conversation-stephen-harper/p30723
2. Stephen Harper, "Address to Council on Foreign Relations" (speech), New York, September 25, 2007. http://www.cfr.org/canada/conversation-stephen-harper-rush-transcript-federal-news-service/p14315 (accessed June 6, 2016).
3. Wolin, *Presence of the Past*, 183. Also, Brown, *Undoing the Demos*, 17–46.
4. Max Weber, "Politics as a Vocation," in *From Max Weber: Essays in Sociology*, eds. H. H. Gerth and C. Wright Mills (New York: Oxford University Press, 1958), 77–128.

5. Wolin, *Presence of the Past*, 183.
6. Elisabeth R. Anker, *Orgies of Feeling* (Durham, NC: Duke University Press, 2014), 128.
7. Note I use the terms aboriginal and indigenous interchangeably throughout this chapter.
8. Section 35 of Canada's Constitution Act of 1982 reads:

   (1) The existing aboriginal and treaty rights of the aboriginal peoples of Canada are hereby recognized and affirmed.
   (2) In this Act, "aboriginal peoples of Canada" includes the Indian, Inuit and Métis peoples of Canada.
   (3) For greater certainty, in subsection (1) "treaty rights" includes rights that now exist by way of land claims agreements or may be so acquired.
   (4) Notwithstanding any other provision of this Act, the aboriginal and treaty rights referred to in subsection (1) are guaranteed equally to male and female persons.

9. As will become clear in the next section, it is important to note however that not all First Nations recognize the legitimacy of this negotiated settlement, arguing that it wrongly validates the sovereign authority of the Canadian state. For the same reason, some reject the term "aboriginal" as an external imposition upon them.
10. House Government Bill C-45 (41–42): Jobs and Growth Act, 2012: A Second Act to Implement Certain Provisions of the Budget Tabled in Parliament on March 29, 2012 and Other Measures. Ottowa: Public Works and Government Services Canada, 2012. Available online: http://www.parl.gc.ca/LegisInfo/BillDetails.aspx?Language=E&Mode=1&Bill=C45&Parl=41&Ses=1
11. Quoted in Brooke Jarvis, "Idle No More: Native-Led Protest Takes on Canadian Government," *Rolling Stone*, February 4, 2013. Available online: http://www.rollingstone.com/politics/news/idle-no-more-native-led-protest-movement-takes-on-canadian-government-20130204 (accessed June 6, 2016)
12. Ryan McMahon, "Everything You Do Is Political, You're Anishinaabe. Or, What Idle No More Is To Me" in *The Winter We Danced*, edited by The Kino-nda-niimi Collective (Winnipeg: ARP Books, 2014),142; emphasis in original.
13. Chickadee Richard, "'Waking Up To The Beauty': An Interview with Chickadee Richard," Chickadee Richard with Leah Gazan in *The Winter We Danced*, 137.
14. McMahon, "Everything You Do Is Political, You're Anishinaabe" in *The Winter We Danced*, 139.
15. Glen Coulthard, "Subjects of Empire," *Contemporary Political Theory*, 6 (2007): 451.
16. Ibid., 444.
17. McLeod, "Nothing Will Ever Be The Same," in *The Winter We Danced*, , edited by The Kino-nda-niimi Collective, 127–129 (Winnipeg: ARP Books, 2014).
18. Mary Elizabeth Anderson, "Oprah Feelin': Technologies of Reception in the Commercial Flash Mob," in *Embodied Consciousness*, eds. Jade Rosina McCutcheon and Barbara Sellers-Young (New York: Palgrave-Macmillan, 2013): 162.
19. Ibid., 163.
20. Ibid., 169.

21. Cristina Beltrán, "Going Public: Hannah Arendt, Immigrant Action, and the Space of Appearance," *Political Theory* 37 (2009): 607.
22. Simon Critchley, *Infinitely Demanding: Ethics of Commitment, Politics of Resistance* (London: Verso, 2007), 109–110.
23. S. E. Wilmer, ed., *Native American Performance and Representation* (Tucson: The University of Arizona Press, 2009), 1–10.
24. Janice Esther Tulk, "Localizing Intertribal Traditions: The Powwow as Mi'kmaw Cultural Expression," in *Aboriginal Music in Contemporary Canada*, eds., Anna Hoefnagels and Beverly Diamond (Montreal: McGill-Queen's University Press, 2012), 71–72.
25. Pamela Green and Norman Moyah, "Join the Circle: History and Lore of the Round Dance," *Aboriginal Multi-Media Society* 16, no. 2 (1998), 29. Available online: http://www.ammsa.com/publications/windspeaker/join-circle-history-and-lore-round-dance-0, accessed June 6, 2016, and Kay L. Carlson, "Origin of the Round Dance Ceremony," *Women Against Violence Against Women* (blog), April 13, 2015, http://www.wavaw.ca/blogsround-dance-ceremony/
26. W. Richard West, Jr., "Foreword," in Charlotte Heth, ed., *Native American Dance: Ceremonies and Social Traditions* (Washington: National Museum of the American Indian, Smithsonian Institute, with Fulcrum Publishers, 1992), ix-x.
27. John Protevi, "Semantic, Pragmatic, and Affective Enactment at OWS," *Theory & Event* 14, no. 4 (2011 Supplement), available online only: https://muse.jhu.edu/article/459210 (accessed June 6, 2016), and William McNeil, *Keeping Together in Time* (Cambridge: Harvard University Press, 1995), 1–11.
28. Michel Foucault, *Discipline and Punish*, trans. Alan Sheridan, (New York: Vintage Books, 1995), 135–169.
29. James Sinclair, "Dancing in a Mall," *The Winter We Danced*, 148–150.
30. Taiaike Alfred, *Wasase* (Petersborough, ON: Broadview Press, 2005), 447.
31. Ibid., 62.
32. Ibid., 128.
33. Kevin Bruyneel explains that the source of tension is whether indigenous sovereignty depends on recognition from the colonial state (in Canada, Section 35) or whether indigenous sovereignty is inherently independent of such recognition. The tension between the two understandings has unfolded across the history of colonial and indigenous encounters, from open conflict and assimilatory policies in the past to more opportunities for limited self-governance in recent decades and it remains an unresolved question in the current Idle No More movement. As Bruyneel's work makes clear, Idle No More should be understood within a long trajectory of indigenous movements for solidarity where what it means to contest sovereignty has itself been the subject of debate and disagreement. This means that Idle No More represents less a stable subject position and more an example of an active effort to think beyond a statist notion of sovereignty. That alternative concept of sovereignty emerges from within and alongside that of the Canadian government as well as within a debate among First Nations bands over the degree of focus on land, sovereignty, and nationhood. See Kevin Bruyneel,

The Third Space of Sovereignty (Minneapolis: University of Minnesota Press, 2007), *xi–xxiv*.

34. Glen Coulthard, *Red Skin, White Masks* (Minneapolis: University of Minnesota Press, 2014).
35. Stout, *Blessed Are the Organized*, 260–277.

CHAPTER 2

1. George Shulman, "Interpreting Occupy," *Possible Futures*, December 20, 2011. Available online only: http://www.possible-futures.org/2011/12/20/interpreting-occupy/ (Accessed June 7, 2016).
2. Mattathais Schwartz, "Pre-occupied" *New Yorker*, November 28, 2011. Available online: http://www.newyorker.com/magazine/2011/11/28 (Accessed June 7, 2016).
3. Anker writes:

   > Felt legitimacy is as powerful and meaningful as any formal consent, even when nothing procedural or deliberative has occurred to instantiate that feeling. People often participate in politics through felt legitimacy; they feel the legitimacy of the policies up for consideration, even as their judgment or legitimacy can occur outside procedural or deliberative channels that compose conventional authorizing channels . . . Melodramatic tactics in twenty-first century discourse depicted war and state surveillance as necessary for healing the nation's pain and for practicing freedom, which solicited the felt sense that these actions were necessarily legitimate. Felt legitimacy that is cultured by melodramatic modes of political discourse incorporates the sense that feeling the pain of national injury is equivalent to feeling the legitimacy of state power that will respond to it. Anker, *Orgies of Feeling*, 111.

4. Ibid., 170.
5. Ibid., 77.
6. Ibid., 83.
7. Ibid., 120.
8. Ibid., 123.
9. Mirowski, *Never Let a Serious Crisis Go to Waste*, 226–230.
10. My understanding of how common sense limits the range of the sayable and thinkable is drawn from Cavell's writing on the ordinary as uneventful. See Cavell, "The Ordinary As Uneventful."
11. Ibid., 55.
12. William Connolly, *Capitalism and Christianity, American Style* (Durham: Duke University Press, 2008), 94–95.
13. Ibid., 63–64.
14. My discussion of Occupy's documentary practices builds on Connolly's crucial insight while sidestepping the criticism that Connolly has aestheticized politics by overstating the political potential of popular film.
15. This is most visible in Stephen White's *Ethos of a Late-Modern Citizen* (Cambridge: Harvard University Press, 2009), a book which both bears the influence of and complements Connolly's work on ethos.

16. Foucault, "What is Critique?" in *The Politics of Truth*, trans. Sylvere Lotringer (Los Angeles: Semiotext(e), 2007), 61–63.
17. Chris Hartman, *Zombie Capitalism* (Chicago: Haymarket Press, 2010).
18. These scholars are concerned primarily but not exclusively with theorizing documentary filmmaking. As will become clear, I am interested in applying their insights in documentary film to a larger category of activities and artifacts. I will use the term documentary film and documentary filmmaking in this section to refer to this more capacious understanding.
19. Bill Nichols, *Introduction to Documentary*, 2nd ed. (Bloomington: Indiana University Press, 2010), 10.
20. This paragraph was informed by Chapter 1 of Elizabeth Cowie's *Recording Reality, Desiring the Real* (Minneapolis: University of Minnesota Press, 2011), 19–45.
21. Hannah F. Pitkin, *Representation* (New York: Atherton Press, 1969), 2.
22. Examples of such documentaries include *Harlan County USA,* directed by Barbara Kopple (1976); *Thin Blue Line,* directed by Errol Morris (1988); *Roger & Me*, directed by Michael Moore (1989); *Hoop Dreams*, directed by Steve James (1994); and *Fog of War*, directed by Errol Morris (2003).
23. John Corner, "Performing the Real: Documentary Diversions," *Television and New Media* 3, no. 3 (August 2002): 259–260.
24. Ibid., 258.
25. http://blog.piconetwork.org/?p=478, accessed April 15, 2012.
26. In addition to documenting the activities of participants via blog posts, photos, and videos, many of the Occupy sites took care to archive materials such as posters or songs produced by the protesters as well as those sources, such as books in the lending libraries that sprang up in each of the sites, which served as strategic resources and inspiration for those involved.
27. For an overview of these activities see Marina Sitrin, "One No, Many Yeses" in *Occupy! Scenes from Occupied America*, ed. Astra Taylor, Keith Cessen, et al. (New York: Verso, 2012), 7–11.
28. Marco Roth, "Letters of Resignation from the American Dream" in *Occupy! Scenes from Occupied America*. ed. Astra Taylor, Keith Cessen, et al. (New York: Verso, 2012), 23–30.
29. http://wearethe99percent.tumblr.com/post/14640212866
30. Timothy Recuber, "Occupy Empathy?" Online Politics and Micro-Narratives of Suffering," *New Media & Society* 17, no. 1 (January 2015): 62–77.
31. Cowie, *Recording Reality*, 168.
32. Ibid., 168.
33. For a discussion of the Occupy Movement's general relationship to homelessness and in Philadelphia see Christopher Herring and Zoltán Glück, "The Homeless Question" in *Occupy! Scenes from Occupied America* ed. Astra Taylor, Keith Cessen, et al. (New York: Verso, 2012), 163–169; and Nikil Saval, "Scenes from Occupied Philadelphia" in *Occupy! Scenes from Occupied America* ed. Astra Taylor, Keith Cessen, et al. (New York: Verso, 2012), 157–169. The material in this paragraph draws on these two accounts.

34. Curtis Smith, Ernesto Castaneda, and Josiah Heyman describe a collaboration among Occupy El Paso activists and the homeless men and women who joined their encampments. After initial efforts by activists to exclude members of the city's homeless population from their camps, the authors write that attitudes changed as homeless people took lead roles in keeping the camp running. Smith, Castaneda, and Heyman, "The Homeless and Occupy El Paso: Creating Community Among the 99%," *Social Movement Studies* 11, no. 3–4, 2012, 356–366.
35. Camilla Mortensen, et al., "Keeping Occupied: Who Are These People and What Do They Want?" *Eugene Weekly*, November 10, 2011, http://eugeneweekly.com/2011/11/10/coverstory.html, accessed April 17, 2012.
36. Associated Press. *OregonLive.com*, "Occupy Eugene's downtown camp turns into homeless haven," December 8, 2011, http://www.oregonlive.com/pacific-northwest-news/index.ssf/2011/12/occupy_eugenes_downtown_camp_t.html, accessed April 17, 2012.
37. See Michael D. Anderson, "Occupy Wall Street Re-Occupies Foreclosed Home in East New York: A Report from the Scene" in *Occupy Your Homes* (blog), *Village Voice*, http://blogs.villagevoice.com/runninscared/2011/12/occupy_wall_str_37.php, accessed April 20, 2012.
38. Emahunn Raheeem Ali Campbell, "A Critique of the Occupy Movement from a Black Occupier," *Black Scholar* 41, no. 4 (Winter 2011): 44–45; emphasis in original.
39. Farrow, "Occupy Wall Street's Race Problem."
40. Montano, "Open Letter to Occupy Wall Street Activists"
41. Adrienne Keene, "Representing the Native Presence in 'Occupy Wall Street' Narrative," *Native Appropriations* (blog), October 12, 2011.
42. Campell, "A Critique," 45.
43. Ibid., 48.
44. David Zlutnick, "How Are Racial Justice Activists Making Occupy Work For Everyone?" *Colorlines* (blog) video, March 13, 2012: http://www.colorlines.com/articles/how-are-racial-justice-activists-making-occupy-work-everyone-video, accessed June 7, 2016.
45. Manissa McCleave Maharawal, "So Real It Hurts: Notes on Occupy Wall Street," *Racialicious* (blog), October 3, 2011, http://www.racialicious.com/2011/10/03/so-real-it-hurts-notes-on-occupy-wall-street/. (Accessed June 6, 2016)
46. Keene, "Representing the Native Presence."
47. Keene quotes from the Occupy Denver statement of purpose:

    If this movement is serious about confronting the foundational assumptions of the current U.S. system, then it must begin by addressing the original crimes of the U.S. colonizing system against indigenous nations. Without addressing justice for indigenous peoples, there can never be a genuine movement for justice and equality in the United States. Toward that end, we challenge Occupy Denver to take the lead, and to be the first "Occupy" city to integrate into its philosophy, a set of values that respects the rights of indigenous peoples, and that recognizes the importance of employing indigenous visions and models in restoring environmental, social, cultural, economic and political health to our homeland. See Keene "Representing the Native Presence"

48. Brown, *Undoing the Demos*, 214–215.
49. Idid., 216.
50. Idid., 218.
51. David Zlutnick, "How Are Racial Justice Activists Making Occupy Work for Everyone?" http://colorlines.com/archives/2012/03/how_are_nyc_racial_justice_activists_making_occupy_work_for_everyone_video.html

CHAPTER 3

1. Butler, *Precarious Life*, xiv.
2. Butler, *Notes Towards A Performative Theory of Assembly* (Cambridge, MA: Harvard University Press, 2015), 66–98.
3. According to Nathan J. Brown, a diversely constituted group of activists agreed on a reform agenda focused on reducing the powers of the president; securing an independent judiciary; guaranteeing fair and free elections; eliminating exceptional courts; ending the country's state of emergency in effect since nearly 1939 and limiting the situations that would warrant emergency powers; protecting individual rights and freedoms; and allowing pluralist political parties. Brown, N. "Egypt's Constitutional Revolution?" in Nathan Brown, ed., *The Rule of Law, Islam, and Constitutional Politics in Egypt and Iran* (New York: State University of New York Press, 2013), 308.
4. Further supporting the idea of a prior shared vulnerability to police violence and surveillance Brown notes, "Egyptians living under Mubarak talked of living in a *dawla bulisiyya* (police state), a *mukhabarat* (intelligence state) or even a state of thugs (*baltagiyya*). . . ." Brown, N. "Egypt's Constitutional Revolution?" 309.
5. Michael Chwe. *Rational Rituals* (Princeton: Princeton University Press, 2003), 3–18.
6. Norval, *Aversive Democracy*, 114.
7. Sheldon Wolin, *Democracy Incorporated* (Princeton: Princeton University, 2010), 65.
8. Butler, *Precarious Life*, 61.
9. Butler explains the relationship between sovereignty and the suspension of the law in the following passage:

   Given that the military tribunal is itself extra-legal, we seem to be witnessing the replication of a principle of sovereign state prerogative that knows no bounds. At every step of the way, the executive branch decides the form of the tribunal, appoints its members, determines the eligibility of those to be tried, and assumes power over final judgment; it imposes the trial selectively; it dispenses with conventional evidentiary procedure. And it justifies all this through recourse to a determination of "dangerousness" which it alone is in the position to decide. A certain level of dangerousness takes a human outside the bounds of law, and even the bounds of the military tribunal itself, makes that human into the state's possession, infinitely detainable. What counts as "dangerous" is what is deemed dangerous by the state, so that once again, the state posits what is dangerous, and in so positing it, establishes the conditions for its own preemption and usurpation of the law, a notion of law that has already been usurped by a tragic facsimile of a trial.

Ibid., 75–76.

10. Ibid., 55.
11. Ibid., 65.
12. Ibid., 24.
13. Ibid., 27–31.
14. Judith Butler, *Giving an Account of Oneself* (New York: Fordham University Press, 2005), 43.
15. Though her critics accused Butler of trying to develop a new universal foundation for ethical action that depoliticizes the motives that drive human action. See Ella Myers, *Worldly Ethics*, 76–82.
16. Butler, *Giving an Account*, 114.
17. David McIvor, "Bringing Ourselves to Grief: Judith Butler and the Politics of Mourning," *Political Theory* 40 (2012):409–436.
18. Butler, "Bodies in Alliance."
19. Butler, *Notes Towards A Performative Theory of Assembly*, 140.
20. Ibid., 110.
21. Michel Foucault, *Security, Territory, Population*, trans. Graham Burchell (New York: Picador, 2007), 311–322.
22. Salwa Ismail, "The Egyptian Revolution against the Police," *Social Research* 79, no. 2 (2012): 437.
23. Bayat, *Life as Politics* (Palo Alto, CA: Stanford University Press, 2010), 56.
24. Ismail, "The Egyptian Revolution against the Police," 445.
25. Mavelli, "Postsecular Resistance, the Body, and the 2011 Egyptian Revolution," *Review of International Studies* 38 (2012): 1072.
26. Bayat, *Life as Politics*, 22.
27. Ibid., 24.
28. Elshahed, "Breaking the Fear Barrier of Mubarak," Social Science and Research Council. http://www.ssrc.org/pages/breaking-the-fear-barrier-of-mubarak-s-regime/, accessed November 4, 2015.
29. Tweets from antigovernment protesters from the opening days of the revolution make clear how vital clearing Tahrir Square of protesters was. These tweets testify to the heavy police presence in Tahrir Square and their regular attempts to set up barricades and to intimidate and beat protestors. Nadia Idle and Alex Nunns, eds., *Tweets from Tahrir* (New York: OR Books 2011), 34–35.
30. David D. Kirkpatrick, "Mubarak Orders Crackdown, With Revolt Sweeping Egypt." *New York Times*, January 28, 2011, online edition: http://www.nytimes.com/2011/01/29/world/middleeast/29unrest.html?pagewanted=all&_r=0, accessed November 4, 2015.
31. David D. Kirkpatrick, "Mubarak's Foes and Allies Clash in Egypt," *New York Times*, February 2, 2011, online edition: http://www.nytimes.com/2011/02/03/world/middleeast/03egypt.html?pagewanted=all, accessed November 4, 2015.

32. Notably, both the Mufti of Al-Azhar and the Pope of the Coptic Church, leaders of Egypt's two largest religious groups, urged protestors to return to their homes, stopping short of endorsing the revolution. See Nathan J. Brown, *Post-Revolutionary Al-Azhar*, (New York: Carnegie Endowment for International Peace: September 2011), 9, http://carnegieendowment.org/files/al_azhar.pdf , accessed May 1, 2015.
33. Alaa Al-Aswany, *On the State of Egypt* (New York: Vintage, 2011), 153.
34. Mavelli, "Postsecular resistance," 1071.
35. Zeinab Abu-Magd, "Occupying Tahrir Square: The Myths and Realities of the Egyptian Revolution," *South Atlantic Quarterly*, 111, no. 3 (2012): 256.
36. Wael Khairy's tweets from February 11, 2011, point to the size and significance of the Friday prayers that week compared with previous weeks. He wrote: "The most crowded Friday prayer just ended. Some are headed to Tahrir and others to the presidential palace. Lines and lines of people." Less than half an hour later, he tweeted: "Friday after Friday I keep saying it's the biggest protest yet, but today it's truly epic. This is as massive as they come." Idle and Nunns, *Tweets from Tahrir*, 209.
37. Idle and Nunns, *Tweets from Tahrir*, 139.
38. Kim Badawi, "Egypt: The Day of the Martyrs," Photograph, Getty Images. ID: 08901284KB007_martyrs.
39. Wael Khairy's blog post "Letter from Cairo on February 11, 2011" offers a firsthand account of how Muslims and Christians reciprocated in protecting one another by forming human chains during congregational services. Posted online: http://www.rogerebert.com/far-flung-correspondents/a-letter-from-cairo-on-february-11-2011, accessed November 4, 2015.
40. An American blogger, Jayson Casper, living in Cairo reports on the unity of these services, espoused in the cry "Eid Wahida!" (one hand), referring to the unity among Christians and Muslims. He reports that the Sunday Mass was distinctively Christian, but that Muslims joined in the singing of a chorus identified with Christians, "Bless my country," and even sang lyrics that asserted "Son of God, you are our king" despite the Muslim belief that God has no son and Jesus was only a prophet. Jayson Casper, "A Christian Face to the Protests," Arab West Report Blog, http://www.arabwestreport.info/year-2011/week-6-week-glory/13-christian-face-protests.
41. "Egypt: A New Turning Point for the Revolution," *The Atlantic*, February 10, 2011, online edition: http://www.theatlantic.com/photo/2011/02/egypt-a-new-turning-point-for-the-revolution/100007/, accessed November 4, 2015. Source of estimated crowd, Pedro Ugarte/Associated Press/Getty Images.
42. Shaykh Yusuf Al-Qaradawi, *Khutba*, February 18, 2011, Tahrir Square, translated by Yahya Michot, http://www.beliefnet.com/columnists/cityofbrass/2011/03/the-khutbah-sermon-of-yusuf-al.html (accessed May 14, 2014).
43. Patrick Gaffney, *The Prophet's Pulpit: Islamic Preaching in Contemporary Egypt* (Berkeley: University of California Press, 1994), 122.
44. Aghar Fathi, "The Islamic Pulpit as a Medium of Political Communication," *Journal for the Scientific Study of Religion*, 20, no. 2 (1981): 169.
45. Michael Chwe, *Rational Rituals* (Princeton: Princeton University Press, 2003), 19–29.

46. McNeil, *Keeping Together in Time.*
47. Elshahed, "Breaking the Fear Barrier of Mubarak."
48. Saba Mahmood, *The Politics of Piety* (Princeton: Princeton University Press, 2005), 12.
49. Ibid.
50. Mahmood invokes Pierre Bourdieu's well-known work, *Outline of a Theory of Practice.* Trans. Richard Nice (Cambridge: Cambridge University Press, 1977), in her discussion of *salat*. For Bourdieu, practice refers to the dynamic relationship between structural factors (the distribution of natural resources and geography, for instance) and the subject positions, including gesture, affect, and culture, that develop within these constraints. These practices reflect and reinforce what Bourdieu terms a *habitus*: the objective conditions inscribed upon the bodies and dispositions of subjects who, in turn, *unconsciously* reproduce and naturalize their social position within those objective conditions as a result of those practices.
51. Saba Mahmood, "Rehearsed Spontaneity and the Conventionality of Ritual: Disciplines of *Salat*," *American Ethnologist* 28, no. 4 (2001): 831–832.
52. Khaled Abou El Fadl, "The Language of Age: Shari'a and Natural Justice in the Egyptian Revolution," *Harvard Internal Law Journal* (online), 52 (2011): 313, http://www.harvardilj.org/2011/04/online_52_el-fadl/.
53. Charles Hirschkind, "Beyond Secular and Religious: An Intellectual Genealogy of Tahrir Square," *American Ethnologist* 39, no. 1 (2012): 49–53. Hirschkind does note the controversy surrounding al-Bishri's claims.
54. Gaffney, *The Prophet's Pulpit*, 51.
55. See Cristina Beltrán, "Going Public: Hannah Arendt, Immigrant Action and the Space of Appearance," *Political Theory* 37, no. 5 (October 2009): 595–622, for an account of the traditions that support public appearance.
56. Moya Lloyd, "Towards a Cultural Politics of Vulnerability," *Judith Butler's Precarious Politics*, ed. Samuel Chambers and Terrell Carver (New York: Routledge, 2008), 103–104.
57. George Shulman, "Acknowledgement and Disavowal as an Idiom for Theorizing Politics." *Theory & Event* (online), 14, no. 1, (2011): https://muse.jhu.edu/article/423098, accessed June 7, 2016.
58. *The Square* (Al Midan), directed by Jehane Noujaim, (Cairo: Noujaim Films, 2013), DVD.
59. Brown, "Egypt's Constitutional Revolution?" 304.
60. Kouddos, "Voting After Mubarak: What Can Egyptians Expect?" *The Nation*, October 21, 2011, http://www.thenation.com/article/164114/voting-after-mubarak-what-can-egyptians-expect#, accessed November 4, 2015.
61. "Protestors Flood Cairo in Competing Rallies," Al-Jazeera America, July 26, 2013, http://www.aljazeera.com/news/middleeast/2013/07/2013726164710914498.html
62. David D. Kirkpatrick, "Egyptian Leader Apologizes to Victim of Mass Sexual Assault in Tahrir Square," *New York Times*, June 11, 2014, http://www.nytimes.com/2014/06/12/world/middleeast/president-sisi-of-egypt-apologizes-to-victim-of-mass-sexual-assaults.html?

module=Search&mabReward=relbias%3Ar%2C%5B%22RI%3A11%22%2C%22RI%3A14%22%5D

63. David D. Kirkpatrick, "Coming to Mourn Tahrir Square's Dead, and Joining Them Instead," *New York Times* (online edition), February 3, 2015: http://www.nytimes.com/2015/02/04/world/middleeast/shaimaa-el-sabbagh-tahrir-square-killing-angers-egyptians.html?emc=eta1, accessed November 4, 2015

CHAPTER 4

1. Wolin, *Democracy Incorporated*, 288–289.
2. Amy Spencer, *DIY: The Rise of Lo-Fi Culture* (New York: Marion Books, 2005), 16.
3. Warner, *Publics and Counterpublics*, 62.
4. Ibid., 62–63.
5. Reinhardt Koselleck, *Critique and Crisis* (Cambridge: MIT Press, 1988), 103.
6. Berlant, *Cruel Optimism*, 255.
7. Ibid., 255.
8. Ibid., 259.
9. Ibid., 260.
10. Ibid., 262.
11. George McKay, ed., *DiY Culture: Party & Protest in Nineties Britain* (New York: Verso, 1998).
12. Kyle Bravo, ed., *Making Stuff and Doing Things: A Collection of DIY Guides to Doing Just About Everything*, 3rd ed. (Bloomington, IN: Microcosm Publishing, 2008). Chris Carlsson, *Nowtopia: How Pirate Programmers, Outlaw Bicyclists, and Vacant-Lot Gardeners Are Inventing the Future Today* (Oakland, CA: AK Press, 2008).
13. Bravo, *Making Stuff and Doing Things*, 4.
14. Ibid., 7.
15. Elaine Brass and Sophie Polewski Koziell, *Gathering Force: DIY Culture—Radical Action for Those Tired of Waiting* (London: The Big Issue Writers, 1997), 7.
16. Ibid.
17. Carlsson, *Nowtopia*, 3–4.
18. McKay, *DiY Culture*, 3.
19. Fred Turner, *From Counterculture to Cyberculture* (Chicago: University of Chicago Press, 2006), 1–10.
20. In *The Female Complaint*, Berlant's point is to indicate that "women's literature," is a category of writing that acknowledges the powerlessness that women feel yet because women's literature is recognized as a less serious form of writing the complaint is merely expressive. It holds no chance at changing the conditions that maintain women as powerless. Lauren Berlant, *The Female Complaint* (Durham: Duke University Press, 2008).
21. Deborah Gould. *Moving Politics* (University of Chicago Press, 2009), 188.
22. Sarah Schulman, *The Gentrification of the Mind* (Berkeley: University of California Press, 2013).
23. Josh Fox, *Occupy Sandy*, released on VIMEO.com November 30, 2012, 8:34–8:46.

24. Nastaran Mohrit, "On The Margins of Disaster, Revolutionary Acts of Care," *Tidal: A Journal of Occupy Theory*, February 2, 2013, 24–25.
25. Nick Pinto. "Hurricane Sandy is New York's Katrina," *Village Voice*, November 12, 2012, http://www.villagevoice.com/2012-11-21/news/hurricane-sandy-is-new-york-s-katrina/ (Accessed November 1, 2015)
26. Luc Boltanski and Eve Chiapello, *The New Spirit of Capitalism*, trans. Gregory Elliot (New York: Verso, 2007), 18.
27. Today we could add the rise of "social entrepreneurship" as another example of how capitalism, as a system, has responded to concerns for the common good. Or in the frequently heard claims by tech executives that their newly launched products and digital platforms will benefit humanity at large by reducing processing speeds or adding choice and convenience, which represents a confusing and narcissistic entwinement of profit motive and commitment to the public good that has been satirized in episodes of the television show *Silicon Valley*.
28. The latter explains why technologies companies like Google are willing look past their commitments to making information publicly accessible and cooperate with the US government's cyber surveillance program.
29. Boltanski and Chiapello, *New Spirit of Capitalism*, 37–38.
30. Ibid., 105.
31. Ibid., 154.
32. Ibid., 353. In short, the authors conclude, humanitarian groups working to address the social misery generated by capitalist production by protesting its "exclusions" were organized according to the model of capitalist production (353). The prevalence of the network metaphor across the economy means that the line between inclusion and exclusion has grown fuzzy, however; it is more accurate to speak in terms of more or less networked, not included or excluded. Those who are marginalized within the network are pitied for their suffering and lack of human capital, but ultimately, they are responsible for their own circumstances.
33. Ibid., 349.
34. Pinto, "Hurricane Sandy is New York's Katrina."
35. See Klein, *This Changes Everything* (New York: Simon & Schuster, 2014), and Andrew Ross, *Creditocracy* (New York: OR Books, 2013).
36. Fox, *Occupy Sandy*, 8:34–8:46.
37. In order, the closing messages read "END FOSSIL FUELS," "Climate Crisis is Real," "End Climate Silence," "Climate Silence=Death," Fox, *Occupy Sandy*.
38. The film also suggests the role that a "democratic elite" committed to promoting democratic values and power among citizens can play in furthering critiques that enable public knowledge and action. Bonnie Honig's discussion of Louis Post's actions during the Red Scare suggests a similar democratic elite; see Honig, *Emergency Politics*, 40–64. I borrow the term "democratic elite" from Wolin, *Democracy Incorporated*, 291. For a longer treatment of the role of leadership in democratic organizations, see Stout, *Blessed Are the Organized*, 93–113.
39. My argument for resisting neoliberalism on the basis of a desire not to be human capital dovetails with the argument made by Michel Feher. My analysis and path

to this conclusion differs from Feher's, however, consistent with my goal of engaging in public philosophy. Whereas Feher proceeds by a close examination of the theoretical writings of Ordoliberal economists like Gary Becker who developed the concept of human capital, I have relied first on Boltanski and Chiapello's arguments about shifts in the labor market toward short-term projects and, second, a work of popular documentary film to suggest that resistance is already present. See Feher, "Self-Appreciation," 21–41.

40. In chapter 5, I argue that immanent critiques originating in the ordinary experience of citizens as creditors offers a more promising basis of solidarity than those post-capital models articulated by Marxist-Leninist thinkers like Jodi Dean and Slavoj Zizek. My claim is that alternatives that are unfamiliar to the norms and practices that constitute citizens in their day-to-day relations feel abstract and will be unlikely to resonate with citizens for that reason.
41. Mirowski points to the promotion of cap and trade programs and green jobs and technologies as examples of how neoliberalism rests final authority in markets, not political processes. Mirowski, *Never Let a Serious Crisis Go to Waste*, 336–343.
42. Boltanski and Chiapello, *New Spirit of Capitalism*, 378.
43. Ibid., 376–377.
44. Berlant, *Cruel Optimism*, 261.

CHAPTER 5

1. Wendy Brown, *Walled States, Waning Sovereignty* (New York: Zone Books, 2010), 66.
2. Wendy Brown, "We are all Democrats now . . . ," in *Democracy in What State?* ed. Amy Allen (New York: Columbia University Press, 2011), 4.
3. I thank Patchen Markell for encouraging me to seek out and appreciate this other side of Dean's public philosophy.
4. I am not the first to name the undemocratic character of the contemporary economy or to explore the idea of democratizing some part of it through a combination of worker cooperatives, shareholder democracy, and public corporations. Recent works in this area include Tom Malleson's *After Occupy* (New York: Oxford University Press, 2014); J. K. Gibson-Graham's *Take Back the Economy* (Minneapolis: University of Minnesota Press, 2013); and Gar Alperovitz's *America Beyond Capitalism* (Hoboken, NJ: Wiley, 2006). While Gibson-Graham and Alperovitz tend to focus on smaller-scale initiatives to democratize the economy, such as cooperatives, Malleson's attention to features like national capital controls and public community banks operating at the regional level set his work apart. The focus on debt resistance as a means of democratizing the sovereign-like character of debt profiled in this chapter supplements and can complement those on-going efforts.
5. Dean does not believe that democratic theorists who advocate ethical generosity are actually dealing with any kind of ideological difference. She writes:

   What can be said about a political response to those who reject this ethics? What about those who prioritize preservation of a narrowly conceived self and nation over acknowledgment of common vulnerability? Butler's account of the context of address seems to presume an other who shared this context or who will accept her account of it, as if the other answers the call to an account in necessarily the same way, without a fundamentally different ethics of his own. Jodi Dean, *Democracy and Other Neoliberal Fantasies* (Durham: Duke University Press, 2009), 142.

6. Dean, *Democracy and Other Neoliberal Fantasies*, 47.
7. Ibid., 59.
8. Ibid., 62.
9. Jodi Dean, *The Communist Horizon*. (London: Verso, 2012), 5.
10. Dean, *Democracy and Other Neoliberal Fantasies*, 79.
11. Ibid., 78.
12. Ibid., 131.
13. Ibid., 133.
14. Dean, *The Communist Horizon*, 34.
15. Dean, *Democracy and Other Neoliberal Fantasies*, 135.
16. Ibid., 174.
17. Dean, *The Communist Horizon*, 217–218.
18. Ibid., 224–229.
19. Ibid., 227.
20. Ibid., 220.
21. Ibid., 234.
22. Ibid., 87; emphasis in original.
23. Ibid., 185.
24. Ibid., 2–3.
25. Ibid., 9.
26. A number of works have explored Occupy Wall Street as an experiment in non-hierarchical direct democracy operating according to the principles of *horizontalidad* or horizontalism developed in Argentina in the period following the 2001 economic collapse. These scholars emphasize the participatory, consensus-driven decision-making process within Occupy. See A. J. Bauer, Cristina Beltran, Andrew Ross, and Rana Jaleel, eds., *Is This What Democracy Looks Like?* http://what-democracy-looks-like.com; and Marina Sitrin, Dario Azzellini, and David Harvey, eds., *They Can't Represent Us!* (New York: London, 2014).
27. Keith Glesson, "Laundry Day," in *Occupy!* eds. Carla Blumenkrantz and Keith Glesson. (New York: N+1, 2011), 195–212.
28. Max Weber, "Politics as a Vocation" in *From Max Weber*, eds. C. Wright Mills and H.H. Gerth, (New York: Oxford University Press, 1946), 77–128; and Jean-Paul Sartre, "Dirty Hands" *in No Exit and Three Other Plays*, trans. Lionel Abel (New York: Vintage, 1989), 125–242.
29. Maurizio Lazzarato, *The Making of Indebted Man*, trans. David Joshua Jordan (Cambridge, MA: MIT Press, 2012).
30. Feher, "Self-Appreciation," 21–41.
31. *The Debt Resistors' Operations Manual* (2012), 1, available online at: strikedebt.org/The-Debt-Resistors-Operations-Manual.pdf, accessed February 1, 2013.

32. Creditors angry over the seizure of farms by Boston bankers for unpaid debts organized behind the leadership of Massachusetts farmer Daniel Shays in 1786 to stop magistrates from foreclosing properties and liberate those jailed because they had defaulted on their loans. Several scholars argue that the delegates to the Constitutional Convention were motivated to establish stronger central powers by Shays Rebellion and similar episodes of civil unrest. See David P. Szatmary, *Shays' Rebellion: The Making of an Agrarian Insurrection* (Amherst, MA: University of Massachusetts Press, 1980), and Leonard Richards, *Shays's Rebellion: The American Revolution's Final Battle* (Philadelphia, PA: University of Pennsylvania Press, 2003).
33. Friedrich Nietzsche, *On the Genealogy of Morality* (Cambridge: Cambridge University Press, 1997), 2nd essay, 36.
34. Ibid., 46.
35. Ibid., 2nd Essay Section 3.
36. Ibid., 2nd Essay, Section 12.
37. Ibid., 50.
38. Ibid., 2nd essay, sections 1–6.
39. Lazzarato, *Making of Indebted Man,* 153. Thomas Dumm also names consumer debt's ability to circumscribe the horizon of choice as a major political threat in his *A Politics of the Ordinary*.
40. Nietzsche, *On the Genealogy of Morals*, 36.
41. Ibid., 38.
42. Ibid., 41.
43. Reckoning with habits of personal consumption and the debt it has created begs the question of the larger historical circumstances that made the accumulation and pursuit of such pleasures possible. Specifically, it would involve acknowledging the unpaid and underpaid labor and resources extracted from slavery, women in the household, colonialism, and current practices of exploitation between the Global North and South.
44. For a discussion of efforts to cultivate alternative subjectivities, see J. K. Gibson-Graham, *A Post-Capitalist Politics* (Minneapolis: University of Minnesota Press, 2006), 127–164.
45. *Operations Manual*, 105–106.
46. "An Update on the Rolling Jubilee," Strike Debt http://strikedebt.org/rjupdate/, accessed February 8, 2013.
47. Anna Altman, "Occupy Returns with a New Idea," *New Yorker*, November 21, 2012, http://www.newyorker.com/online/blogs/newsdesk/2012/11/occupy-returns-with-a-new-idea.html, accessed January 2014.
48. John Bringardiner, "A Robin Hood for the Debt-Crisis?" *New Yorker*, November 27, 2013, http://www.newyorker.com/online/blogs/currency/2013/11/a-robin-hood-for-the-debt-crisis.html, accessed January 25, 2014.
49. Anne Johnson, Tobin Van Ostern, and Abraham White, *The Student Debt Crisis* (Center for American Progress, 2012), http://www.americanprogress.org/wp-content/uploads/2012/10/WhiteStudentDebt-5.pdf, accessed February 2, 2013.

50. Walter Hamilton, "Student-Delinquency Rate Hits Danger Zone, Report Says," *Los Angeles Times* (online edition), January 20, 2013, http://www.latimes.com/business/money/la-fi-mo-student-loan-delinquency-20130129,0,548490.story, accessed February 8, 2013.
51. *Operations Manual*, 41–42.
52. On June 4, 2013, Jefferson County, Alabama, reached an agreement with creditors that would allow it to declare bankruptcy on its loans of more than $4.2 billion, the largest municipal bankruptcy in US history. See Mary Williams Walsh, "A County in Alabama Strikes a Deal," *New York Times*, June 4, 2013, online: http://dealbook.nytimes.com/2013/06/04/a-county-in-alabama-strikes-a-bankruptcy-deal/?hp, accessed June 9, 2013. Michigan's Governor Rick Snyder appointed an emergency manager to oversee Detroit in the wake of that city's precarious financial position. See Bill Vlasic and Steven Yaccino, "Detroit Waits, Apprehensive, for Manager to Take Over," *New York Times*, March 23, 2013, http://www.nytimes.com/2013/03/24/us/defiant-anxious-detroit-gets-an-emergency-manager.html?pagewanted=all, accessed June 9, 2013.
53. "Hello to All Who Love Gardens and Post Offices," Strike Debt Bay Area http://strike-debt-bay-area.tumblr.com/post/109123140922/hello-to-all-who-love-gardens-and-post-offices
54. "Strike Debt has a Song . . . And A Radio Slot to Sing It On!" Occupy Oakland, https://occupyoakland.org/2013/12/strike-debt-song/
55. *Operations Manual*, 103.
56. B. Marke, "15-M Utopia: Protests in Spain grow into massive popular movement," *San Francisco Bay Guardian Online*, May 25, 2011, http://www.sfbg.com/politics/2011/05/25/m-15-utopia-protests-spain-grow, accessed February 2, 2013.
57. Daniel Chávez, "El Barzón: Performing Resistance in Contemporary Mexico," *Arizona Journal of Hispanic Cultural Studies*, 2 (1998): 87–112.
58. *Operations Manual*, 103. For more on the protests in Quebec, see: Olivier Asselin and Laura Balladur, "Red Square: A Colored Form's Political Destiny." *Theory & Event* (online)15, no. 3 (2012): https://muse.jhu.edu/article/484443 accessed February 2, 2013.
59. Maritza Stanchich, "A University Besieged: Initial Impressions of a Student Strike." *Qui Parle: Critical Humanities and Social Sciences* 20, no. 1 (2011): 233–239: https://muse.jhu.edu/article/454337/pdf, accessed February 2, 2013.
60. Tyler Kingkade, "Cooper Union, CUNY Students Rally, Hoping for Spark of Larger Movement," *Huffington Post*, December 8, 2012, http://www.huffingtonpost.com/2012/12/08/cooper-union-cuny-students-rally_n_2260732.html, accessed June 7, 2013.
61. David Graeber, *Debt: The First 5,000 Years* (New York: Melville, 2011).
62. For more on the link between democracy and Christian religious tradition in the United States and the idea that democracy itself represents an inheritance and tradition, see Jeffrey Stout, *Democracy and Tradition*, (Princeton: Princeton University Press, 2004).
63. They explain, "It is an assault on our homes, our families, our communities and on the planet's fragile ecosystem—all of which are being destroyed by endless

production to pay back creditors who have done nothing to earn the wealth they demand we make for them," *Operations Manual*, 2.

64. Kim Severson, "At Vacant Homes, Foraging for Fruit," *New York Times*, August 14, 2011, http://www.nytimes.com/2011/08/15/us/15forage.html. accessed November 4, 2015.
65. Tina Rosenberg, "Where All Work is Created Equal," *New York Times*, September 15, 2011, http://opinionator.blogs.nytimes.com/2011/09/15/where-all-work-is-created-equal/, accessed November 4, 2015.
66. For a longer discussion of downshifting see Gibson-Graham, *Take Back the Economy*.
67. Consider, for example, the magazine *Real Simple*.
68. Patrick Caldwell, "Elizabeth Warren Slams Regulators for Keeping Banks 'Too Big to Fail,'" *Mother Jones*, November 12, 2013 (online edition): www.motherjonescom/politics/2013/11/elizabeth-warren-dodd-frank-too-big-fail-speech-regulators, accessed November 7, 2015.
69. Timothy Williams, "Seeking New Start, Finding Steep Costs," *New York Times*, August 17, 2014, http://www.nytimes.com/2014/08/18/us/workforce-investment-act-leaves-many-jobless-and-in-debt.html?ref=topics, accessed November 4, 2015.
70. "Students Speak Out at DOE Hearing to Demand Debt Cancellation and Free Education," Debt Collective Blog, November 6, 2014 http://blog.debtcollective.org/students-speak-out-at-doe-hearing-to-demand-debt-cancellation-and-free-education/, accessed November 4, 2015.
71. "Corinthian Students Lured by Job Prospects Get Loan Break," *New York Times*, February 3, 2015, http://www.nytimes.com/aponline/2015/02/03/us/politics/ap-us-cfpb-corinthian.html, accessed November 4, 2015.
72. Plutarch, "Solon" *Plutarch's Lives*, Vol. 1, ed. Arthur Hugh Clough. (New York: Modern Library Classics, 2001), 106–128.
73. Josiah Ober, "The Original Meaning of 'Democracy': Capacity to Do Things, not Majority Rule," *Constellations*, 15, no. 1 (March 2008): 3–9.

CONCLUSION

1. David Neiwert, "'He Thinks He's Going to Save the World': The Making of a 'Sovereign Citizen,'" *Salon*, June 21, 2014, http://www.salon.com/2014/06/21/he_thinks_he's_going_to_save_the_world"_the_making_of_a_sovereign_citizen/ [accessed March 25, 2015].
2. Liz Keller, "Attempted Murder Suspect: 'They Were Trying to Silence Me,'" *The Union*, June 28, 2014, http://www.theunion.com/news/11996510-113/cole-ranger-shot-rights accessed March 25, 2015.
3. Doktor Zoom, "Here is Possibly (Totally) the 'Sovereign Citizen' Who Shot A BLM Officer and Cop, For Freedom," *Wonkette*, June 17, 2014, http://wonkette.com/551950/here-is-possibly-totally-the-sovereign-citizen-who-shot-a-blm-officer-and-cop-for-freedom#oKCMjAAVgPpIrLVo.99, accessed March 15, 2015.
4. "Sovereign Citizens Movement," Southern Poverty Law Center: http://www.splcenter.org/get-informed/intelligence-files/ideology/sovereign-citizens-movement, accessed March 25, 2015.

5. In 2010, a father and son identifying as sovereigns shot and killed two highway patrol officers during a traffic stop in Arkansas. Idaho Brothers Doug and Craig Broderick killed one police officer and wounded another before being killed by police in a similar incident in 1997.
6. David Neiwart, "'Sovereign Citizen' Is Suspected in Georgia Courthouse Shooting," Hatewatch, June 6, 2014, http://www.splcenter.org/blog/2014/06/06/sovereign-citizen-is-suspected-in-georgia-courthouse-shooting/, accessed March 15, 2015.
7. "Sovereign Citizen Movement," Southern Poverty Law Center.
8. Tully, *Public Philosophy in a New Key,* Vol. 2, 284.
9. Hiroko Tabuchi, "Next Goal for Walmart Workers: More Hours," *New York Times*, February 25, 2015, http://www.nytimes.com/2015/02/26/business/next-goal-for-walmart-workers-more-hours.html?hp&action=click&pgtype=Homepage&module=photo-spot-region&region=top-news&WT.nav=top-news, accessed March 4, 2015.
10. Kathi Weeks, *The Problem With Work*, (Durham: Duke University Press, 2011), 4.
11. In September 24, 2014, a thirty-two-year old New Jersey woman named Maria Fernandes died from carbon monoxide poisoning. Fernades worked three jobs, at three different Dunkin Donuts franchises. Fernades regularly slept in the car in the few hours between shifts with the motor running, one reason why she kept a full plastic gas container in her car. She died in her sleep, unaware the container had fallen over and spilled. Coverage of her death drew attention to the conditions many workers face trying to make a living, working multiple low-wage jobs. Rachel Swarns, "For a Worker With Little Time Between 3 Jobs, a Nap Has Fatal Consequences," *The New York Times*, September 28, 2014. Available online: http://www.nytimes.com/2014/09/29/nyregion/3-jobs-plenty-of-dreams-and-the-fatal-consequences-of-one-dangerous-decision.html?_r=0 accessed March 4, 2015.
12. Rancière, *Disagreement*, trans. Julie Rose (Minneapolis: University of Minnesota Press, 1999), 27.
13. Ibid., 29.
14. Arun Gupta, "Fight for $15 Confidential," In These Times, November 13, 2013, http://inthesetimes.com/article/15826/fight_for_15_confidential, accessed November 2, 2015.
15. Julie Carrie Wong, "Oakland-Area Protests Disrupt Sunday Shoppers," *USA Today*, January 19, 2015, http://www.usatoday.com/story/news/2015/01/18/oakland-protests-blacklivesmatter-walmart/21952971/, accessed March 4, 2015.

WORKS CITED

Abu-Magd, Zeinab. "Occupying Tahrir Square: The Myths and Realities of the Egyptian Revolution." *South Atlantic Quarterly* 111, no. 3 (2012).565–572.

Al-Aswany, Alaa. *On the State of Egypt*. New York: Vintage, 2011.

Al-Jazeera. "Protesters Flood Cairo in Competing Rallies." July 26, 2011, http://www.aljazeera.com/news/middleeast/2013/07/2013726164710914498.htm.

Allen, Danielle S. *Talking to Strangers*. Chicago: University of Chicago Press, 2004.

Alperovitz, Gar. *America Beyond Capitalism*. Hoboken, NJ: Wiley, 2006.

Al-Qaradawi, Shaykh Yusuf. *Khutba*, Tahrir Square. Translated by Yahya Michot, February 18, 2001, http://www.beliefnet.com/columnists/cityofbrass/2011/03/the-khutbah-sermon-of-yusuf-al.html.

Altman, Anna. "Occupy Returns with a New Idea." *New Yorker*, November 21, 2012.

Anderson, Michael D. "Occupy Wall Street Re-Occupies Foreclosed Home in East New York: A Report from the Scene." *Occupy Your Homes*, blog, *Village Voice*.

Anderson, Mary Elizabeth. "Oprah Feelin': Technologies of Reception in the Commercial Flash Mob." In *Embodied Consciousness*, edited by Jade Rosina McCutcheon and Barbara Sellers-Young, 159–178. New York: Palgrave-Macmillan, 2013.

Anker, Elisabeth R. *Orgies of Feeling*. Durham, NC: Duke University Press, 2014.

Asselin, Olivier, and Laura Balladur. "Red Square: A Colored Form's Political Destiny." *Theory & Event* (online)15, no. 3 (2012).https://muse.jhu.edu/issue/26026.

Associated Press. "Corinthian Students Lured by Job Prospects Get Loan Break." *New York Times*, February 3, 2015. http://www.nytimes.com/aponline/2015/02/03/us/politics/ap-us-cfpb-corinthian.html.

———. "Occupy Eugene's Downtown Camp Turns into Homeless Haven." *Oregonlive.com*, December 8, 2011. http://www.oregonlive.com/pacific-northwest-news/index.ssf/2011/12/occupy_eugenes_downtown_camp_t.html.

Badawi, Kim. "Egypt: The Day of the Martyrs." Photograph, Getty Images. ID: 08901284KB007_martyr.

Bauer, A. J., Cristina Beltran, Andrew Ross, and Rana Jaleel, eds. *Is This What Democracy Looks Like?* 2013 http://what-democracy-looks-like.com.

Bayat, Asef. *Life as Politics*. Palo Alto, CA: Stanford University Press, 2010.

Beltrán, Cristina. "Going Public: Hannah Arendt, Immigrant Action and the Space of Appearance." *Political Theory* 37, no. 5 (October 2009): 595–622.

Berlant, Lauren. *Cruel Optimism*. Durham: Duke University Press, 2011.
———. *The Female Complaint*. Durham: Duke University, 2008.
Bodin, Jean, *On Sovereignty: Four Chapters from The Six Books of the Commonwealth*, edited and translated by Julian H. Franklin (Cambridge, UK: Cambridge University Press, 1992).
Boltanski, Luc, and Eve Chiapello. *The New Spirit of Capitalism*. Translated by Gregory Elliot. New York: Verso, 2007.
Bourdieu, Pierre. *Outline of a Theory of Practice* (Translated by Richard Nice). Cambridge: Cambridge University Press, 1977.
Brass, Elaine, and Sophie Poklewski Koziell, eds. *Gathering Force: DIY Culture—Radical Action for Those Tired of Waiting*. London: The Big Issue Writers, 1994.
Bravo, Kyle, ed. *Making Stuff and Doing Things*, 3rd ed. Bloomington, IN: Microcosm Press, 2008.
Bringardiner, John. "A Robin Hood for the Debt-Crisis?" New Yorker, November 27, 2013.
Brown, Nathan J. "Egypt's Constitutional Revolution?" In *The Rule of Law, Islam, and Constitutional Politics in Egypt and Iran*, edited by Nathan J. Brown, 303–312. New York: State University of New York Press, 2013.
———. *Post-Revolutionary Al-Azhar*. Carnegie Endowment for International Peace: September 2011, http://carnegieendowment.org/files/al_azhar.pdf.
Brown, Wendy. *Undoing the Demos*. New York: Zone Books, 2015.
———. *Walled States, Walled Sovereignty*. New York: Zone Books, 2010.
———. "We Are All Democrats Now . . ." In *Democracy in What State?* ed. Amy Allen, 44–57. New York: Columbia University Press, 2011.
Bruyneel, Kevin. *The Third Space of Sovereignty*. Minneapolis: University of Minnesota Press, 2007.
Butler, Judith. "Bodies in Alliance and the Politics of the Street (September 2011)." http://eipcp.net/transversal/1011/butler/en/print.
———. *Giving an Account of Oneself*. New York: Fordham University Press, 2005.
———. *Notes Towards a Performative Theory of Assembly*. Cambridge, MA: Harvard University Press, 2015.
———. *Precarious Life*. New York: Verso, 2004.
Caldwell, Patrick. "Elizabeth Warren Slams Regulators for Keeping Banks 'Too Big to Fail.'" *Mother Jones* (online), November 12, 2013, www.motherjonescom/politics/2013/11/elizabeth-warren-dodd-frank-too-big-fail-speech-regulators, accessed November 7, 2015.
Campbell, Emahunn Raheeem Ali. "A Critique of the Occupy Movement from a Black Occupier." *Black Scholar* 41, no. 4 (Winter 2011): 42–51.
Carlson, Kay L. "Origin of the Round Dance Ceremony." *Women Against Violence Against Women* blog, April 13, 2015, http://www.wavaw.ca/blogsround-dance-ceremony/.
Carlsson, Chris. *Nowtopia: How Pirate Programmers, Outlaw Bicyclists, and Vacant-Lot Gardeners Are Inventing the Future Today*. Oakland: AK Press, 2008.
Casper, Jayson. "A Christian Face to the Protests." Online post, February 8, 2011. http://asenseofbelonging.org/2011/02/08/a-christian-face-to-the-protests/.
Cassidy, John. "Signs of the Times." *The New Yorker* October 6, 2015, http://www.newyorker.com/news/john-cassidy/wall-street-protests-signs-of-the-times.

Cavell, Stanley. "The Ordinary as the Uneventful." In *Themes Out of School*. Chicago: The University of Chicago Press, 1984, 184–194.

Chávez, Daniel. "El Barzón: Performing Resistance in Contemporary Mexico." *Arizona Journal of Hispanic Cultural Studies* 2 (1998): 87–112.

Chwe, Michael. *Rational Rituals*. Princeton: Princeton University Press, 2003.

Cocks, Joan. *Sovereignty and Other Political Delusions*. New York: Bloomsbury Academic, 2014.

Coles, Romand. *Beyond Gated Politics*. Minneapolis: University of Minnesota Press, 2005.

Coles and Stanley Hauwerwas. *Christianity, Democracy, and the Radical Ordinary: Conversations between a Radical Democrat and a Christian*. Eugene, OR: Cascade Books, 2008.

Connolly, William. *Capitalism and Christianity, American Style*. Durham: Duke University Press, 2008.

———. *The Ethos of Pluralization*. Durham: Duke University Press, 1995.

———. *The Fragility of Things*. Durham: Duke University Press, 2013.

Corner, John. "Performing the Real: Documentary Diversions." *Television and New Media* 3, no. 3 (August 2002): 259–260.

Coulthard, Glen. *Red Skin, White Masks* (Minneapolis: University of Minnesota Press, 2014).

———. "Subjects of Empire." *Contemporary Political Theory* 6 (2007): 437–460.

Cowie, Elizabeth. *Recording Reality, Desiring the Real*. Minneapolis: University of Minnesota Press, 2011.

Critchley, Simon. *Infinitely Demanding: Ethics of Commitment, Politics of Resistance*. London: Verso, 2007.

Curtis, Ben. "Egypt Protest, February 1, 2011," *The Oregonian* (online)http://photos.oregonlive.com/photoessay/2011/02/egypt_protest_february_1 _2011.html

Dean, Jodi. *Democracy and Other Neoliberal Fantasies*. Durham: Duke University Press, 2009.

———. *The Communist Horizon*. New York: Verso, 2012.

Debt Collective. "Students Speak Out at DOE Hearing to Demand Debt Cancellation and Free Education." *DebtCollective*, November 6, 2014, http://blog.debtcollective.org/students-speak-out-at-doe-hearing-to-demand-debt-cancellation-and-free-education/.

The Debt Resistors' Operations Manual, 2012.

Dumm, Thomas L. *A Politics of the Ordinary*. New York: New York University Press, 1999.

"Egypt: A New Turning Point for the Revolution," *The Atlantic*, February 10, 2011, online edition: http://www.theatlantic.com/photo/2011/02/egypt-a-new-turning-point-for-the-revolution/100007/.

El Fadl, Khaled Abou. "The Language of Age: Shari'a and Natural Justice in the Egyptian Revolution." *Harvard Internal Law Journal* 52 (2011): 311–321.

Elshahed, Mohamed. "Breaking the Fear Barrier of Mubarak's Regime." Social Science Research Council, http://www.ssrc.org/pages/breaking-the-fear-barrier-of-mubarak-s-regime/.

Farrow, Kenneth. "Occupy Wall Street's Race Problem." *The American Prospect*, October 24, 2011. http://prospect.org/article/occupy-wall-streets-race-problem.

Fathi, Asghar. "The Islamic Pulpit as a Medium of Political Communication." *Journal for the Scientific Study of Religion* 20, no. 2 (1981): 163–172.
Feher, Michel. "Self-Appreciation; or the Aspirations of Human Capital." *Public Culture*, 21, no. 1 (2009): 21–41.
Feldman, Leonard. "The Banality of Emergency: On the Time and Space of 'Political Necessity.'" In *Sovereignty, Emergency, Legality*, edited by Sarat, Austin, 136–164. New York: Cambridge University Press, 2010.
Foucault, Michel. *Discipline and Punish*. Translated by Alan Sheridan. New York: Vintage Books, 1995.
———. *Security, Territory, Population: Lectures at the College de France*. Translated by Graham Burchell. New York: Picador, 2007.
———. "What is Critique?" In *The Politics of Truth*. Translated by Sylvere Lotringer. Los Angeles: Semiotext(e), 2007, 41–82.
Fox, Josh. *Occupy Sandy*, short film. Released on Vimeo.com, November 30, 2012.
Gaffney, Patrick D. *The Prophet's Pulpit: Islamic Preaching in Contemporary Egypt*. Berkeley: University of California Press, 1994.
Gibson-Graham, J.K. *Take Back the Economy*. Minneapolis: University of Minnesota Press, 2013.
Gould, Deborah. *Moving Politics*. University of Chicago Press, 2009.
Graeber, David. *Debt: The First 5000 Years*. New York: Melville, 2012.
———. *The Democracy Project*. New York: Speigal & Grau, 2013.
Green, Pamela, and Norman Moyah , "Join the Circle: History and Lore of the Round Dance." *Aboriginal Multi-Media Society* 16, no. 2, 1998, , 29. http://www.ammsa.com/publications/windspeaker/join-circle-history-and-lore-round-dance-0.
Gibson-Graham, J.K. *Take Back the Economy*. Minneapolis: University of Minnesota Press, 2013.
———. *A Post-Capitalist Politics*. Minneapolis: University of Minnesota Press, 2006.
Glesson, Keith. "Laundry Day." In *Occupy!* edited by Carla Blumenkrantz and Keith Glesson, 195–212. New York: N+1, 2011.
Gupta, Arun. "Fight for $15 Confidential." *These Times*, November 13, 2013, http://inthesetimes.com/article/15826/fight_for_15_confidential.
Hamilton, Walter. "Student-Delinquency Rate Hits Danger Zone, Report Says." *Los Angeles Times*, January 20, 2013.
Hardt, Michael and Antonio Negri. *Empire*. Cambridge: Harvard University Press, 2000.
———. *Multitude*. New York: Penguin, 2005.
Harper, Stephen. "Address to Council on Foreign Relations." Speech. New York, September 25, 2007. http://www.pm.gc.ca/eng/news/2007/09/25/pm addresses-council-foreign-relations.
Harper, Stephen, and Bob Rubin. "A Conversation with Stephen Harper." New York, May 16, 2013. http://www.cfr.org/canada/conversation-stephen-harper/p30723
Hartman, Chris. *Zombie Capitalism*. Chicago: Haymarket Press, 2010.
"Hello to All Who Love Gardens and Post Offices." *Strike Debt Bay Area Tumblr*, January 25, 2015, http://strike-debt-bay-area.tumblr.com/post/109123140922/hello-to-all-who-love-gardens-and-post-offices.

Herring, Christopher, and Zoltán Glück, "The Homeless Question" in *Occupy! Scenes from Occupied America* ed. Astra Taylor, Keith Cessen, et al., 163–169, New York: Verso, 2012, 163–169.

Hibbing, John R. and Elizabeth Theiss-Morse. *Stealth Democracy.* New York: Cambridge University Press, 2002.

Hirschkind. Charles. "Beyond Secular and Religious: An Intellectual Genealogy of Tahrir Square." *American Ethnologist* 39, no. 1, (2012): 49–53.

Hoefnagels, Anna. "Renewal and Adaptation: Cree Round Dances." http://www.native-dance.ca/index.php/Renewal/Round_Dances?tp=z accessed November 3, 2015.

Honig, Bonnie. *Antigone, Interrupted.* New York: Cambridge University Press, 2013.

———. *Emergency Politics.* Princeton: Princeton University Press, 2009.

Idle, Nadia, and Alex Nunns, eds. *Tweets from Tahrir.* New York: OR Books, 2011.

Ismail, Salwa. "The Egyptian Revolution against the Police." *Social Research* 79, no. 2 (2012): 435–462.

Jacobs, Karrie. "Strange Bedfellows." *Metropolis Magazine*, December 15, 2011.

Jarvis, Brooke. "Idle No More: Native-Led Protest Takes on Canadian Government." *Rolling Stone*, February 4, 2013.

Jobs and Growth Act, 2012. 2012, c. 31. http://www.parl.gc.ca/LegisInfo/BillDetails.aspx?Language=E&Mode=1&Bill=C45&Parl=41&Ses=1.

Johnson, Anne, Tobin Van Ostern, and Abraham White. *The Student Debt Crisis.* Center for American Progress, 2012.

Khairy, Wael. "Letter from Cairo on February 11." Message posted to: http://www.rogerebert.com/far-flung-correspondents/a-letter-from-cairo-on-february-11-2011.

Keene, Adrienne. "Representing the Native Presence in the 'Occupy Wall Street' Narrative." *Native Appropriations* (blog), October 12, 2011. http://nativeappropriations.com/2011/10/representing-the-native-presence-in-the-occupy-wall-street-narrative.html.

Keller, Liz. "Attempted Murder Suspect: 'They Were Trying to Silence Me.'" *The Union*, June 28, 2014.

Kingkade, Tyler. "Cooper Union, CUNY Students Rally, Hoping for Spark of Larger Movement." *Huffington Post*, December 8, 2012.

Kirkpatrick, David D. "Mubarak Orders Crackdown, With Revolt Sweeping Egypt." *New York Times*, January 28, 2011.

———. "Mubarak's Foes and Allies Clash in Egypt." *New York Times*. February 2, 2011, online edition.

———. "Egyptian Leader Apologizes to Victim of Sexual Assault in Tahrir Square." *New York Times*, June 11, 2014.

———. David D. Kirkpatrick, "Coming to Mourn Tahrir Square's Dead, and Joining Them Instead," *New York Times* (online edition), February 3, 2015: http://www.nytimes.com/2015/02/04/world/middleeast/shaimaa-el-sabbagh-tahrir-square-killing-angers-egyptians.html?emc=eta1.

Klein, Naomi. *Shock Doctrine: The Rise of Disaster Capitalism.* New York: Picador, 2008.

———. *This Changes Everything: Capitalism vs. The Climate*. New York: Simon & Schuster, 2015.

Koselleck, Reinhardt. *Critique and Crisis.* Cambridge: MIT Press, 1988.

Kouddos, Sharif Abdel. "Voting After Mubarak: What Can Egyptians Expect?" *The Nation*, October 21, 2011, http://www.thenation.com/article/164114/voting-after-mubarak-what-can-egyptians-expect#.

Labor Solidarity Committee. "Strike Debt Has a Song . . . And a Radio Slot to Sing It On!" *Occupy Oakland*, December 8, 2013, https://occupyoakland.org/2013/12/strike-debt-song/.

Lazzarato, Maurizio. *The Making of Indebted Man*. Translated by David Joshua Jordan. Cambridge, MA: The MIT Press, 2012.

Lloyd, Moya. "Towards a Cultural Politics of Vulnerability." In *Judith Butler's Precarious Politics*, ed. Samuel Chambers and Terrell Carver, 92–106, New York: Routledge, 2008.

John Locke, "Second Treatise." In *Two Treatises of Government*, ed. Peter Laslett Cambridge, UK: Cambridge University Press, 1994.

Maharawal, Manissa McCleave. "So Real It Hurts: Notes on Occupy Wall Street." *Racialicious* (blog), October 3, 2011. http://www.racialicious.com/2011/10/03/so-real-it-hurts-notes-on-occupy-wall-street/.

Mahmood, Saba. *The Politics of Piety*. Princeton: Princeton University Press, 2005.

———. "Rehearsed Spontaneity and the Conventionality of Ritual: Disciplines of *Salat*." *American Ethnologist* 28, no. 4 (2001): 831–832.

Maharawal, Manissa. "Standing Up." In *Occupy!* edited by Carla Bleumenkranz, Keith Gessen, Mark Grief, Sarah Leonard, and Sarah Resnick. New York: Verso, 2011.

Makar, Farida. "Let Them Have Some Fun": Political and Artistic Forms of Expression in the Egyptian Revolution." *Mediterranean Politics* 16, no. 2 (2011): 307–312.

Malleson, Tom. *After Occupy*. New York: Oxford University Press, 2014.

Marke B., "15-M Utopia: Protests in Spain Grow into Massive Popular Movement." *San Francisco Bay Guardian Online*, May 25, 2011.

Markell, Patchen. "The Rule of the People: Arendt, Archê, and Democracy." *American Political Science Review* 100, no. 1 (February 2006): 1–14.

Martel, James. *Subverting the Leviathan*. New York: Columbia University Press, 2007.

Mavelli, Luca. "Postsecular Resistance, the Body, and the 2011 Egyptian Revolution." *Review of International Studies* 38 (2012): 1057–1078.

Maxwell, Lida. *Public Trials*. New York: Oxford University Press, 2015.

McIvor, David. "Bringing Ourselves to Grief: Judith Butler and the Politics of Mourning." *Political Theory* 40 (2012):409–436.

McKay, George, ed. *DiY Culture: Party & Protest in Nineties Britain*. New York: Verso, 1998.

McNeill, John. *Keeping Together in Time*. Cambridge: Harvard University Press, 1995.

McCleod, . "Nothing Will Ever Be The Same." In *The Winter We Danced*, edited by The Kino-nda-niimi Collective, 142. Winnipeg: ARP Books, 2014.

McMahon, Ryan. "Everything You Do Is Political, You're Anishinaabe. Or, What Idle No More Is To Me." In *The Winter We Danced*, edited by The Kino-nda-niimi Collective, 142. Winnipeg: ARP Books, 2014.

Mills, Charles. *The Racial Contract*. Ithaca: Cornell University Press, 1999.

Mirowski, Philip. *Never Let a Serious Crisis Go to Waste*. New York: Verso, 2013.

Mohrit, Nastaran. "On the Margins of Disaster, Revolutionary Acts of Care." *Tidal: A Journal of Occupy Theory*, February 2, 2013, 24–25.

Montano, John Paul. "An Open Letter to the Occupy Wall Street Activists." *Zashain.com* (blog). http://www.zashnain.com/2011/09/open-letter-to-occupy-wall-street.html.
Montesquieu, Charles Louis de Secondat, Baron de, *Spirit of the Laws* (Amherst, NY: Prometheus Books, 2002).
Mortensen, Camilla, et al. "Keeping Occupied: Who Are These People and What Do They Want?" *Eugene Weekly*, November 10, 2011.
Myers, Ella. *Worldly Ethics: Democratic Politics and Care for the World*. Durham, NC: Duke University Press, 2013.
Neiwert, David. "'He Thinks He's Going to Save the World': The Making of a 'Sovereign Citizen.'" *Salon*, June 21, 2014, http://www.salon.com/2014/06/21/he_thinks_he's_going_to_save_the_world"_the_making_of_a_sovereign_citizen/.
———. "'Sovereign Citizen' Is Suspected in Georgia Courthouse Shooting." *Hatewarch*, June 6, 2014, http://www.splcenter.org/blog/2014/06/06/sovereign-citizen-is-suspected-in-georgia-courthouse-shooting/.
Nichols, Bill. *Introduction to Documentary*. 2nd ed. Bloomington: Indiana University Press, 2010.
Nietzsche, Friedrich. *On the Genealogy of Morality*. Cambridge: Cambridge University Press, 1997.
Norval, Aletta. *Aversive Democracy*. New York: Cambridge University Press, 2007.
Ober, Josiah. "The Original Meaning of 'Democracy': Capacity to Do Things, Not Majority Rule." *Constellations* 15, no. 1 (March 2008): 3–9.
Pinto, Nick. "Hurricane Sandy is New York's Katrina." *Village Voice*, November 12, 2012.
Pitkin, Hannah F. *Representation*. New York: Atherton Press, 1969.
Plutarch, "Solon." *Plutarch's Lives*, Vol. 1, edited by Arthur Hugh Clough. New York: Modern Library Classics, 2001, 106–128.
"Protestors Flood Cairo in Competing Rallies," Al-Jazeera America, July 26, 2013, http://www.aljazeera.com/news/middleeast/2013/07/2013726164710914498.html
Protevi, John. "Semantic, Pragmatic, and Affective Enactment at OWS." *Theory & Event* (online), 14, no. 4 (2011 Supplement), https://www.muse.jhu.edu/article459210.
Rana, Aziz. *The Two Faces of American Freedom*. Cambridge, MA: Harvard University Press, 2010.
Rancèire, Jacques. *Disagreement*. Translated by Julie Rose. Minneapolis: University of Minnesota Press, 1999.
Rankine, Claudia. *Citizen: An American Lyric*. Minneapolis: Greywolf Press, 2014.
Rasmussen, Claire E. *The Autonomous Animal*. Minneapolis: University of Minnesota Press, 2011.
Recuber, Timothy. "Occupy Empathy? Online Politics and Micro-Narratives of Suffering." *New Media & Society* 17, no. 1 (January 2015): 62–77.
Reddy, Chandan. *Freedom With Violence*. Durham, NC: Duke University Press, 2011.
Richard, Chickadee. "'Waking Up to the Beauty': An Interview with Chickadee Richard" (with Leah Gazan). In *The Winter We Danced*, edited by The Kino-nda-niimi Collective, 133–137. Winnipeg: ARP Books, 2014.
Richards, Leonard. *Shays's Rebellion: The American Revolution's Final Battle*. Philadelphia, PA: University of Pennsylvania Press, 2003.

Rosenberg, Tina. "Where All Work is Created Equal." *New York Times*, September 15, 2011.

Ross, Andrew. *Creditocracy*. New York: OR Books, 2013.

Roth, Marco. "Letters of Resignation from the American Dream" in *Occupy! Scenes from Occupied America*. ed. Astra Taylor, Keith Cessen, et al., 23–30, New York: Verso, 2012.

Sartre, Jean-Paul. "Dirty Hands." In *No Exit and Three Other Plays,* trans. Lionel Abel, 125–242. New York: Vintage, 1989.

Saval, Nikil. "Scenes from Occupied Philadelphia" in *Occupy! Scenes from Occupied America* ed. Astra Taylor, Keith Cessen, et al., 157–169, New York: Verso, 2012.

Schulman, Sarah. *The Gentrification of the Mind*. Berkeley: University of California Press, 2013.

Schwartz, Mattathais. "Pre-Occupied." *The New Yorker*, November 28, 2011, http://www.newyorker.com/magazine/2011/11/28/pre-occupied.

Severson, Kim. "At Vacant Homes, Foraging for Fruit." *New York Times*, August 14, 2011.

Sinclair, James. "Dancing in a Mall," *The Winter We Danced*, edited by The Kino-nda-niimi Collective, 148–150. Winnipeg: ARP Books, 2014.

Shulman, George. "Acknowledgement and Disavowal as an Idiom for Theorizing Politics." *Theory & Event* (online), 14, no. 1, (2011): https://muse.jhu.edu/article/423098

———. "Interpreting Occupy." *Possible Futures* (online), December 20, 2011. http://www.possible-futures.org/2011/12/20/interpreting-occupy/.

Sitrin, Marina. "One No, Many Yeses." In *Occupy! Scenes from Occupied America*, edited by Astra Taylor, Keith Cessen, et al., 7–11, New York: Verso, 2012.

Sitrin, Marina, Dario Azzellini, and David Harvey, eds., *They Can't Represent Us!* New York: Verso, 2014.

Smith, Curtis, Ernesto Castaneda, and Josiah Heyman. "The Homeless and Occupy El Paso: Creating Community Among the 99%." *Social Movement Studies* 11, no. 3–4, 2012.

"Sovereign Citizen Movement." Southern Poverty Law Center, 2015. http://www.splcenter.org/get-informed/intelligence-files/ideology/sovereign-citizens-movement.

The Square (Al Midan), directed by Jehane Noujaim, (Cairo: Noujaim Films, 2013), DVD.

Spencer, Amy. *DIY: The Rise of Lo-Fi Culture*. New York: Marion Books, 2005.

Stanchich, Maritza, "A University Besieged: Initial Impressions of a Student Strike." *Qui Parle: Critical Humanities and Social Sciences* 20, no. 1 (2011): 233–239.

Stout, Jeffrey. *Democracy and Tradition*. Princeton: Princeton University Press, 2004.

Stout, Jeffrey. *Blessed Are the Organized*. Princeton: Princeton University Press, 2010.

"Students Speak Out at DOE Hearing to Demand Debt Cancellation and Free Education," Debt Collective Blog, November 6, 2014 http://blog.debtcollective.org/students-speak-out-at-doe-hearing-to-demand-debt-cancellation-and-free-education/.

"Strike Debt has a Song . . . And A Radio Slot to Sing It On!" Occupy Oakland, https://occupyoakland.org/2013/12/strike-debt-song/.

Swarns, Rachel L. "For a Worker With Little Time Between 3 Jobs, a Nap Has Fatal Consequences." *New York Times*, September 28, 2014, http://www.nytimes.com/2014/09/29/nyregion/3-jobs-plenty-of-dreams-and-the-fatal-consequences-of-one-dangerous-decision.html?_r=0.

Szatmary, David P. *Shays' Rebellion: The Making of an Agrarian Insurrection*. Amherst, MA: University of Massachusetts Press, 1980.

Tabuchi, Hiroko. "Next Goal for Walmart Workers: More Hours." *New York Times*, February 25, 2015, http://www.nytimes.com/2015/02/26/business/next-goal-for-walmart-workers-more-hours.html?hp&action=click&pgtype=Homepage&module=photo-spot-region&region=top-news&WT.nav=top-news.

Tocqueville, Alexis de. *Democracy in America*. edited and translated by Harvey C. Mansfield and Delba Winthrop. Chicago: University of Chicago Press, 2000.

Todas-Whitehill, Tara. "Egypt Protest, February 11, 2011", *Oregonian* (online) http://photos.oregonlive.com/photo-essay/2011/02/egypt_protest_february_11_2011.html.

Tully, James. *Public Philosophy in a New Key*, 2 vols. Cambridge: Cambridge University Press, 2008.

———. *Strange Multiplicity*. New York: Cambridge University Press, 1995.

Turner, Fred. *From Counterculture to Cyberculture*. Chicago: The University of Chicago Press, 2006.

Tulk, Janice Esther. "Localixing Intertribal Traditions: The Powwow as Mi'kmaw Cultural Expression." In *Aborginal Music in Contemporary Canada*, edited by Anna Hoefnagels and Beverly Diamond. Montreal: McGill-Queen's University Press, 2012.

Ugarte, Pedro. *Egypt, the wait (photo essay)*. February 18, 2011, http://www.boston.com/bigpicture/2011/02/egypt_the_wait.html.

"An Update on the Rolling Jubilee," Strike Debt http://strikedebt.org/rjupdate/,

Vlasic, Bill, and Steven Yaccino. "Detroit Waits, Apprehensive, for Manager to Take Over." *New York Times*, March 23, 2013.

Walsh, Mary Williams. "A County in Alabama Strikes a Deal." *New York Times*, June 4, 2013.

Warner, Michael. *Publics and Counterpublics*. New York: Zone Books, 2002.

Warren, Mark. *Dry Bones Rattling*. Princeton: Princeton University Press, 2001.

Weber, Max. "Politics as a Vocation." In *From Max Weber*. Edited and translated by H. H. Herth and C. Wright Mills, 77–128. New York: Oxford University Press, 1946.

Weeks, Kathi. *The Problem With Work*. Durham: Duke University Press, 2011.

West, W. Richard, Jr. In *Native American Dance: Ceremonies and Social Traditions*, edited by Charlotte Heth. National Museum of the American Indian, Smithsonian Institute, with Fulcrum Publishers, 1992.

White, Stephen. *The Ethos of a Late-Modern Citizen*. Cambridge: Harvard University Press, 2009.

Williams, Timothy. "Seeking New Start, Finding Steep Costs." *New York Times*, August 17, 2014.

Wilmer, S. E., ed., *Native American Performance and Representation*. Tuscon: The University of Arizona Press, 2009.

Wolin, Sheldon. "Agitated Times." *Parallax* 11 (2005): 2–11.

———. *Democracy Incorporated*. Princeton: Princeton University, 2010.

———. *Politics & Vision*, Expanded Edition. Princeton: Princeton University Press, 2004.

———. *The Presence of the Past*. Baltimore: The Johns Hopkins Press, 1990.

Wong, Julie Carrie. "Oakland-Area Protests Disrupt Sunday Shoppers." *USA Today*, January 19, 2015, http://www.usatoday.com/story/news/2015/01/18/oakland-protests-blacklivesmatter-walmart/21952971/.

Zlutnick, David. "'How Are Racial Justice Activists Making Occupy Work for Everyone?" *Colorlines* (blog) Video. March 13, 2012, http://www.colorlines.com/articles/how-are-racial-justice-activists-making-occupy-work-everyone-video.

Zoom, Doktor. "Here Is Possibly (Totally) The 'Sovereign Citizen' Who Shot A BLM Officer And Cop, For Freedom." *Wonkette*, June 17, 2014. http://wonkette.com/551950/here-is-possibly-totally-the-sovereign-citizen-who-shot-a-blm-officer-and-cop-for-freedom.

INDEX